THE TIMES

MindGames
Word Puzzles & Conundrums

Published by Times Books

An imprint of HarperCollins Publishers
Westerhill Road
Bishopbriggs
Glasgow G64 2QT
www.harpercollins.co.uk
timesbooks@harpercollins.co.uk

First edition 2016

ISBN 978-0-00-819031-6

10 9 8 7 6 5 4 3

A catalogue record for this book is available from the British Library.

If you would like to comment on any aspect of this book, please contact us at the given address or online.
E-mail: puzzles@harpercollins.co.uk

facebook.com/collinsdictionary @collinsdict

Printed and bound in Great Britain by CPI Group (UK) Ltd, Croydon CR0 4YY

Acknowledgements

Codeword	PUZZLER MEDIA
Lexicon	VEXUS PUZZLE DESIGN / LAURENCE MAY
Polygon	ROGER PHILLIPS
Scrabble™ Challenge	ALAN SIMMONS
Wordwatch	JOSEPHINE BALMER

Contents

Introduction

Newspapers are built of words. Often these words are used to convey grave news, challenging opinion and sagacious insights. But they are also used for lighter purposes — and nowhere more delightfully than in the MindGames section of *The Times*.

In this new collection, we bring together five of the best word puzzles from *The Times*: Polygon, Lexica, Word Watch, Scrabble™ Challenge and Codeword. These puzzles have been chosen to appeal to all types of word lover. Polygon probes the boundaries of even the keenest logophile's vocabulary; Lexica and Codeword will give cruciverbalists a whole new perspective on the crossword grid; Word Watch beats a path through some of the less trodden reaches of the dictionary; and Scrabble™ Challenge will richly entertain fans of the ever-popular board game.

Whether you're a dictionary delver, word watcher or Scrabble strategist, you'll find something on every page that exemplifies the joy of words.

David Parfitt
Puzzles Editor of *The Times*

For more MindGames, subscribe to *The Times* at:
store.thetimes.co.uk

T
M
B
U
O
C

Lexica

T O Y

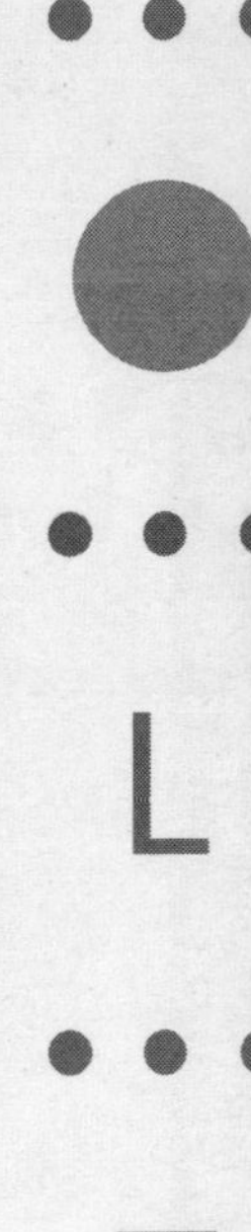

How to Play

- Slide the letters around the outside back into the grid either horizontally or vertically.
- Letters can slide over each other but must stay in their original row or column.

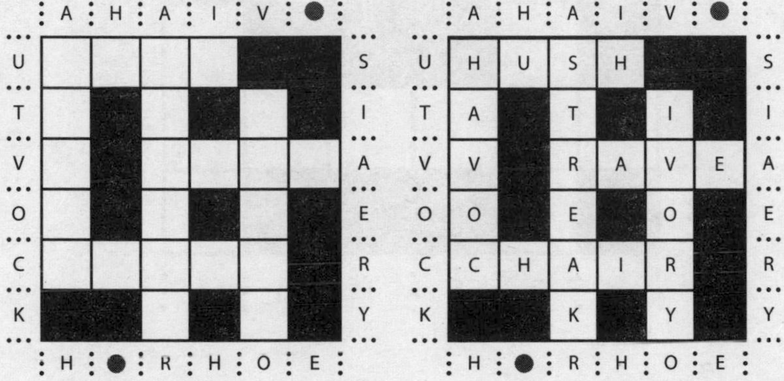

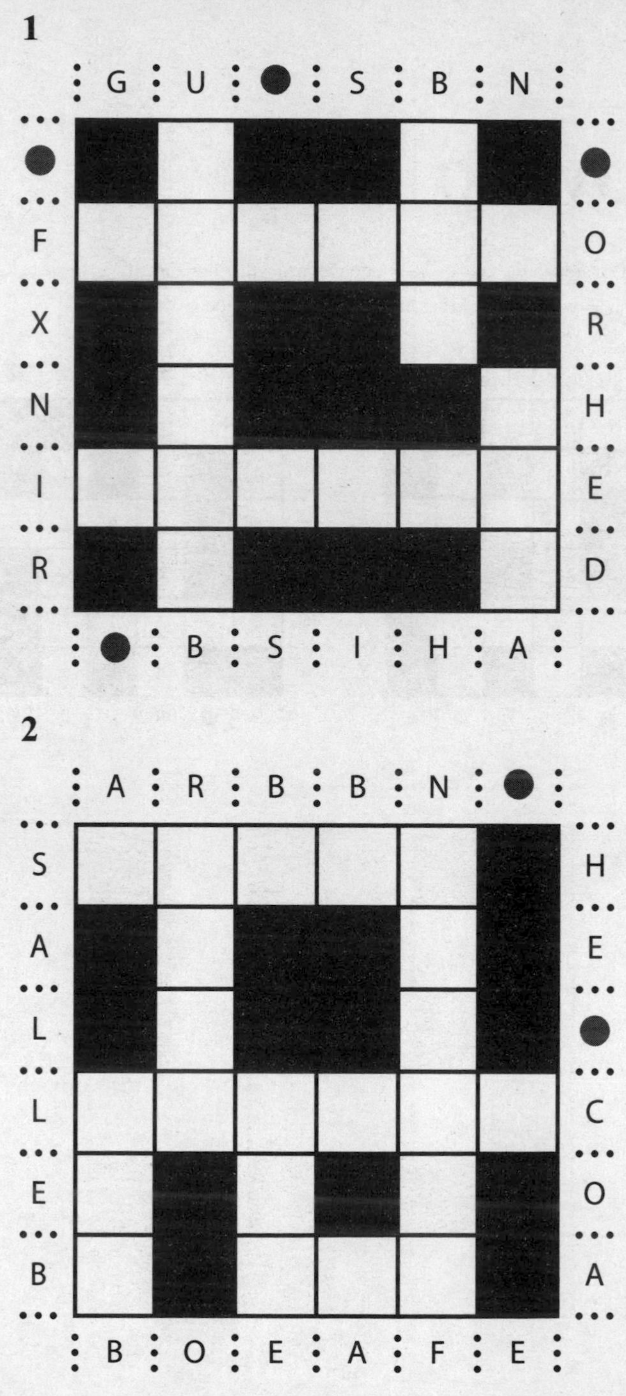
1
G U S B N
F X N I R
O R H E D
B S I H A
2
A R B B N
S A L L E B
H E C O A
B O E A F E

3

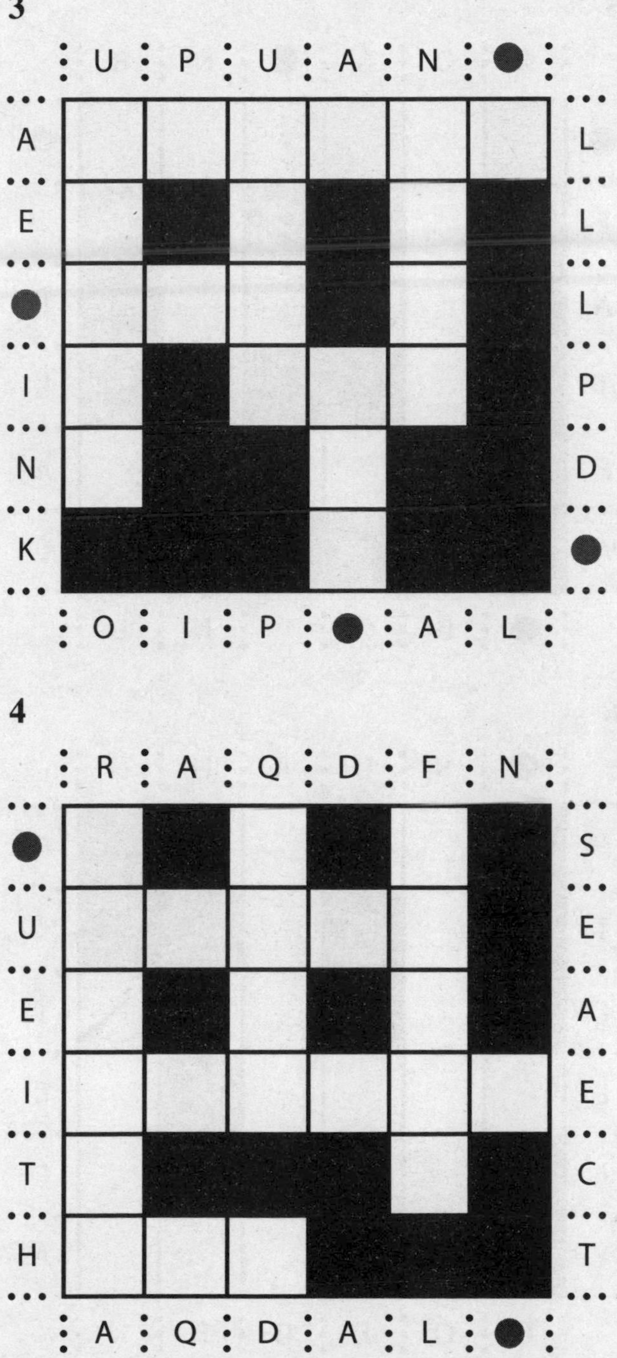

4

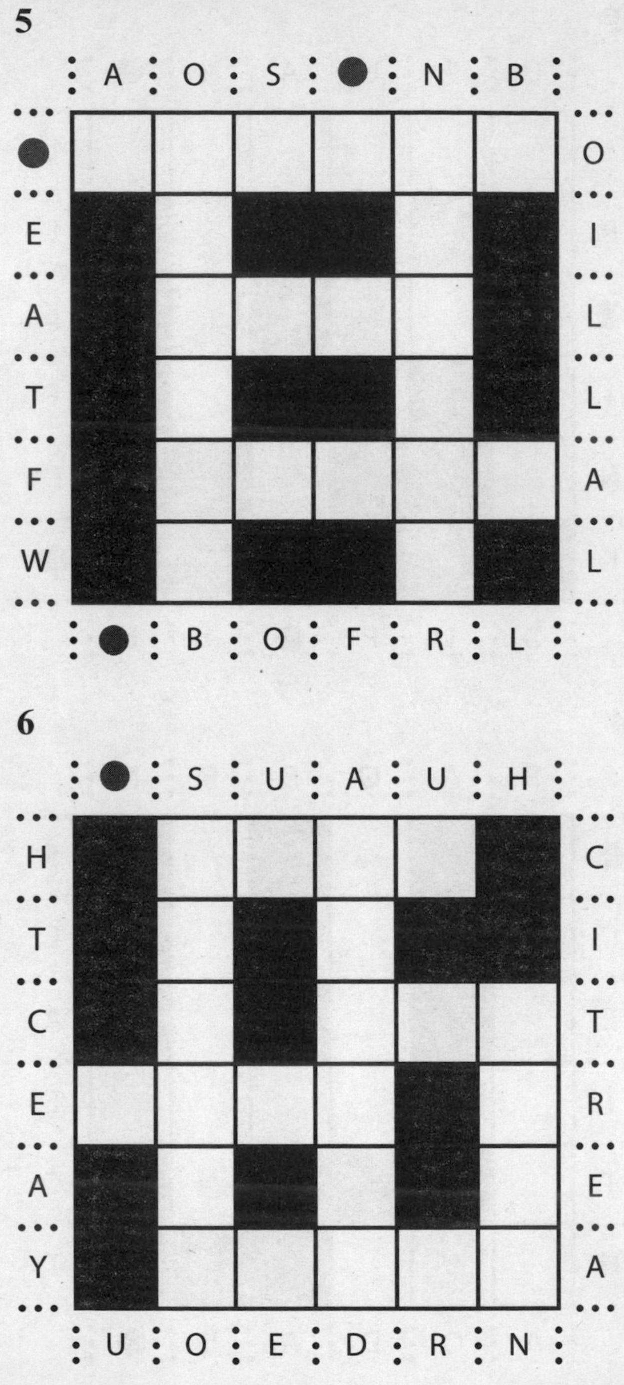
5
A O S N B
E A T F W
O I L L A L
B O F R L
6
S U A U H
H T C E A Y
C I T R E A
U O E D R N

Lexica

Polygon

Scrabble™ Challenge

Word Watch

Codeword

7

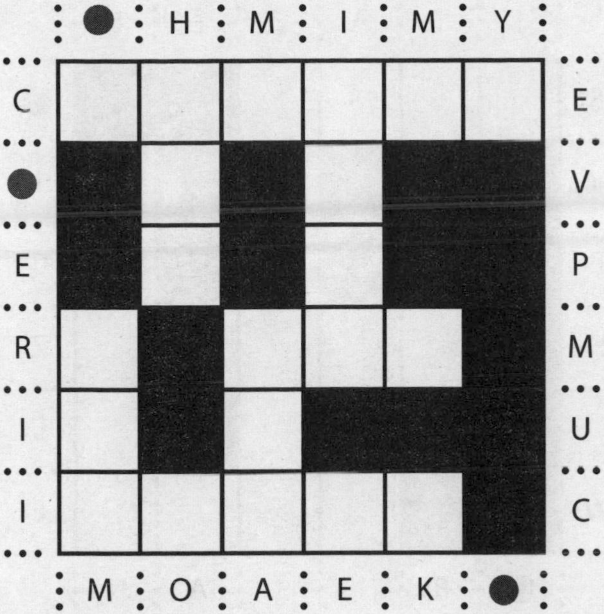

	●	H	M	I	M	Y	
C							E
●	■		■		■	■	V
E	■		■		■	■	P
R		■				■	M
I		■		■	■	■	U
I						■	C
	M	O	A	E	K	●	

8

	D	I	H	S	C	E	
F	■	■		■		■	●
B	■						O
L		■		■		■	C
L						■	A
O		■	■	■		■	E
R							D
	L	E	I	I	R	N	

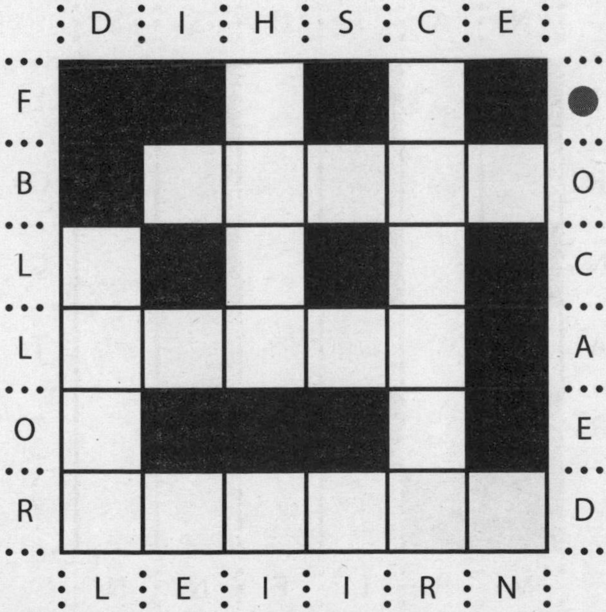

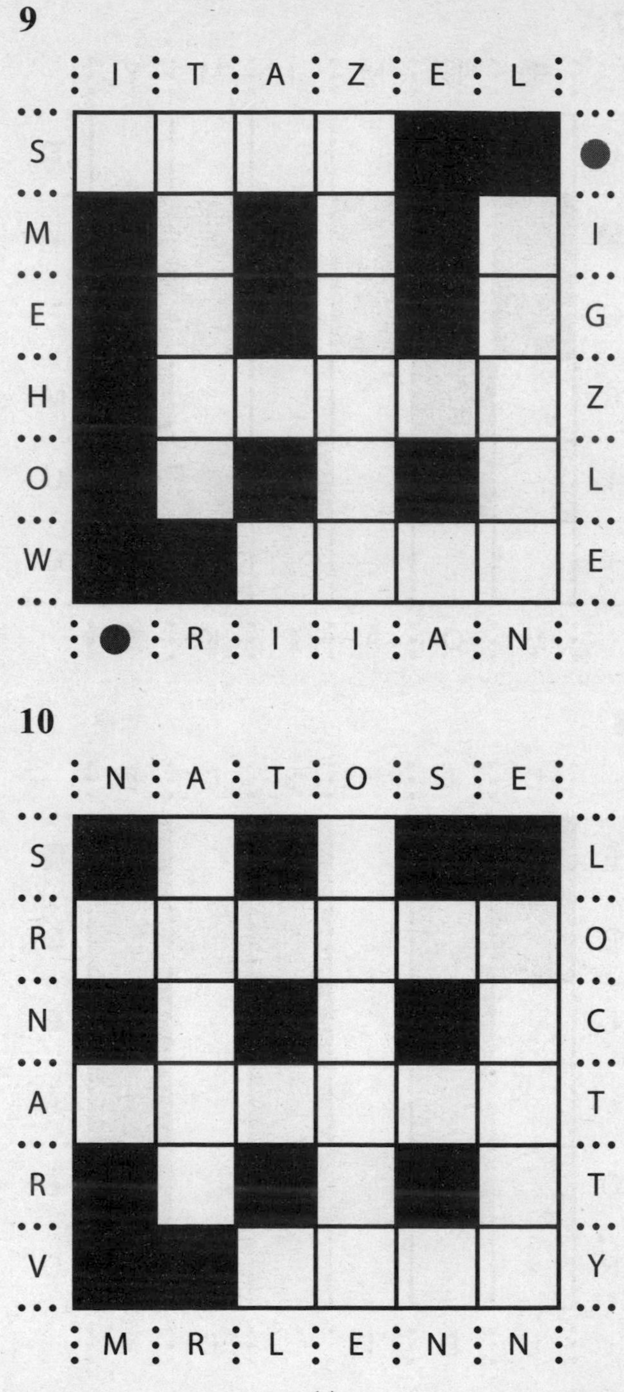
9
I T A Z E L
S M E H O W
I G Z L E
R I I A N
10
N A T O S E
S R N A R V
L O C T T Y
M R L E N N

Polygon

Scrabble™ Challenge

Word Watch

Codeword

11

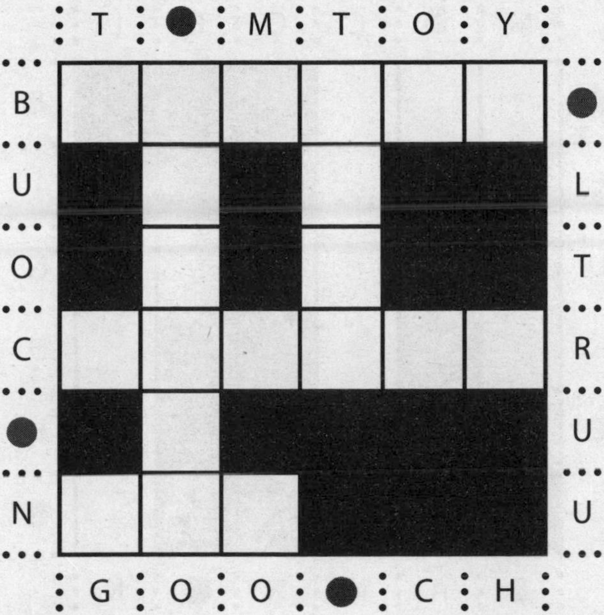

	T	●	M	T	O	Y	
B							●
U							L
O							T
C							R
●							U
N							U
	G	O	O	●	C	H	

12

	U	O	T	E	H	●	
O							C
●							U
C							E
O							F
N							W
H							G
	F	L	I	S	E	T	

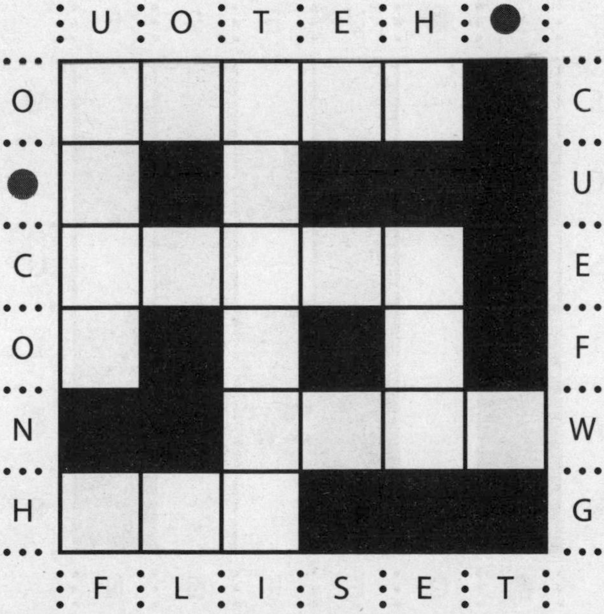

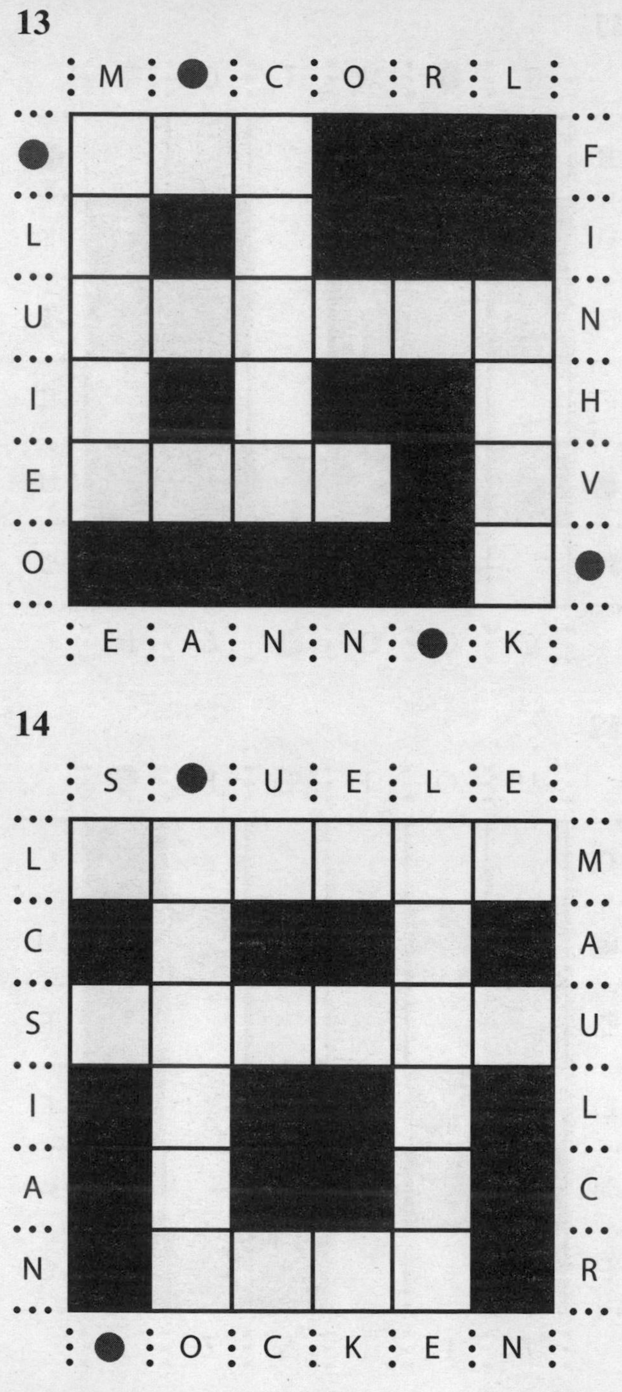
13
M ● C O R L
● L U I E O
F I N H V ●
E A N N ● K
14
S ● U E L E
L C S I A N
M A U L C R
● O C K E N

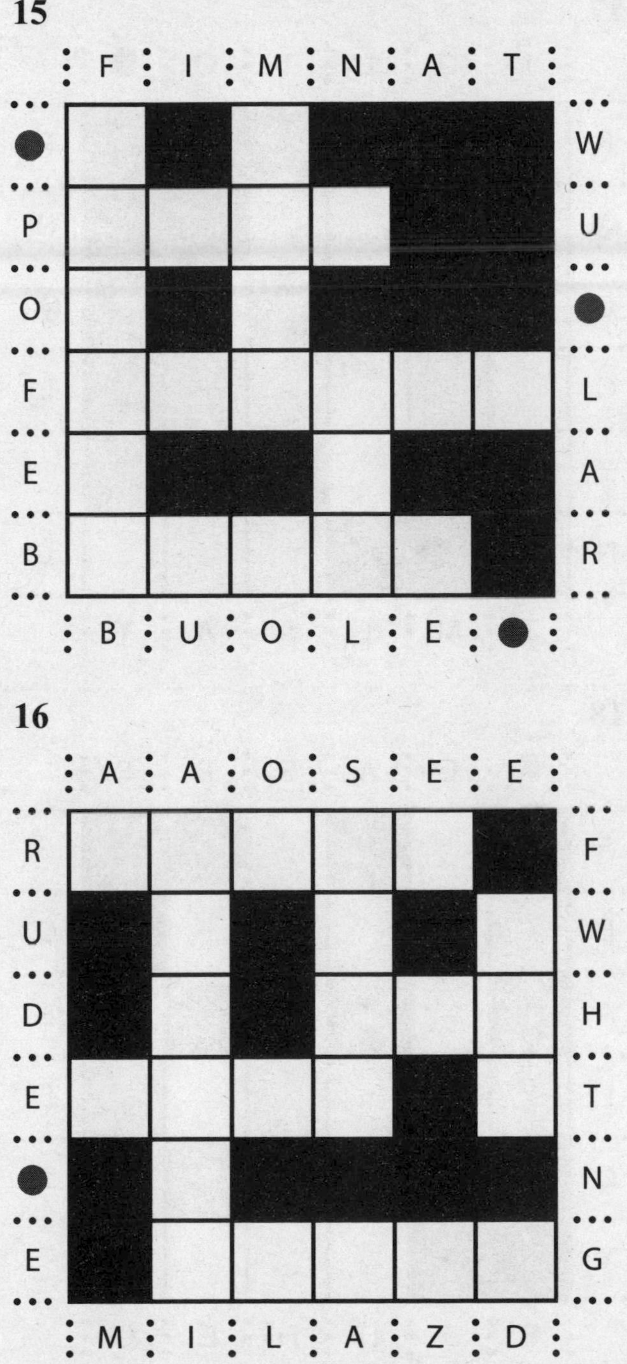
15
F I M N A T
P O F E B
W U L A R
B U O L E
16
A A O S E E
R U D E E
F W H T N G
M I L A Z D

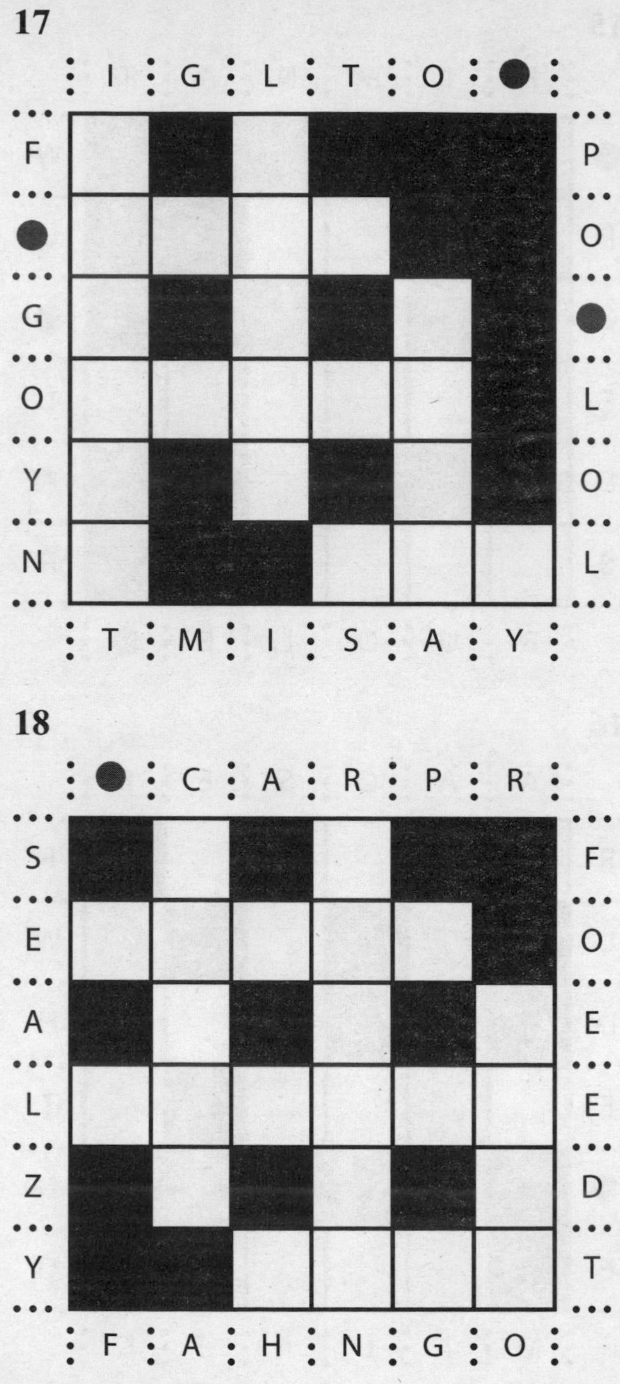
17
I G L T O
F
G
O
Y
N
P
O
L
O
L
T M I S A Y
18
C A R P R
S
E
A
L
Z
Y
F
O
E
E
D
T
F A H N G O

19

	A	N	R	F	Y	●	
●		■	■	■	■	■	B
D					■	■	U
P		■		■		■	R
E						■	L
M		■		■		■	R
A							N
	P	L	A	O	E	T	

20

	T	U	T	R	L	R	
M						■	O
Y		■	■		■		N
I		■					S
E		■	■		■		H
T							F
S		■	■	■	■		H
	O	A	M	B	I	O	

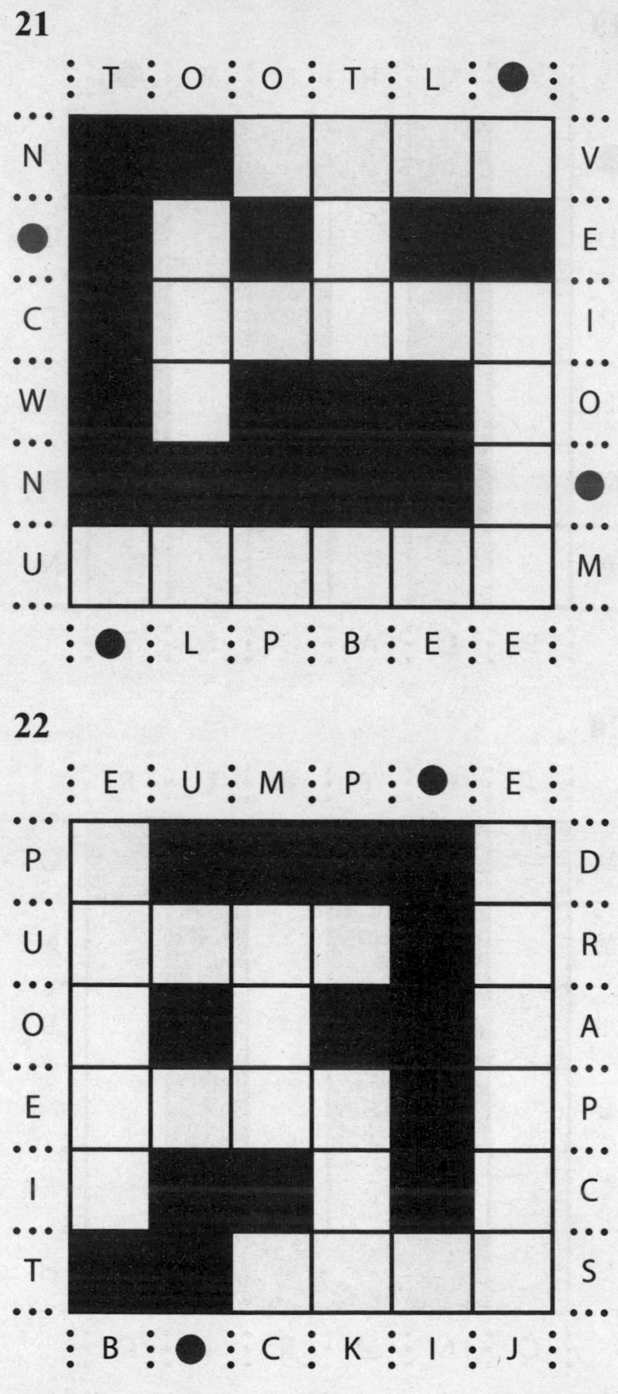
21
T O O T L
N C W N U
V E I O M
L P B E E
22
E U M P E
P U O E I T
D R A P C S
B C K I J

23

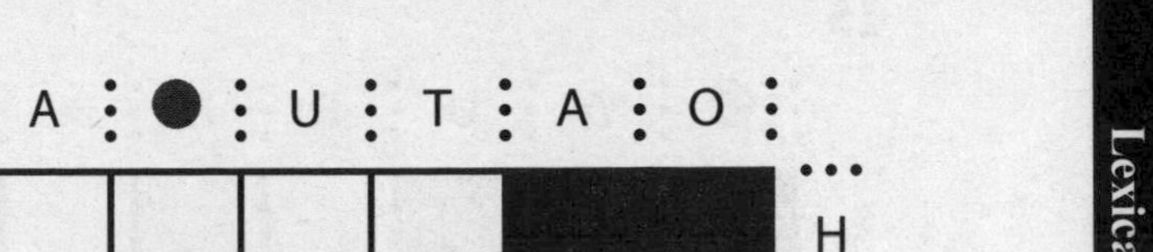

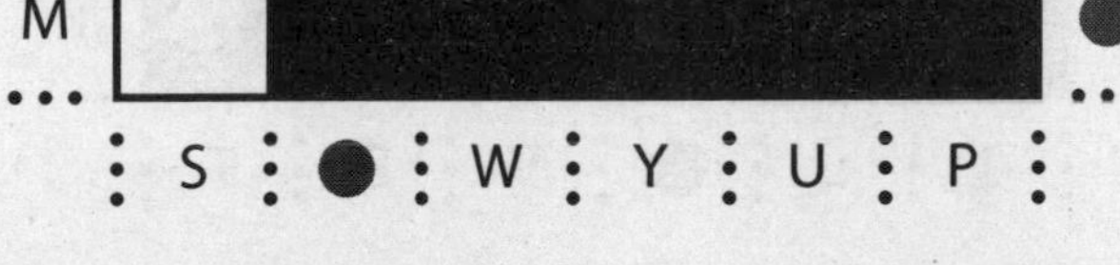

24

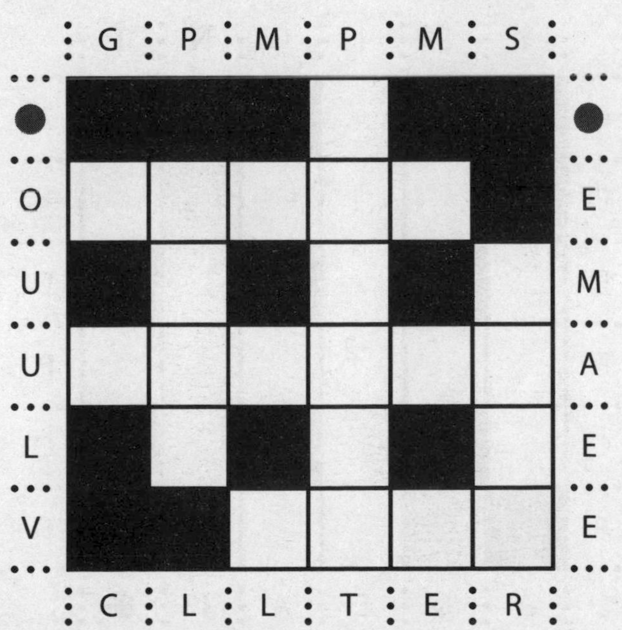

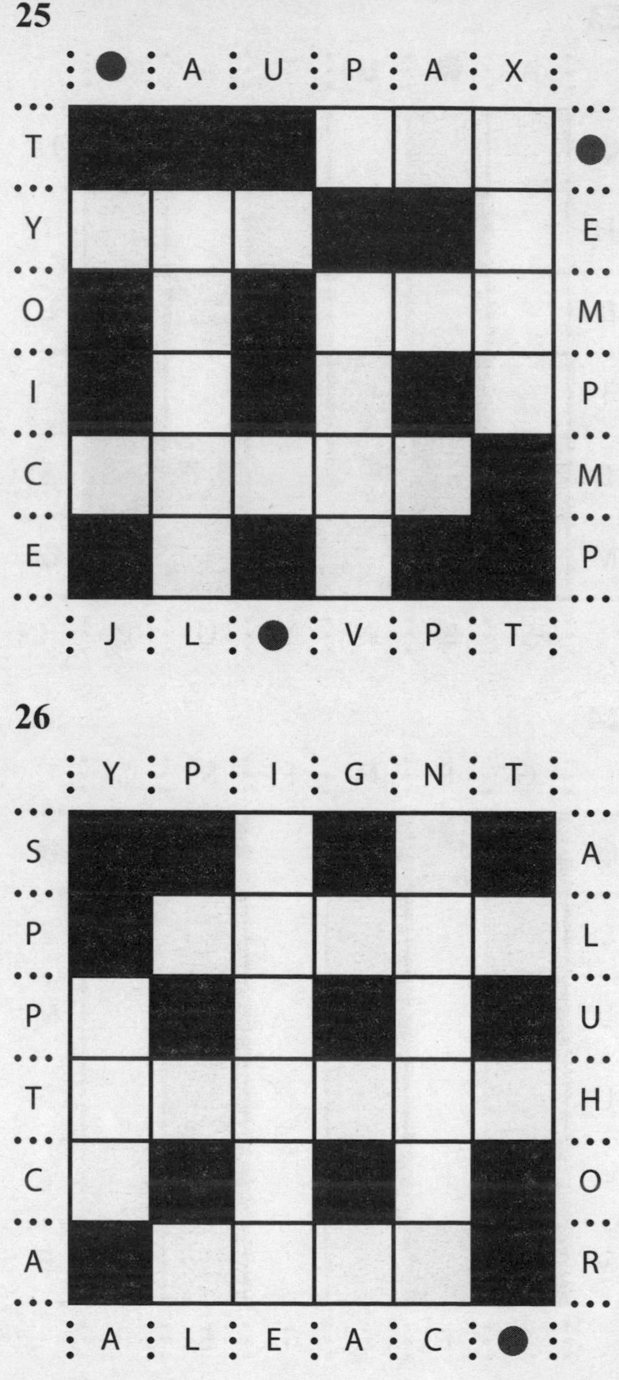
25
A U P A X
T Y O I C E
E M P M P
J L V P T
26
Y P I G N T
S P P T C A
A L U H O R
A L E A C

27

	R	R	E	A	L	●	
U							F
●							U
B							L
B							Y
L							Y
Y							D
	W	E	P	E	F	●	

28

	S	L	I	A	S	T	
N							E
S							U
O							U
K							O
P							N
E							●
	I	Y	V	C	E	S	

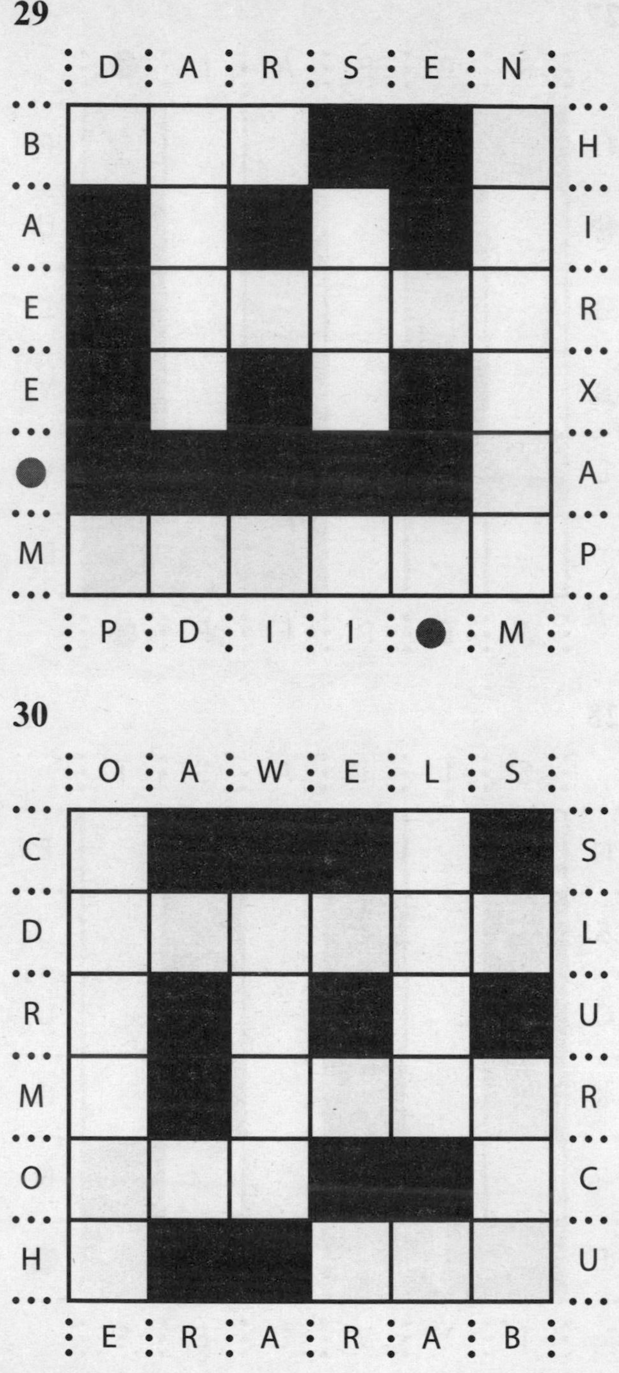
29
D A R S E N
B A E E ● M
H I R X A P
P D I I ● M
30
O A W E L S
C D R M O H
S L U R C U
E R A R A B

31

	T	S	O	C	T	●	
G	■	■	■	■		■	●
P	■					■	R
●	■	■		■		■	O
J		■					A
O		■		■		■	K
H						■	A
	●	E	L	A	W	N	

32

	M	D	G	U	I	H	
●						■	D
A		■		■		■	U
N				■		■	O
F		■	■				E
N	■	■	■	■		■	●
O	■						G
	C	I	O	S	T	X	

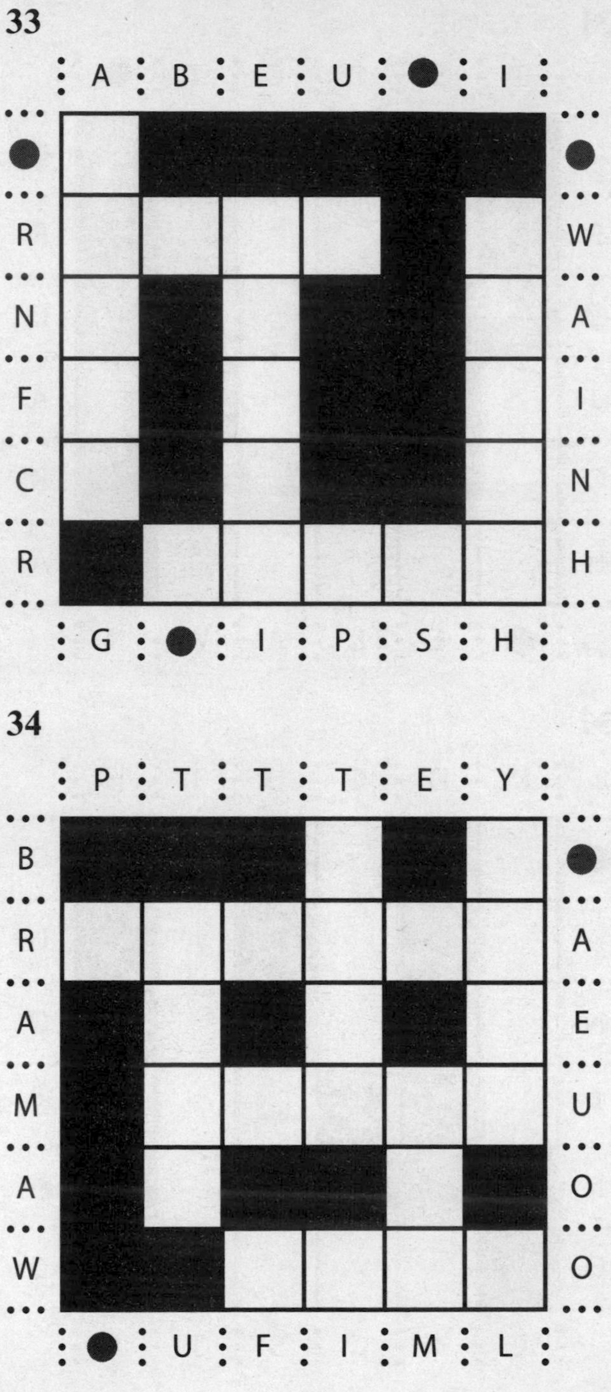
33
A B E U ● I
● R N F C R
● W A I N H
G ● I P S H
34
P T T T E Y
B R A M A W
● A E U O O
● U F I M L

35

	E	N	P	O	T	●	
A							E
O							Y
G							T
R							H
Y							V
●							N
	●	R	I	P	L	Y	

36

	Y	X	L	T	O	N	
●							C
E							I
N							M
L							E
D							R
P							S
	O	B	P	E	G	D	

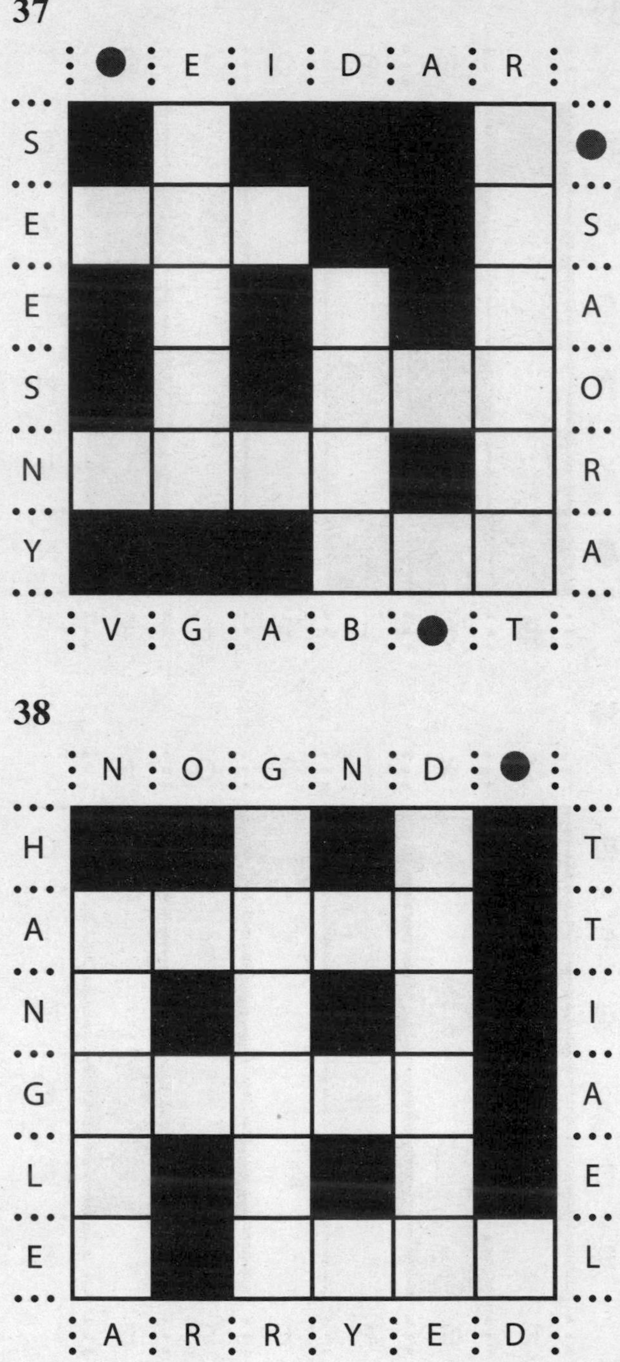
37
● E I D A R
S E E S N Y
● S A O R A
V G A B ● T
38
N O G N D ●
H A N G L E
T T I A E L
A R R Y E D

39

H	V	O	T	L	E

Left: I R E E A

Right: B C K O S

P	E	A	R	E	D

40

E	O	V	N	E	A

Left: V L U O T R

Right: C A S T A Y

P	G	A	I	S	R

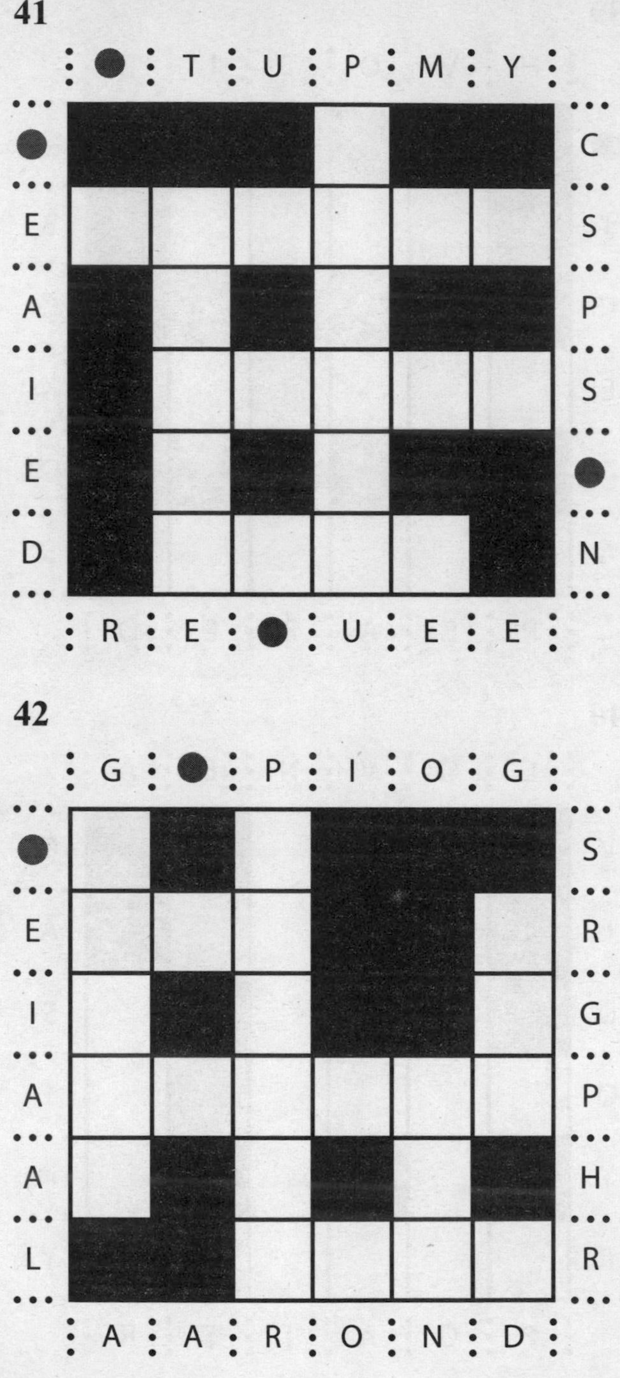
41
T U P M Y
E A I E D
C S P S N
R E U E E
42
G P I O G
E I A A L
S R G P H R
A A R O N D

43

V ● L E N E

●	S
I	T
U	E
L	X
G	●
F	E

● Y A A L Z

44

T R A N I C

B	N
A	I
T	●
O	I
V	G
E	X

N U B M ● K

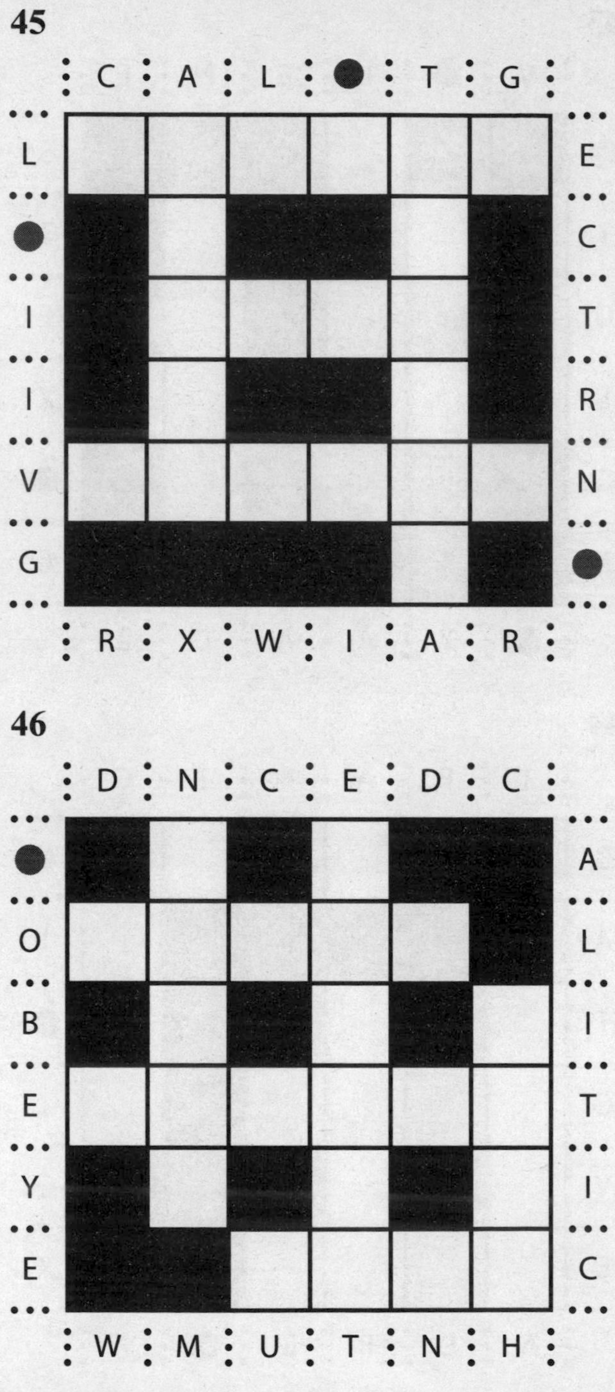
45
C A L T G
L I I V G
E C T R N
R X W I A R
46
D N C E D C
O B E Y E
A L I T I C
W M U T N H

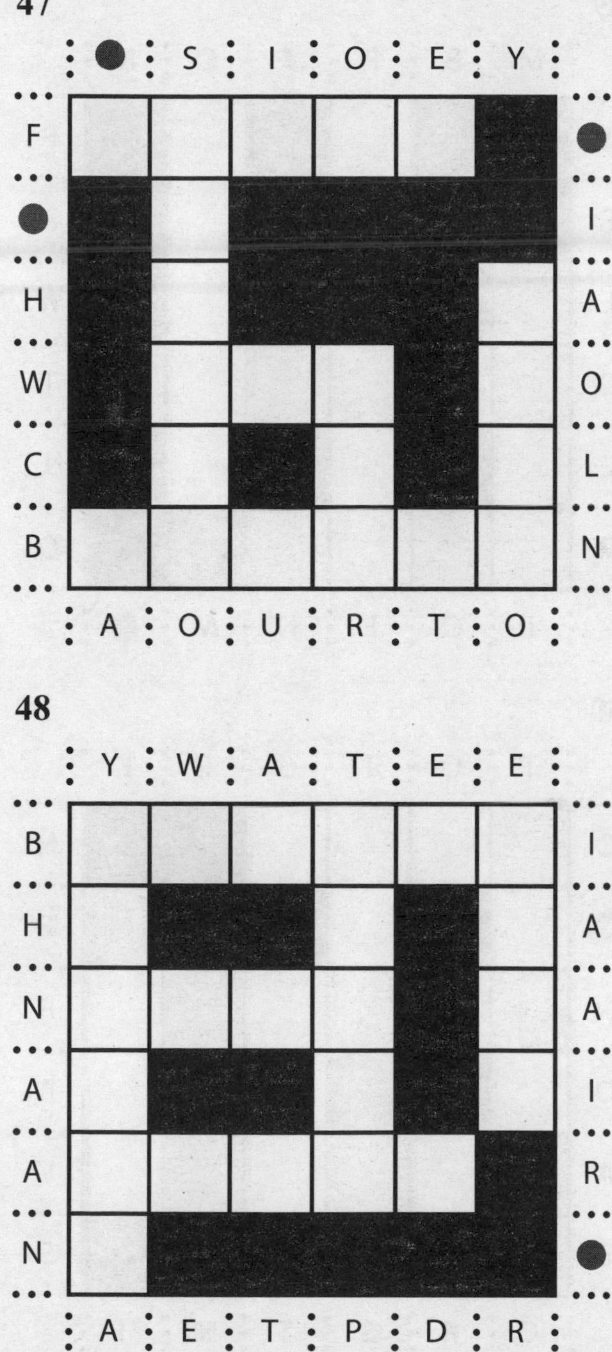
47
S I O E Y
F H W C B
I A O L N
A O U R T O
48
Y W A T E E
B H N A A N
I A A I R
A E T P D R

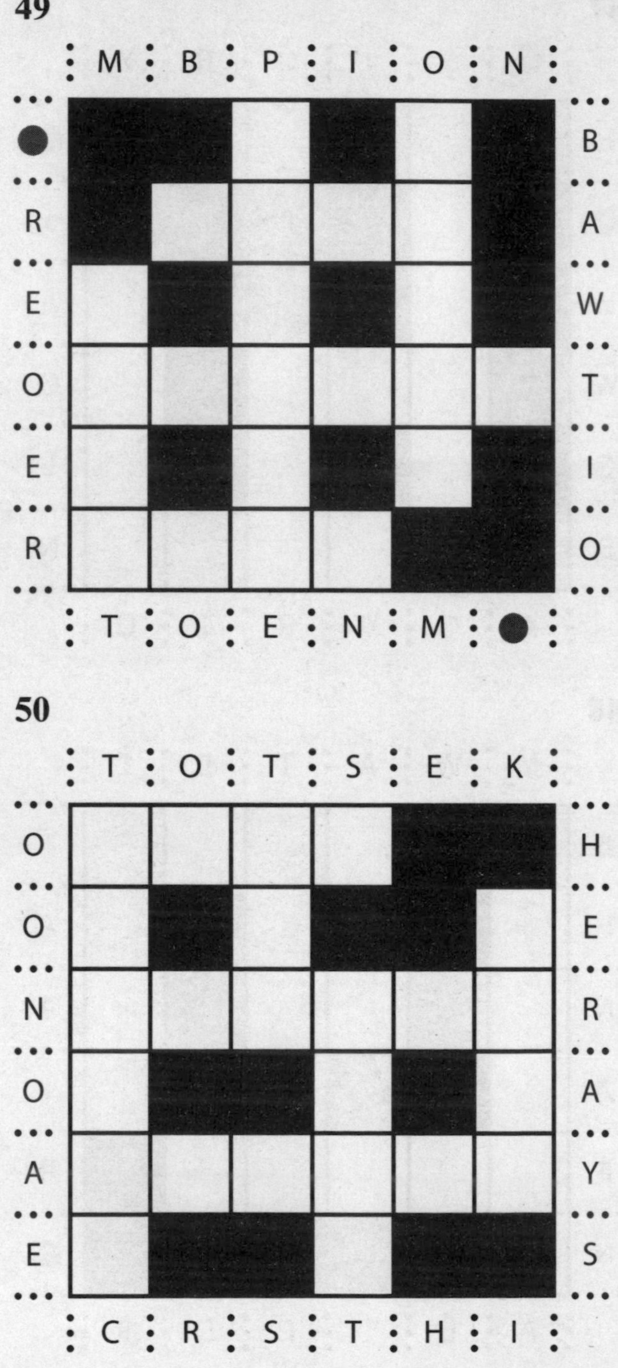
49
M B P I O N
R E O E R
B A W T I O
T O E N M
50
T O T S E K
O O N O A E
H E R A Y S
C R S T H I

51

52

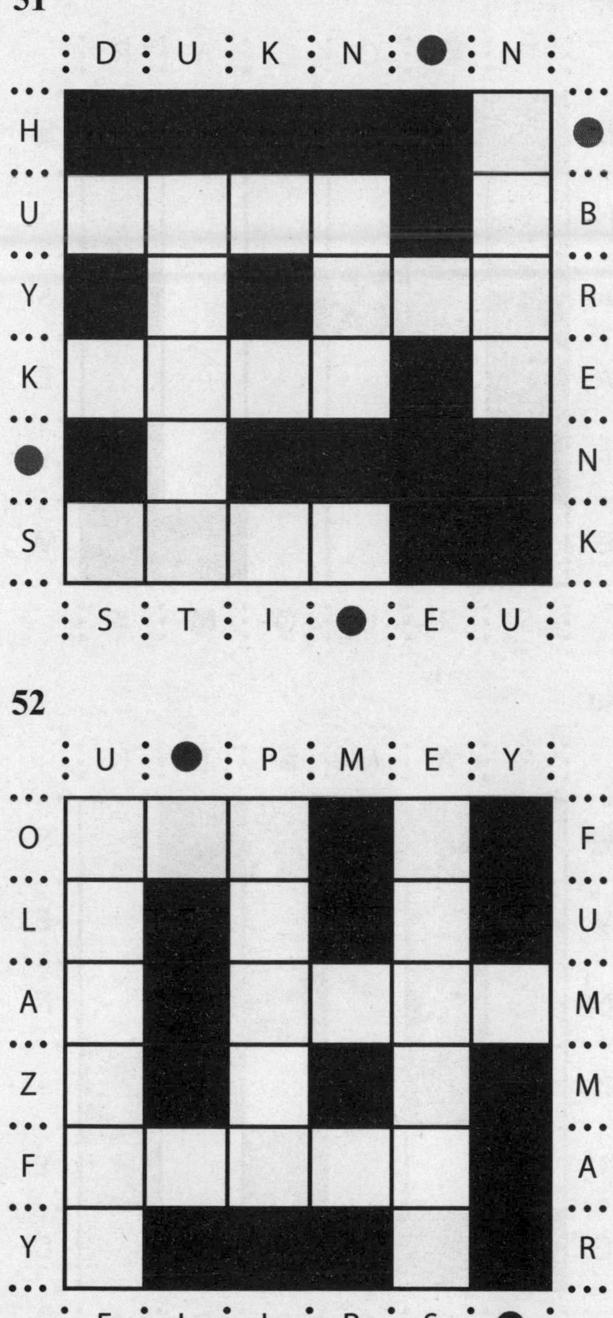

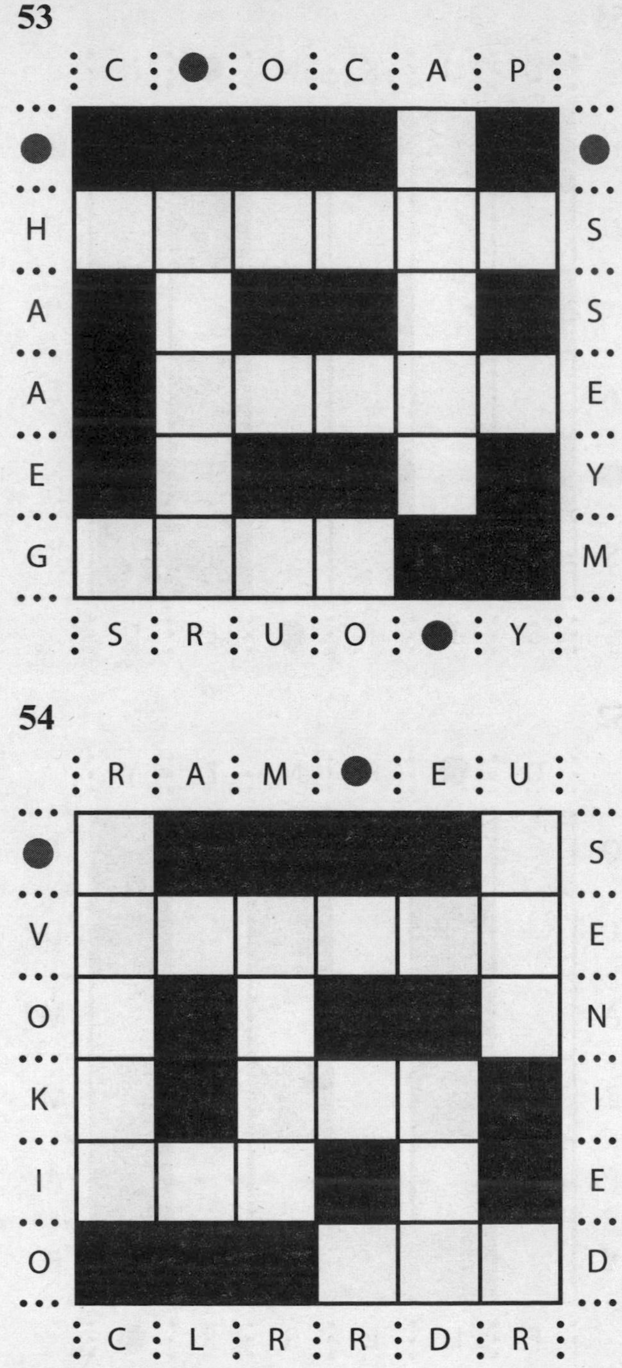
53
C O C A P
H A A E G
S S E Y M
S R U O Y
54
R A M E U
V O K I O
S E N I E D
C L R R D R

55

Top: L U S P ● E

Left: A ● N A T S

Right: ● A O O F T

Bottom: O I T I L D

56

Top: C I E K A M

Left: ● V O O U S

Right: A L E R G E

Bottom: P H N I R L

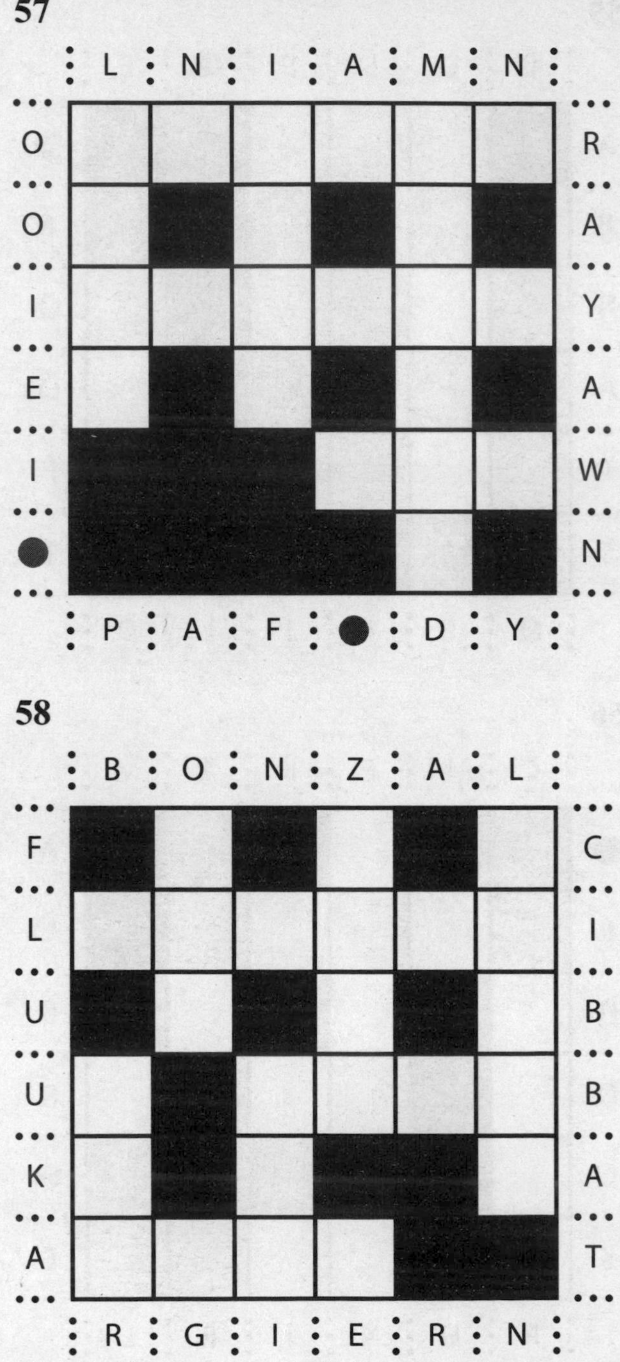
57
L N I A M N
O O I E I
R A Y A W N
P A F D Y
58
B O N Z A L
F L U U K A
C I B B A T
R G I E R N

59

	●	D	U	O	A	L	
●							L
B							R
A							●
R							O
A							U
T							N
	●	R	A	T	Y	P	

60

	I	H	I	U	T	E	
●							W
A							I
A							S
N							K
E							●
K							E
	N	U	T	F	F	V	

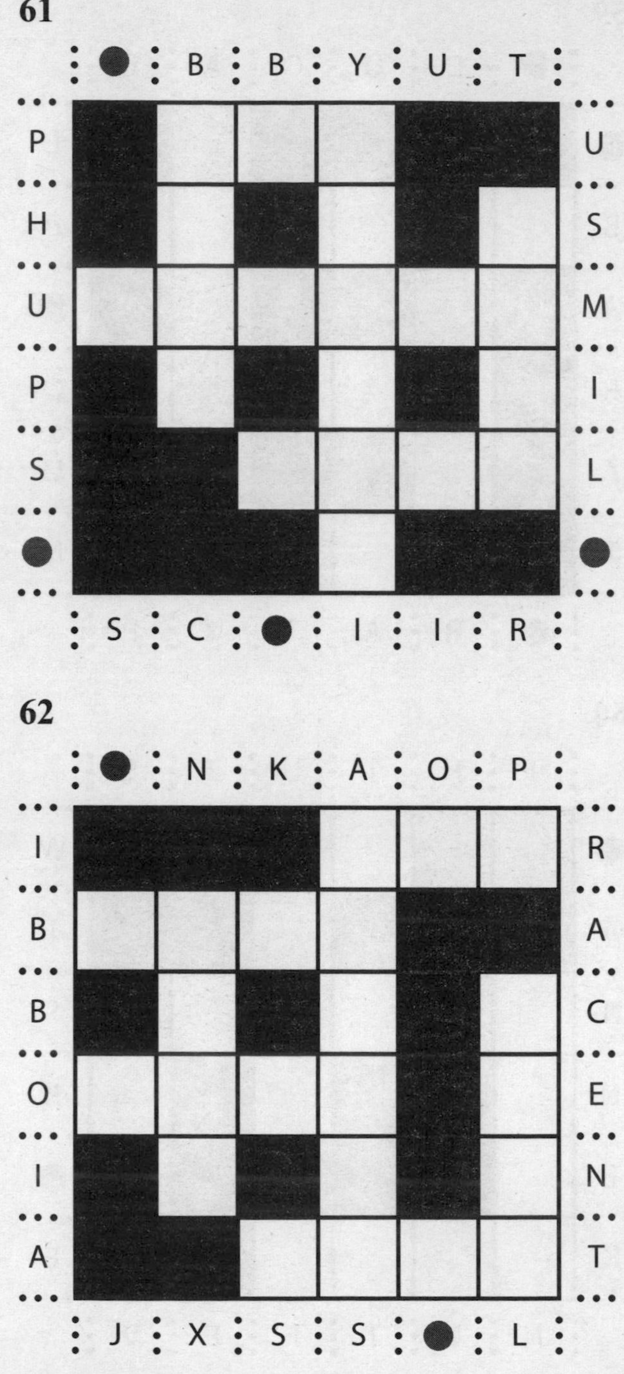
61
B B Y U T
P H U P S
U S M I L
S C I I R
62
N K A O P
I B B O I A
R A C E N T
J X S S L

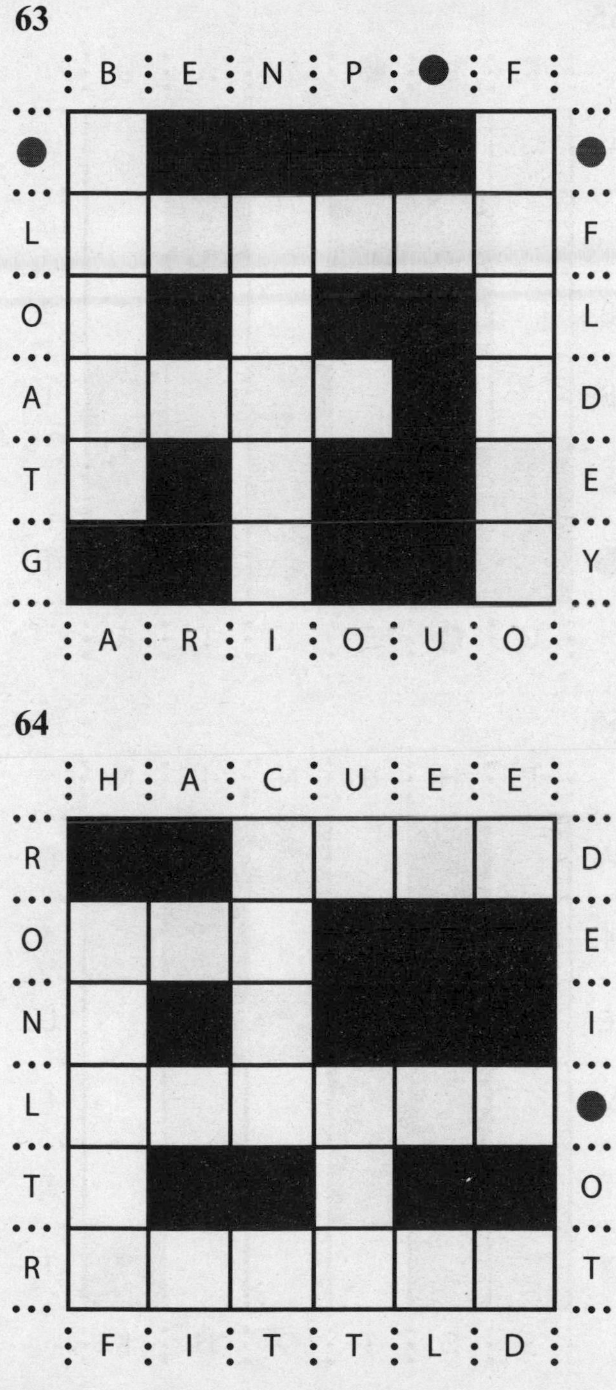
63
B E N P F
L O A T G
F L D E Y
A R I O U O
64
H A C U E E
R O N L T R
D E I O T
F I T T L D

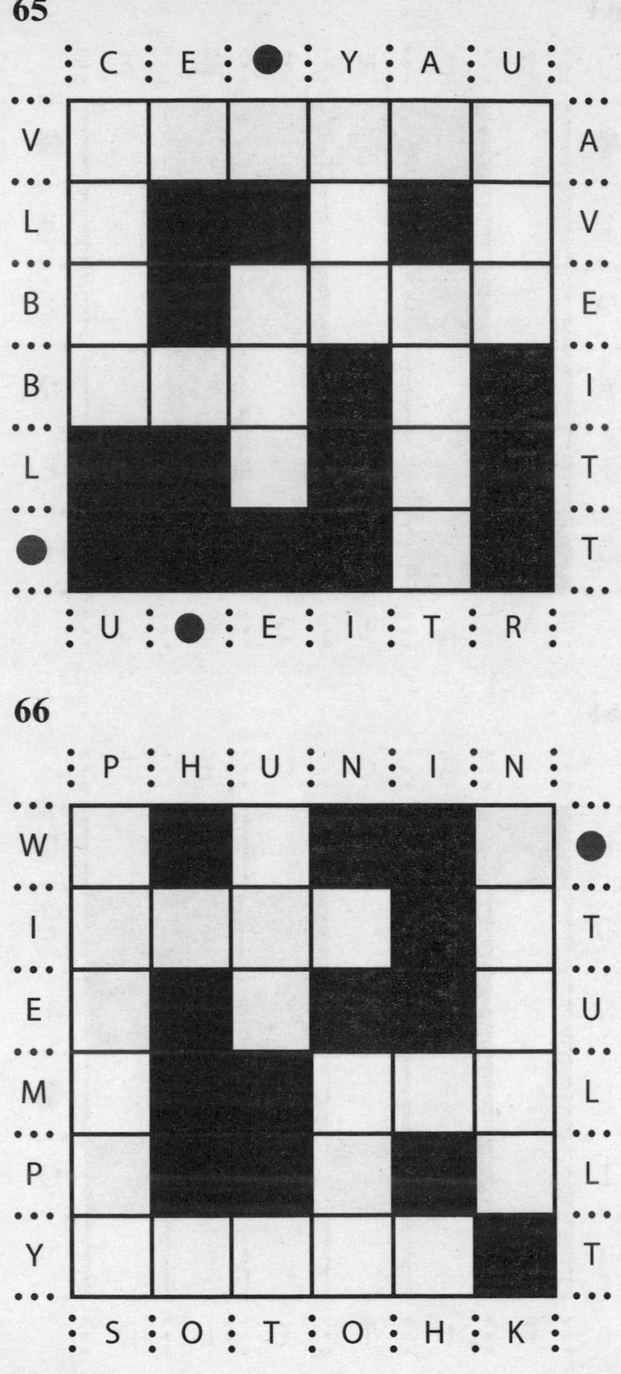
65
C E Y A U
V L B B L
A V E I T T
U E I T R
66
P H U N I N
W I E M P Y
T U L L T
S O T O H K

67

68

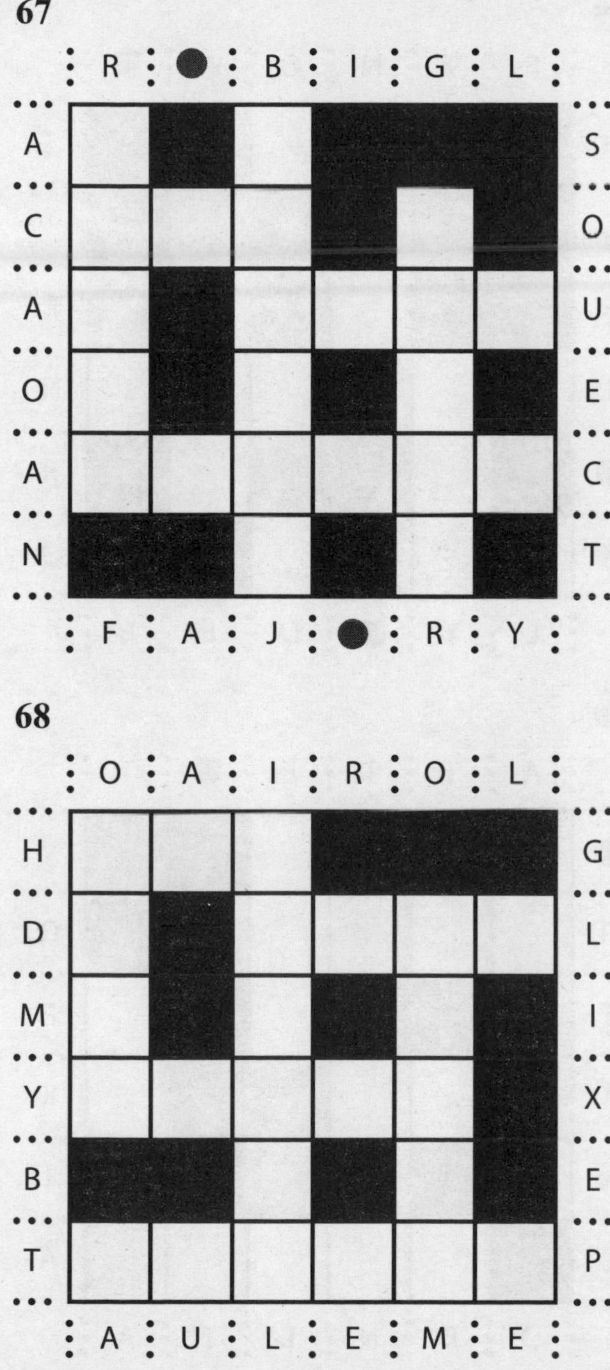

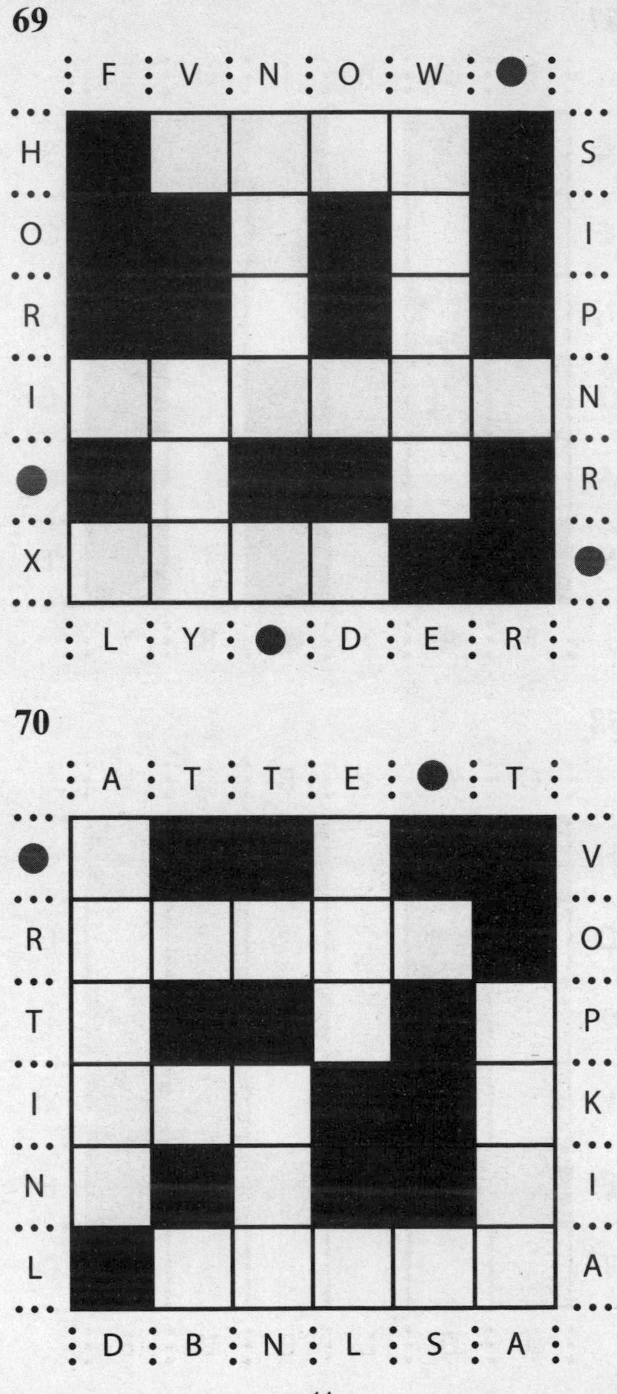
69
F V N O W
H O R I X
S I P N R
L Y D E R
70
A T T E T
R T I N L
V O P K I A
D B N L S A

71

● U A T V E

●							J
E							●
H							R
I							O
S							L
R							L

T ● F I A N

72

B E V P R M

M							S
O							E
O							R
U							M
●							S
T							O

● R E E U B

Lexica

Polygon

Scrabble™ Challenge

Word Watch

Codeword

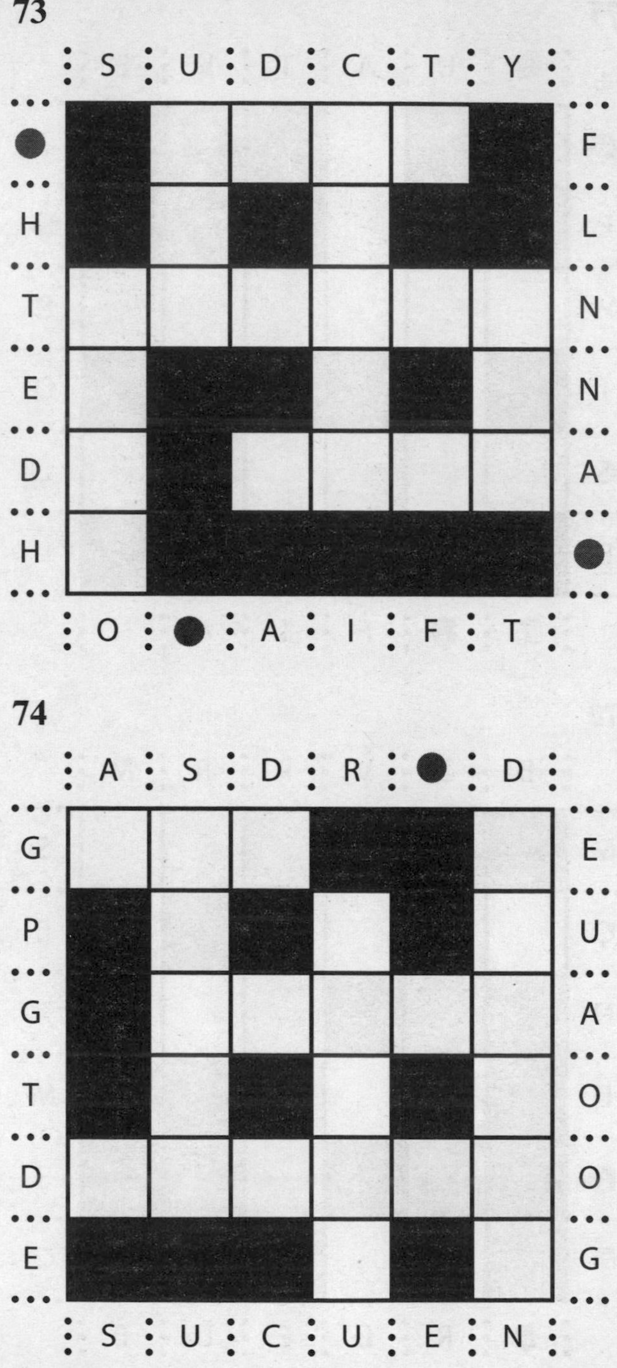

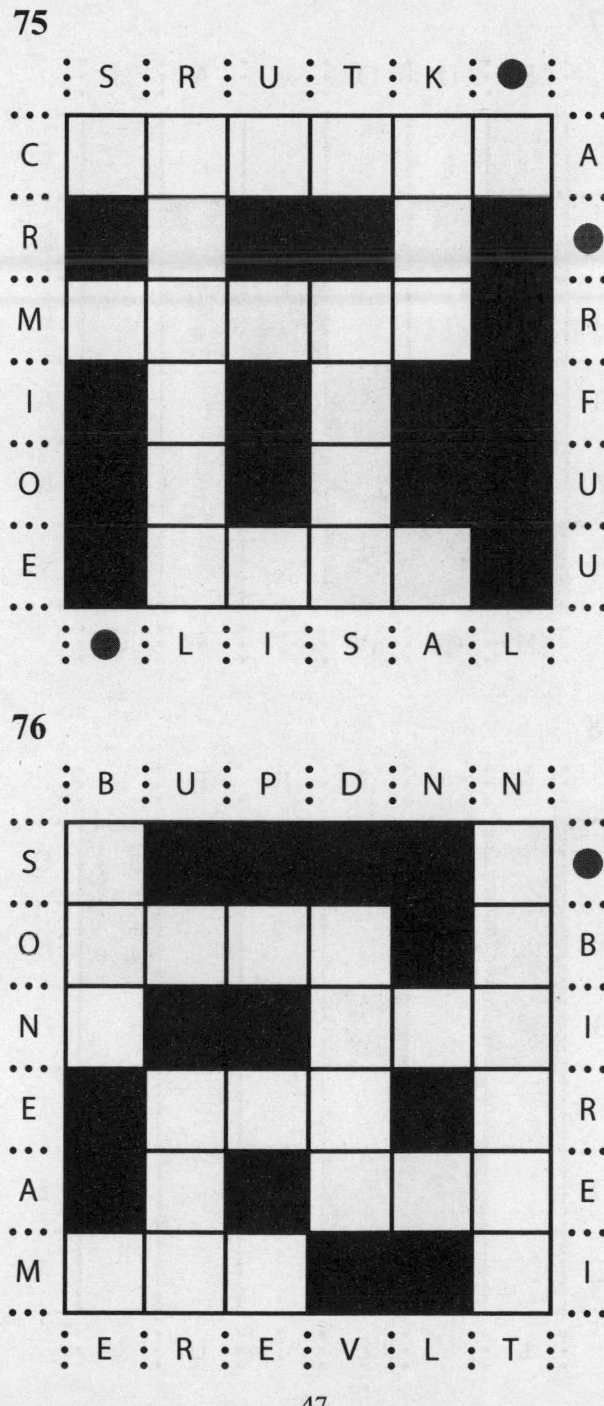
75
S R U T K
C R M I O E
A R F U U
L I S A L
76
B U P D N N
S O N E A M
B I R E I
E R E V L T

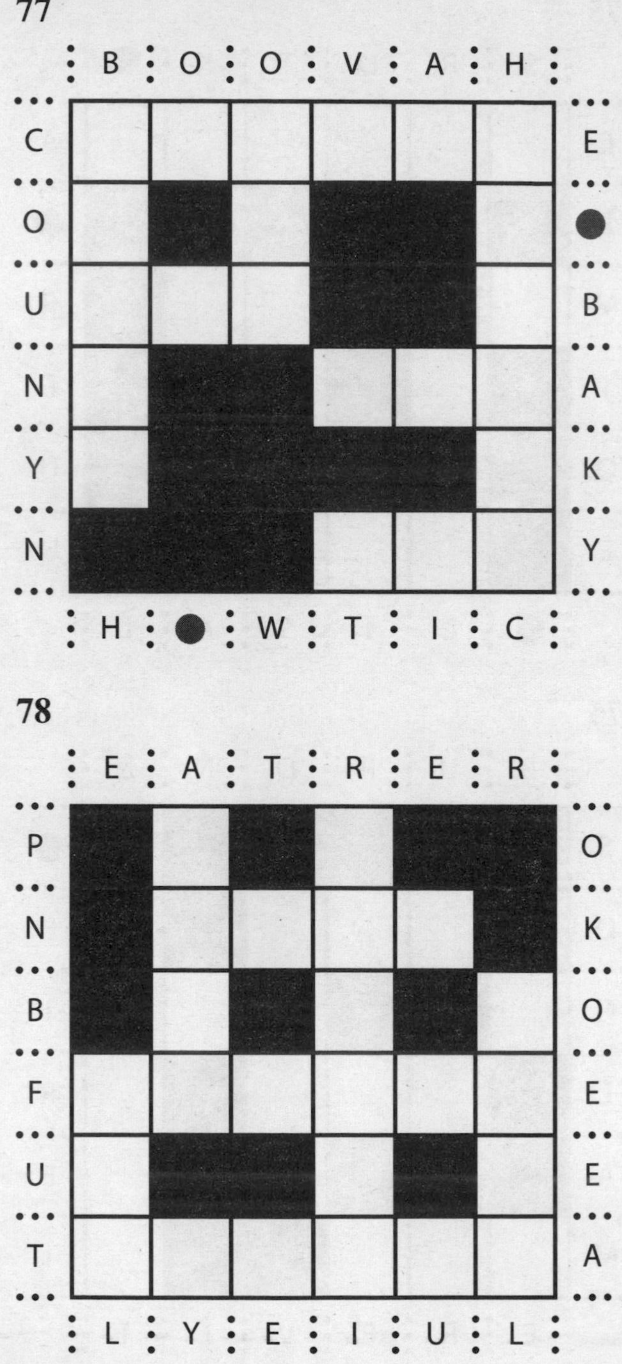
77
B O O V A H
C O U N Y N
E B A K Y
H W T I C
78
E A T R E R
P N B F U T
O K O E E A
L Y E I U L

79

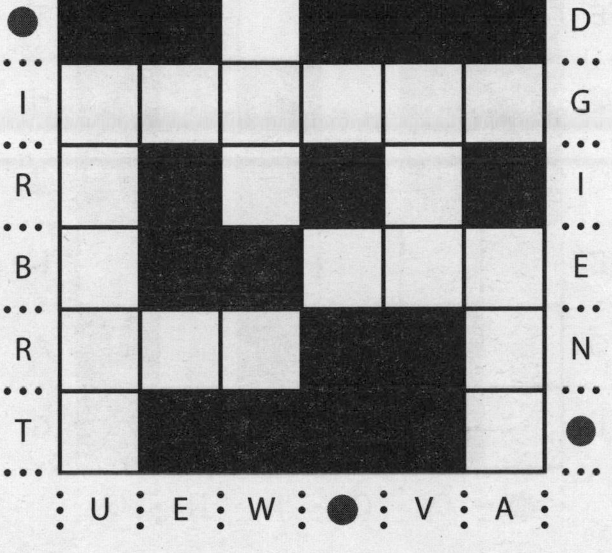

80

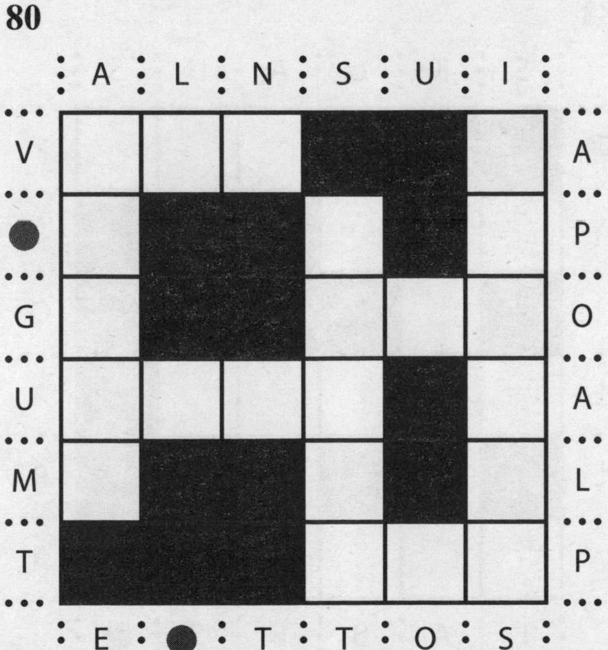

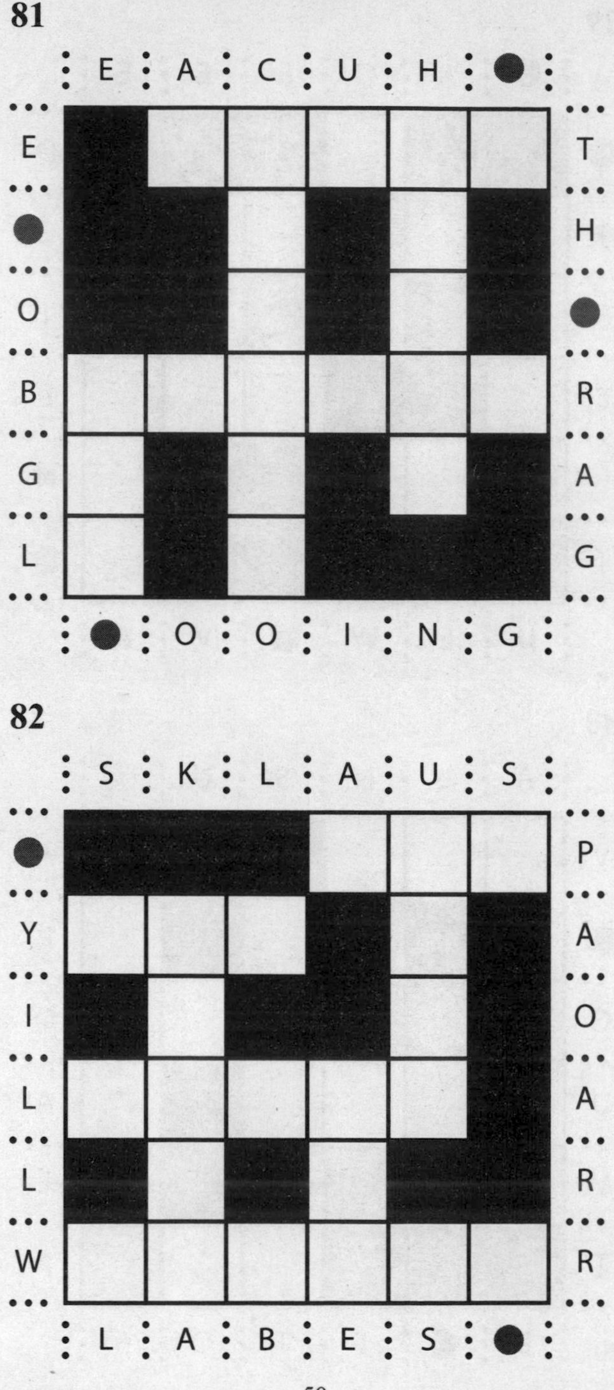
81
E A C U H
E O B G L
T H R A G
O O I N G
82
S K L A U S
Y I L L W
P A O A R R
L A B E S

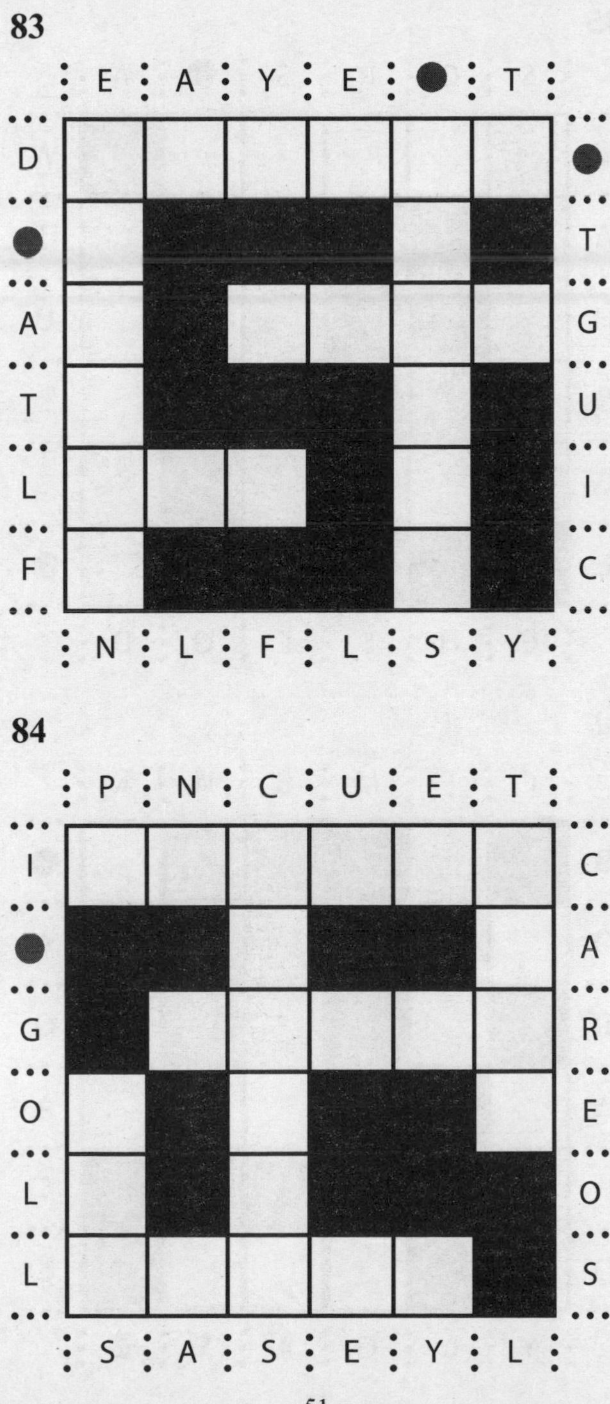

83
E A Y E T
D A T L F
T G U I C
N L F L S Y
84
P N C U E T
I G O L L
C A R E O S
S A S E Y L

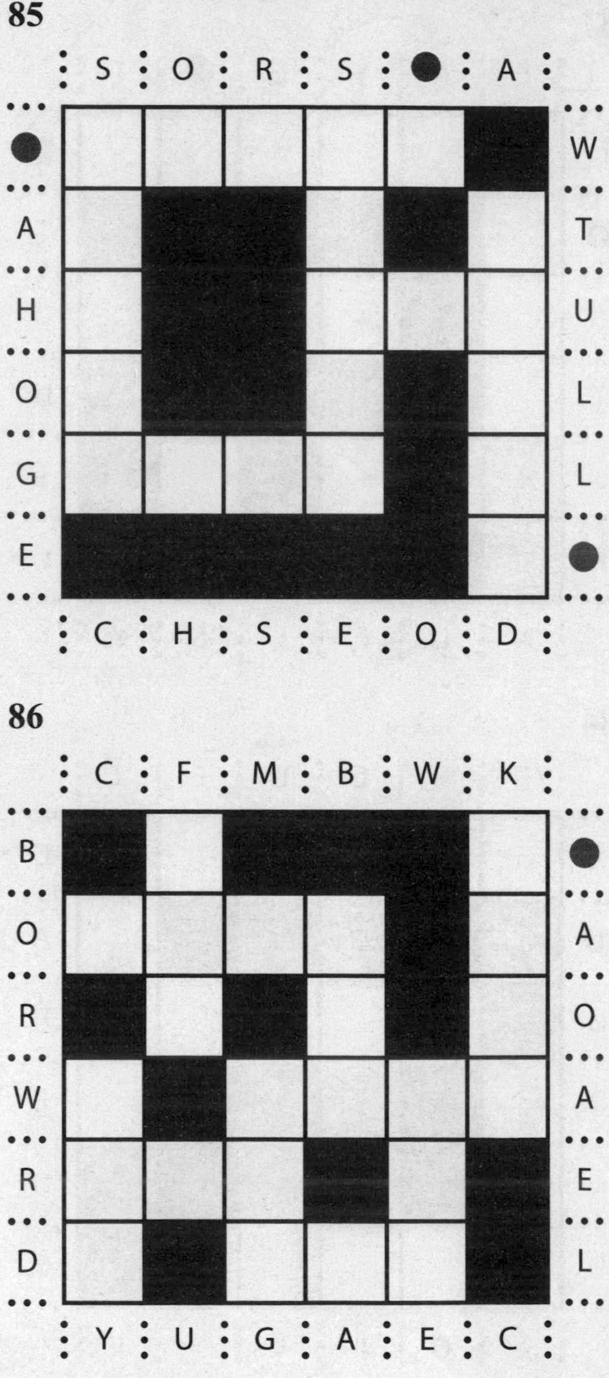
85
S O R S ● A
● A H O G E
W T U L L ●
C H S E O D
86
C F M B W K
B O R W R D
● A O A E L
Y U G A E C

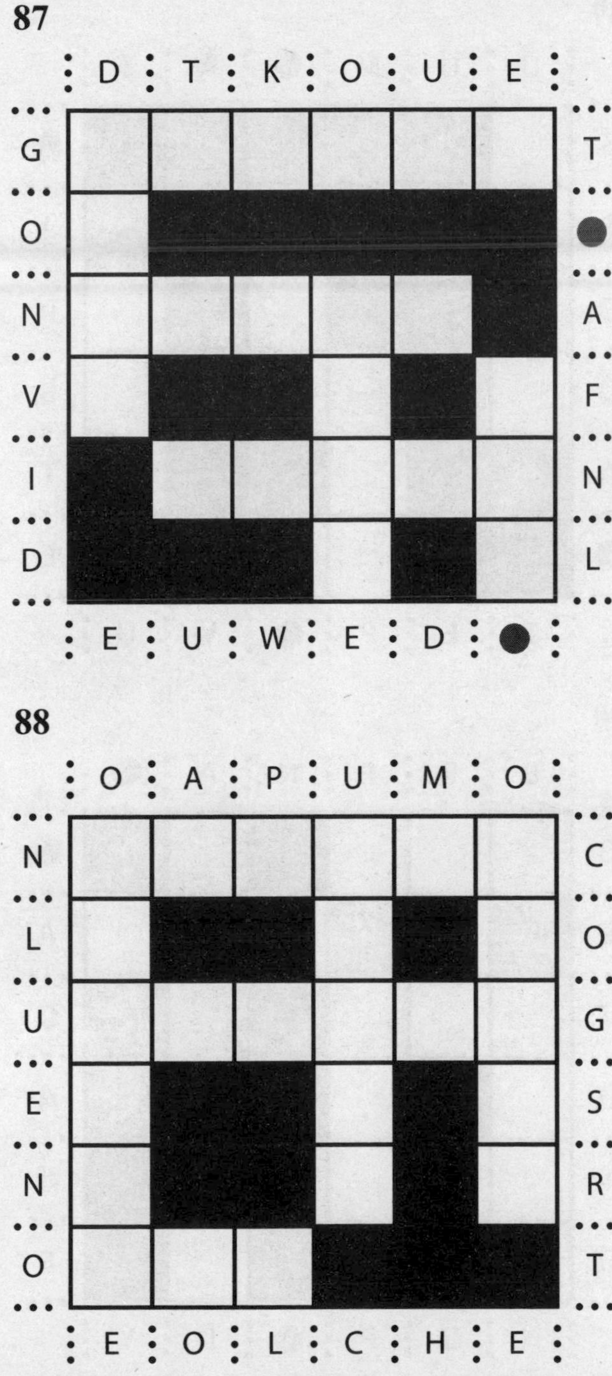
87
D T K O U E
G O N V I D
T A F N L
E U W E D
88
O A P U M O
N L U E N O
C O G S R T
E O L C H E

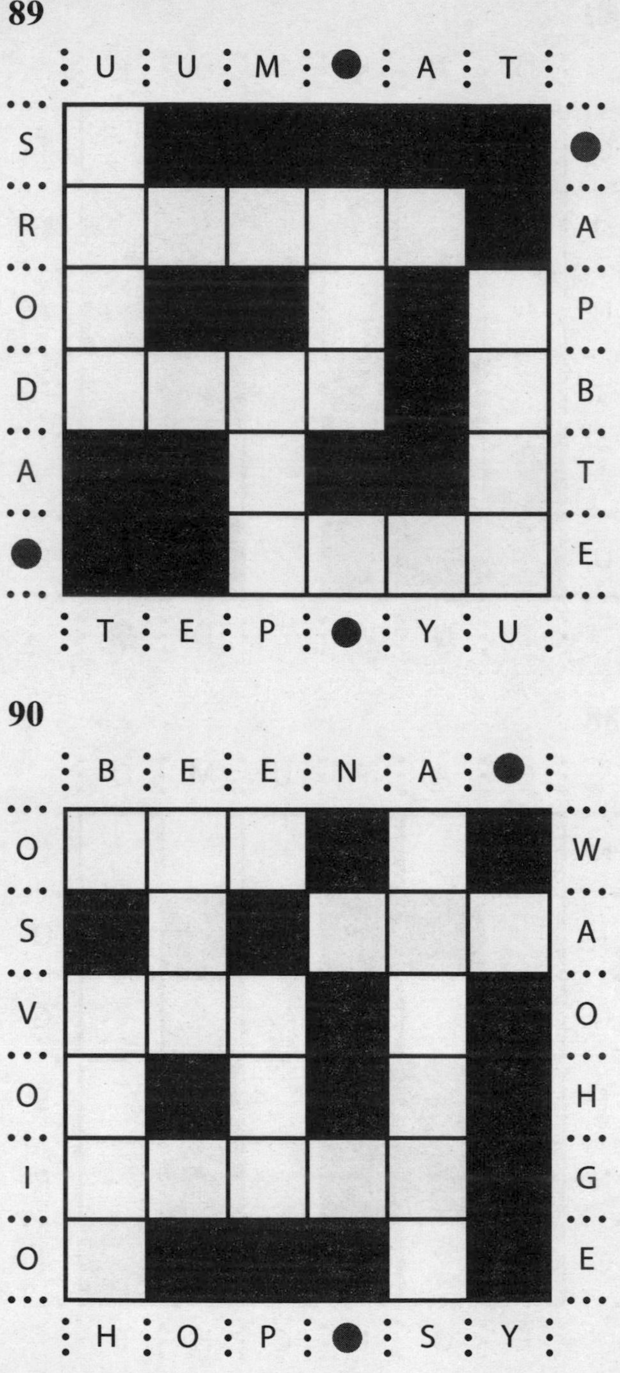
89
U U M A T
S R O D A
A P B T E
T E P Y U
90
B E E N A
O S V O I O
W A O H G E
H O P S Y

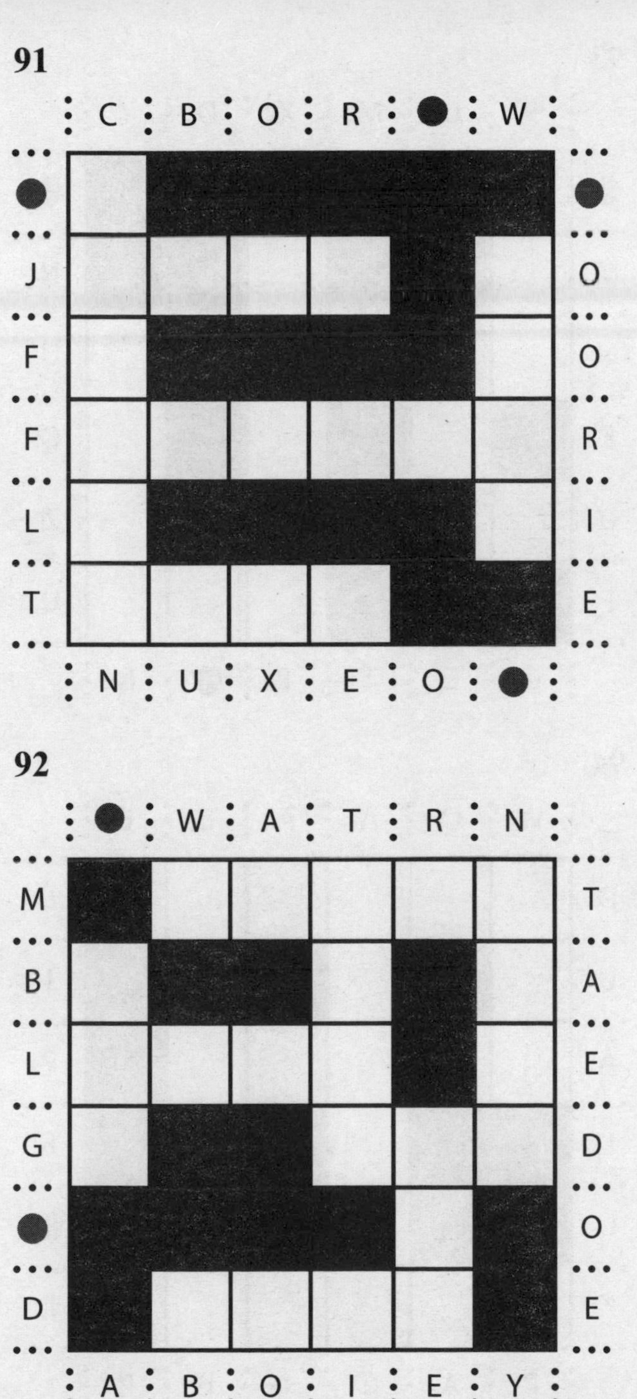
91
C B O R W
J F F L T
O O R I E
N U X E O
92
W A T R N
M B L G D
T A E D O E
A B O I E Y

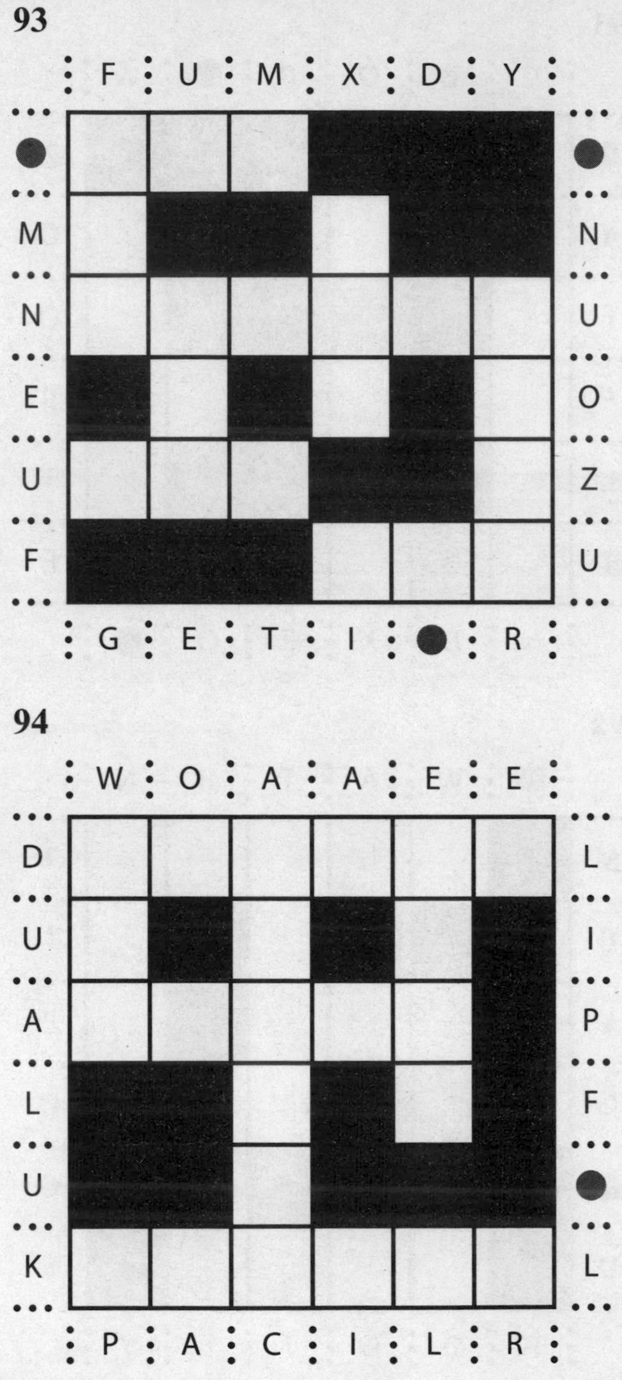
93
F U M X D Y
M N E U F
N U O Z U
G E T I R
94
W O A A E E
D U A L U K
L I P F L
P A C I L R

95

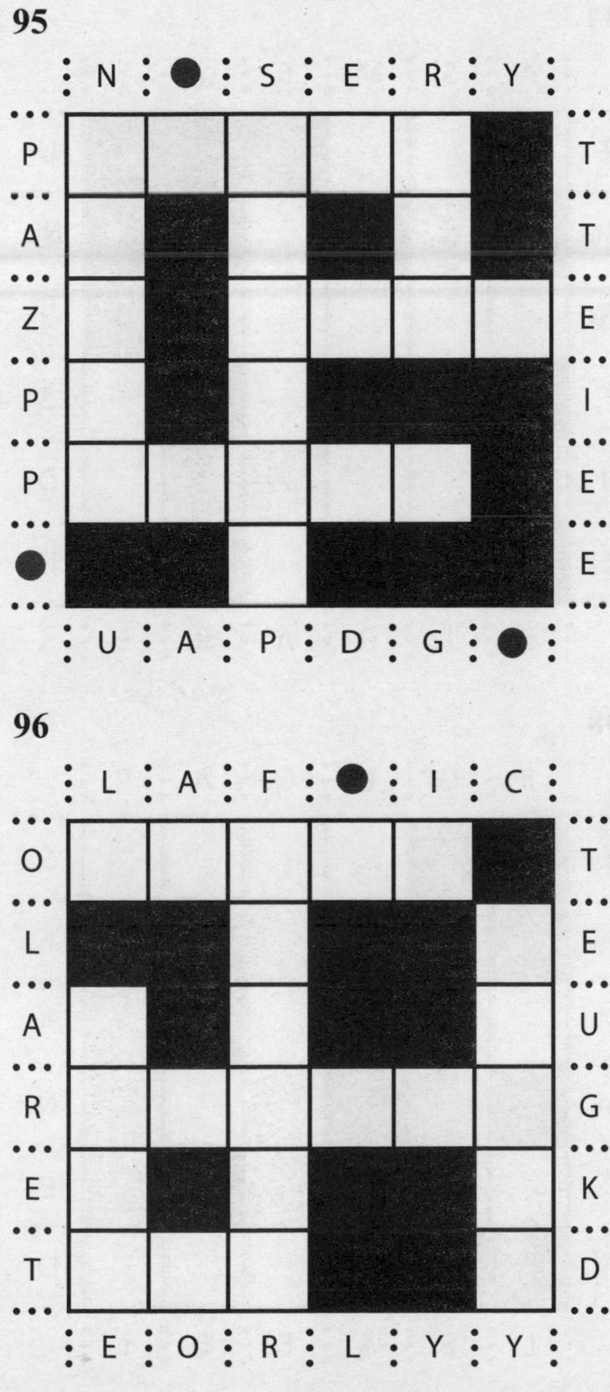

97

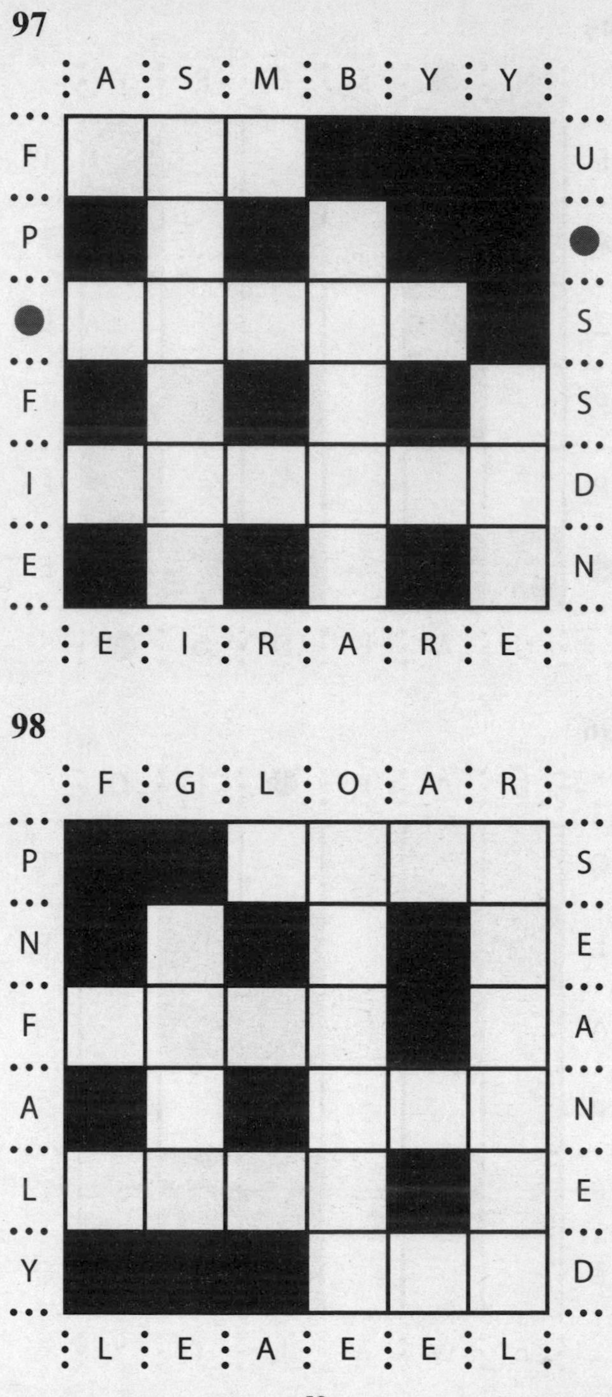

99

	A	●	F	F	C	L	
H				■	■		M
●	■		■	■	■		G
O	■				■		U
E		■		■	■		S
H							T
H		■	■	■	■	■	●
	S	A	E	N	●	B	

100

	S	C	K	T	L	O	
S	■	■	■				U
A				■	■		S
G	■		■	■	■		●
R	■						A
●	■		■	■		■	E
R							L
	A	W	I	J	I	Y	

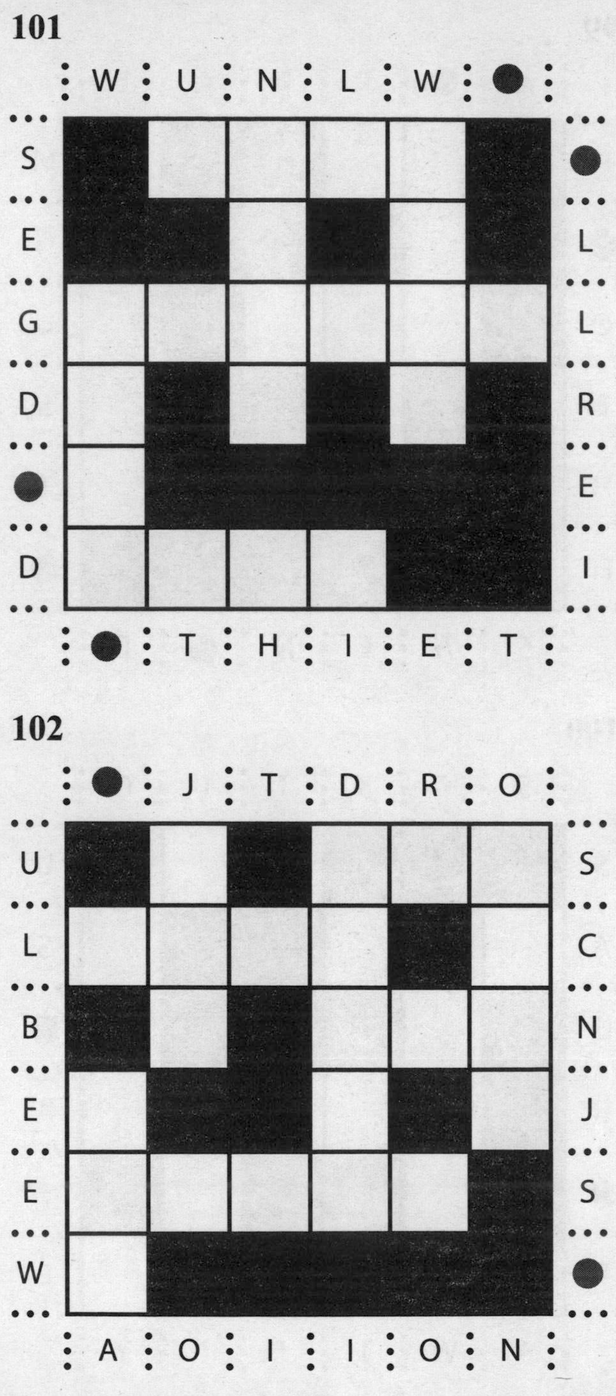
101
W U N L W
S E G D D
L L R E I
T H I E T
102
J T D R O
U L B E E W
S C N J S
A O I I O N

103

M O L C E P

S S ● E R E

● I C A G P

A H E T K ●

104

S K I D L V

R A I I O R

H ● A N E P

W A N A D R

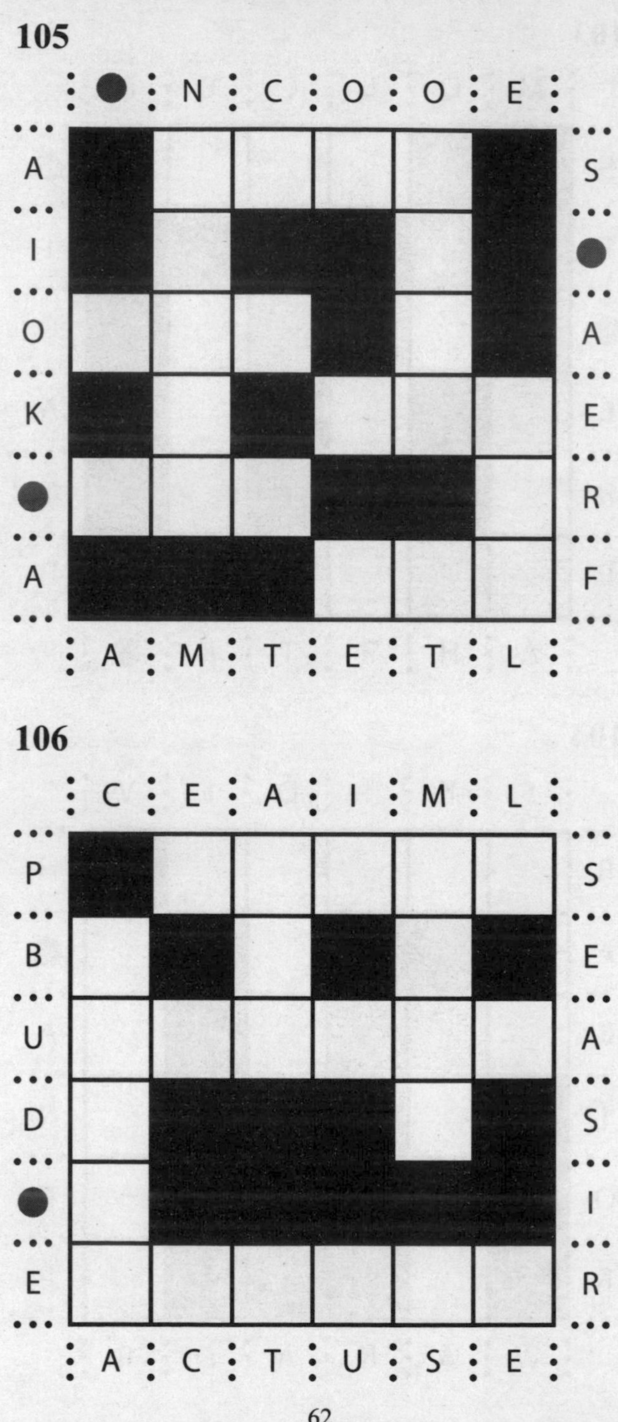
105
N C O O E
A I O K A
S A E R F
A M T E T L
106
C E A I M L
P B U D E
S E A S I R
A C T U S E

107

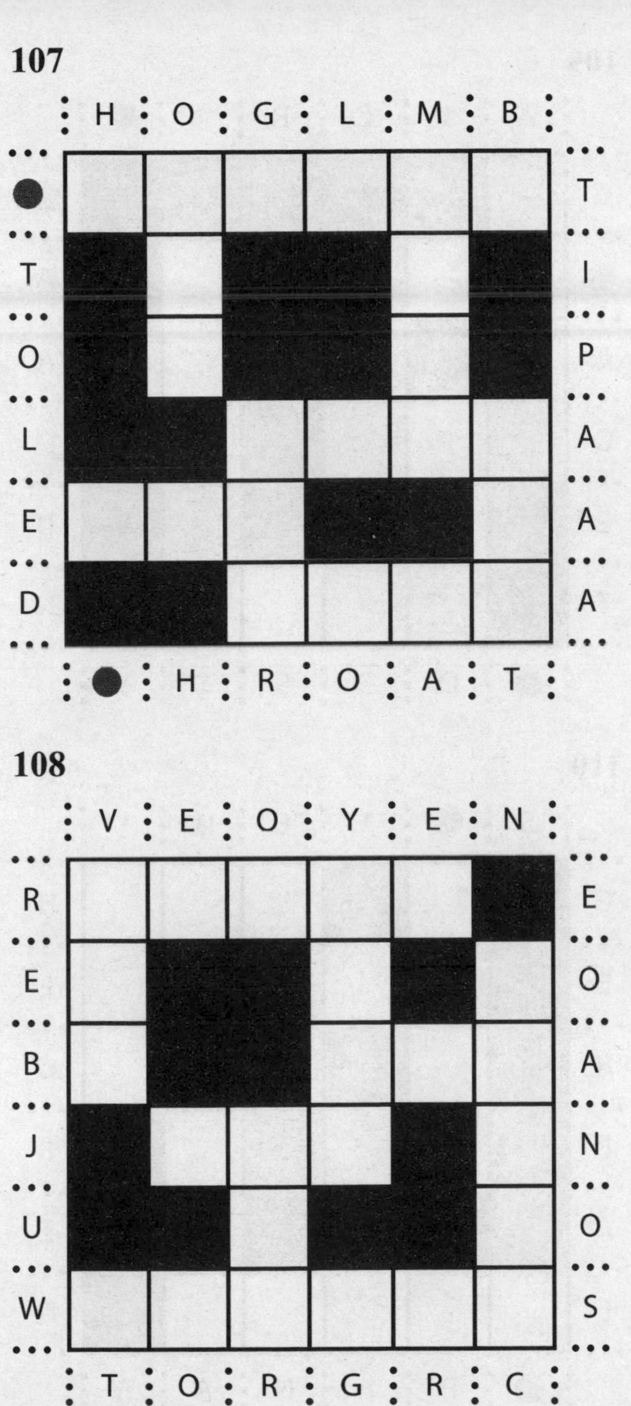

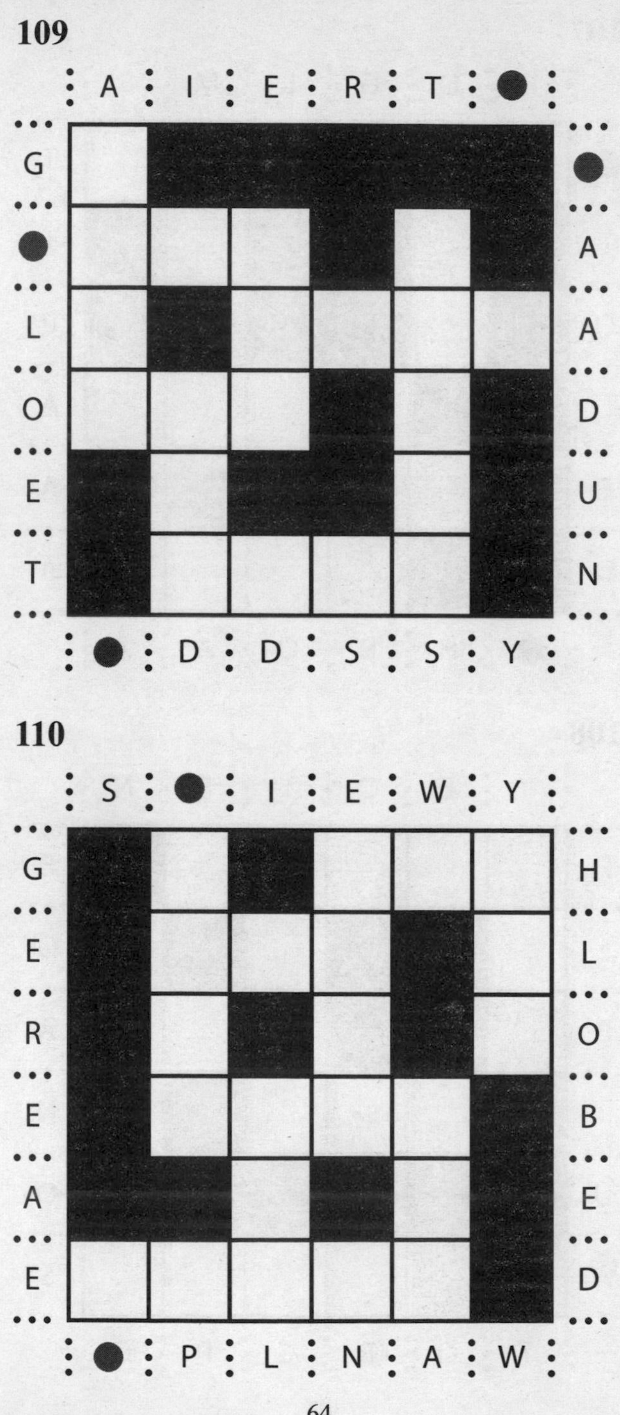
109
A I E R T
G L O E T
A A D U N
D D S S Y
110
S I E W Y
G E R E A E
H L O B E D
P L N A W

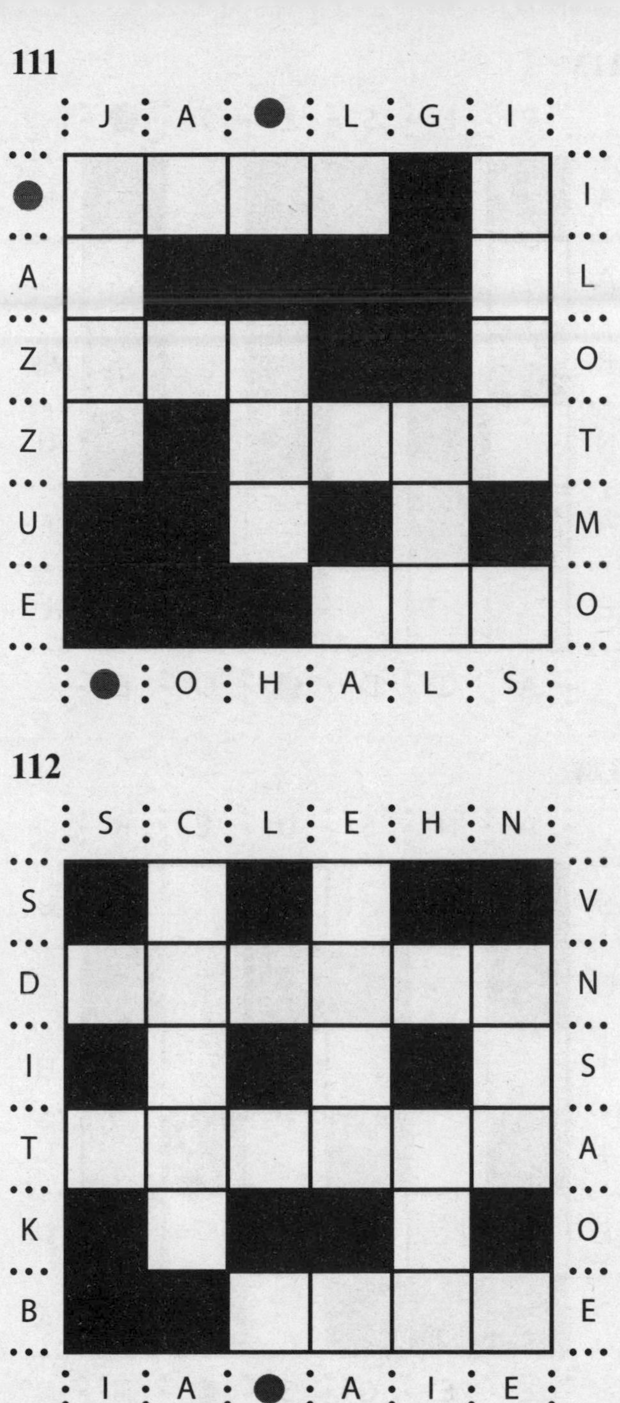
111
J A L G I
A Z Z U E
I L O T M O
O H A L S
112
S C L E H N
S D I T K B
V N S A O E
I A A I E

113

114

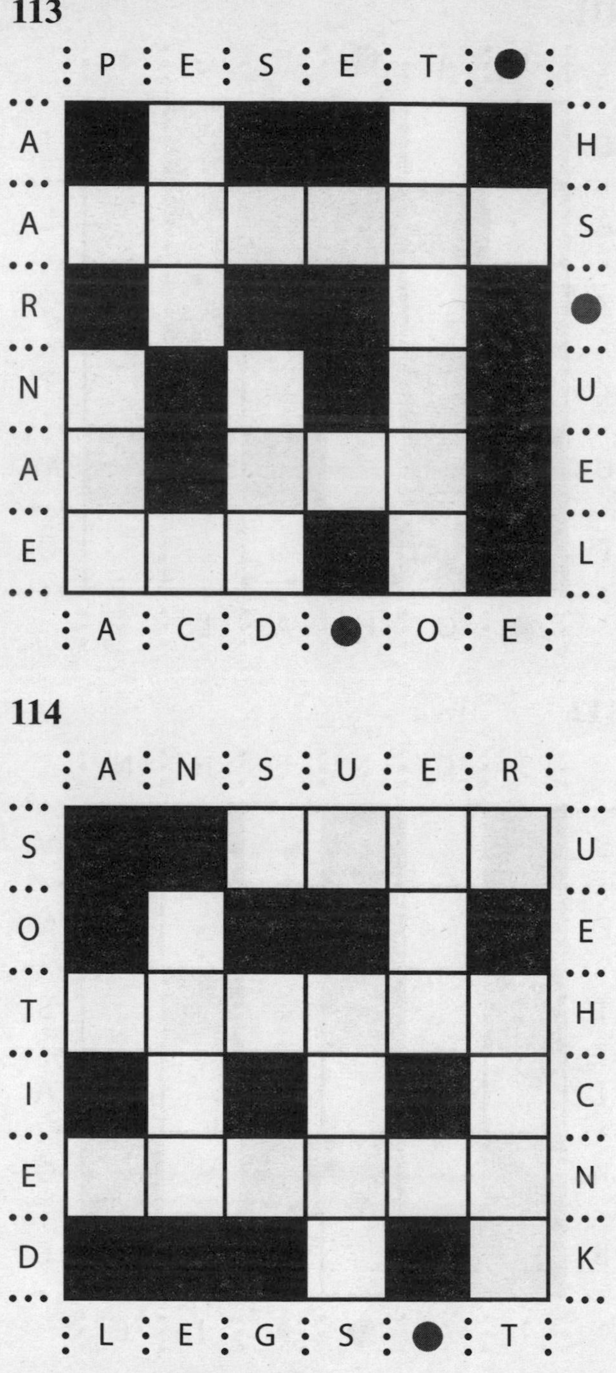

115

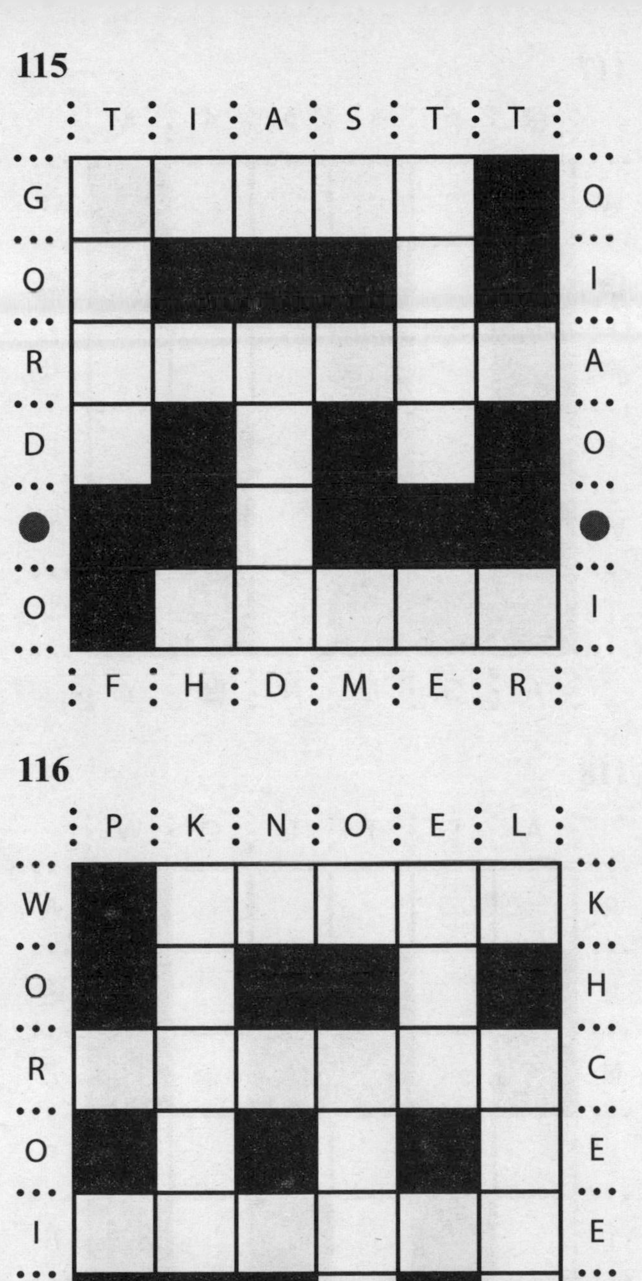

116

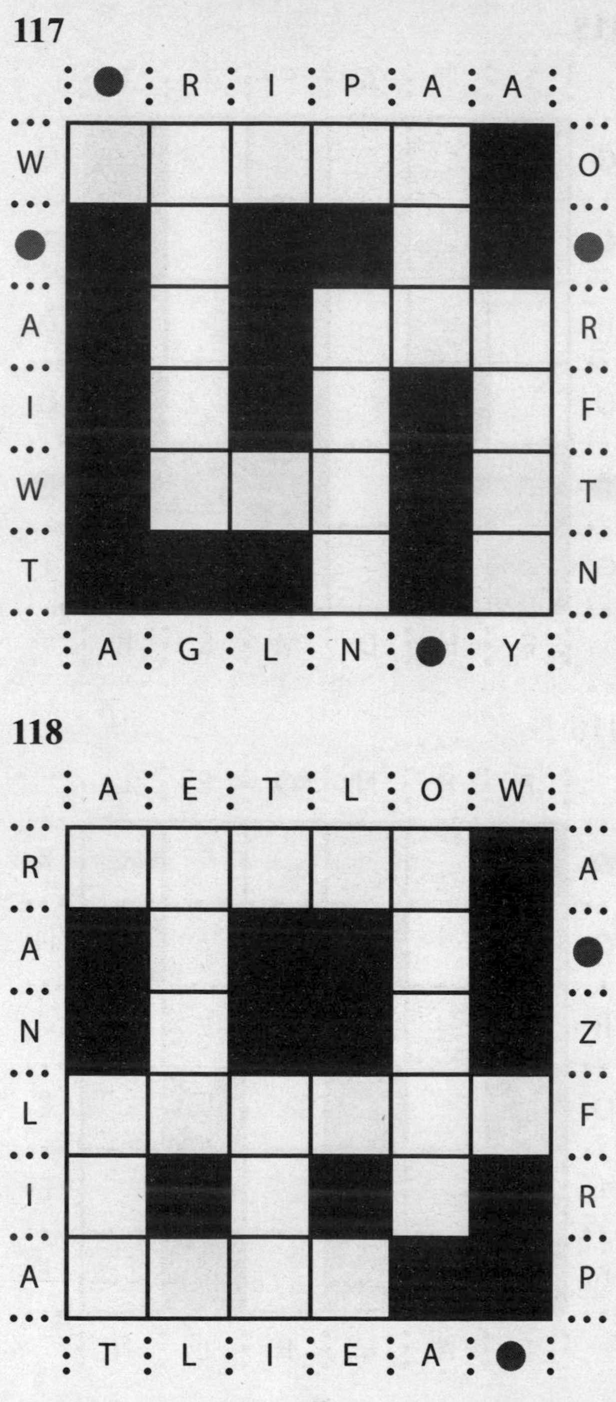
117
R I P A A
W A I W T
O R F T N
A G L N Y
118
A E T L O W
R A N L I A
A Z F R P
T L I E A

119

S D ● P A Y

● L A O E Y

F P H ● H K

O U G A S ●

120

I A T D R U

● S P U L E

N O T C ● L

L N L O A G

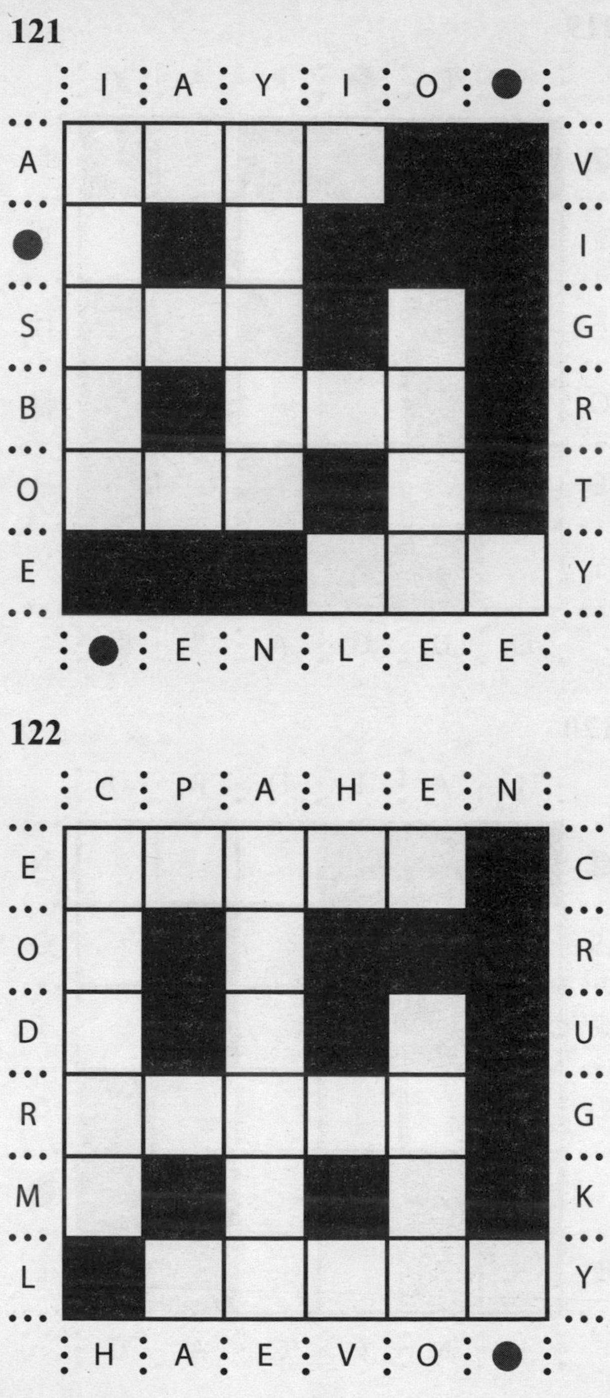
121
I A Y I O ●
A ● S B O E
V I G R T Y
● E N L E E
122
C P A H E N
E O D R M L
C R U G K Y
H A E V O ●

123

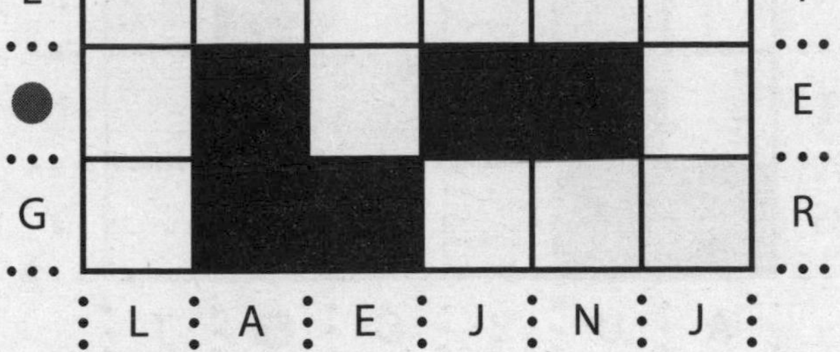

124

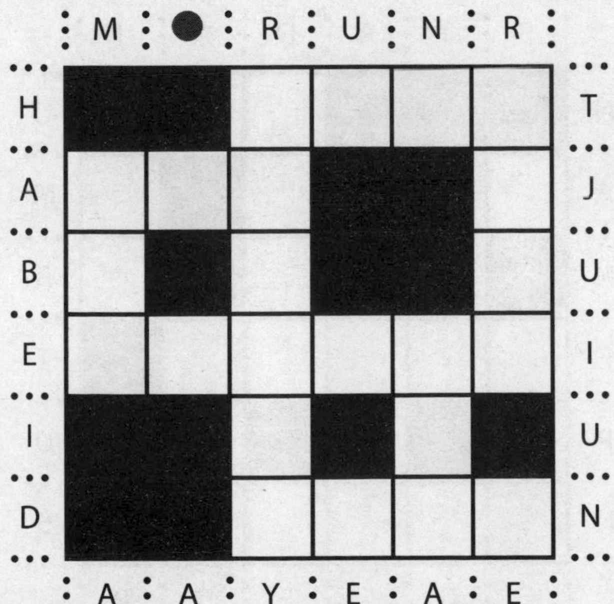

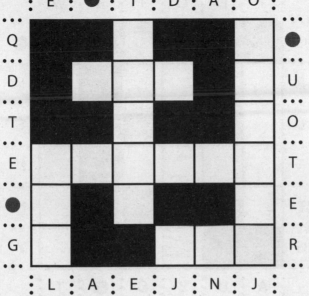

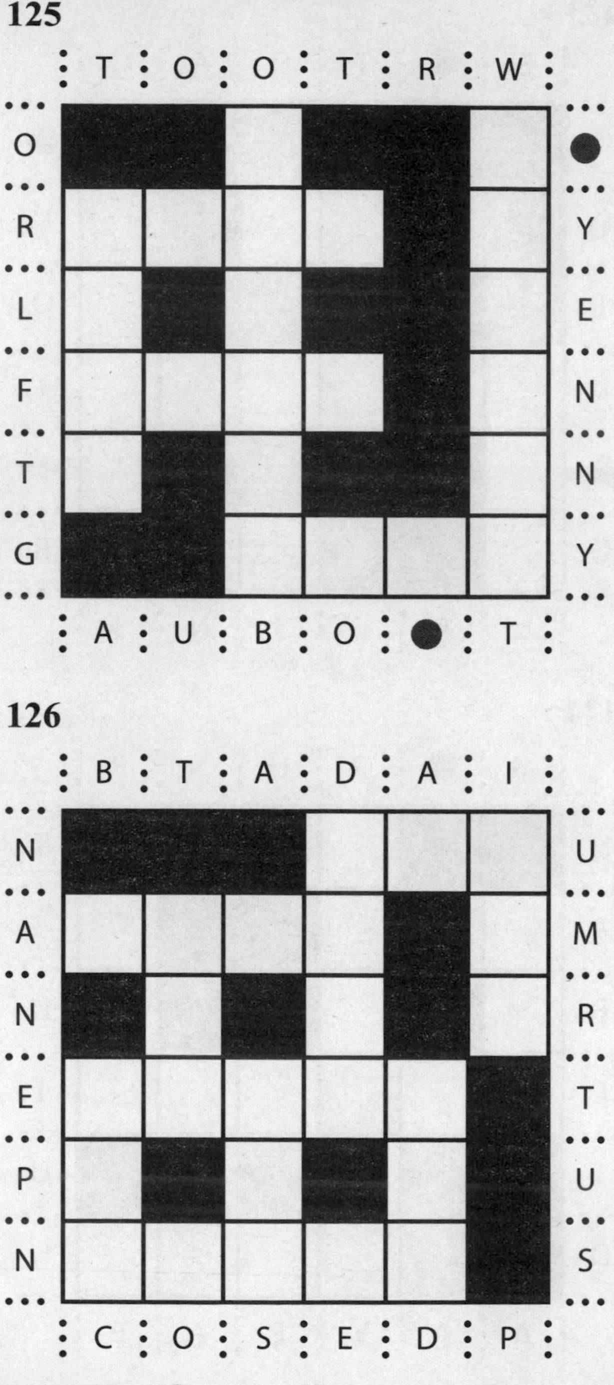
125
T O O T R W
O R L F T G
Y E N N Y
A U B O T
126
B T A D A I
N A N E P N
U M R T U S
C O S E D P

127

128

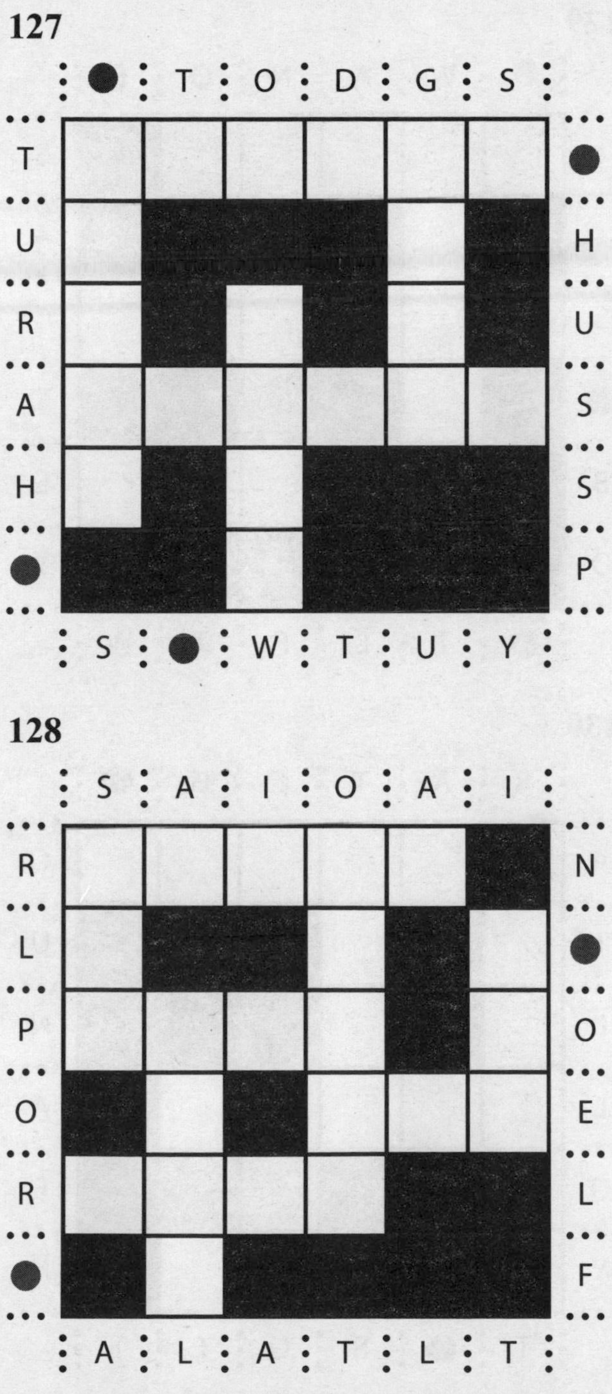

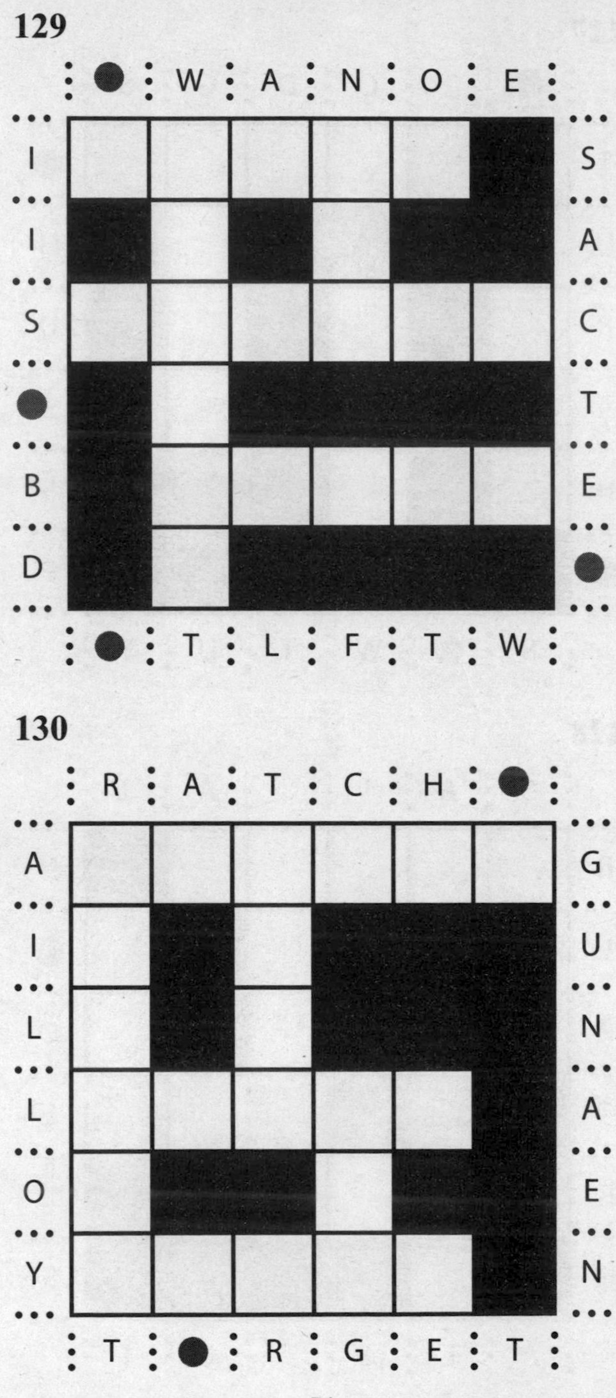
129
W A N O E
I I S B D
S A C T E
T L F T W
130
R A T C H
A I L L O Y
G U N A E N
T R G E T

131

	C	L	A	R	Y	●	
●							●
A							E
Y							Z
E							V
R							A
R							P
	I	P	B	A	V	T	

132

	E	I	C	A	I	G	
M							D
O							I
V							O
E							L
T							O
N							●
	L	E	N	I	N	P	

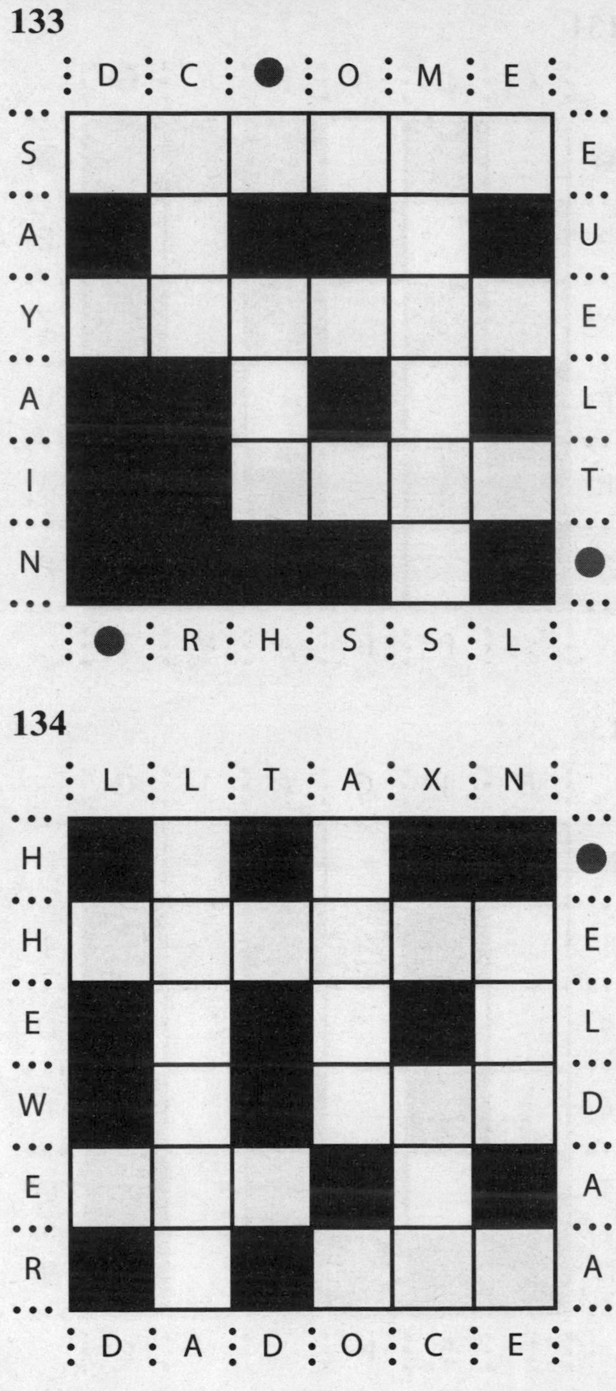
133
D C O M E
S A Y A I N
E U E L T
R H S S L
134
L L T A X N
H H E W E R
E L D A A
D A D O C E

135

	C	O	H	I	N	O	
P							I
O	■		■		■		B
R	■						N
F	■		■		■		T
A	■		■	■	■	■	●
O					■	■	P
	S	L	R	S	●	G	

136

	F	E	P	T	E	D	
O					■		F
I		■	■		■		A
B							R
A		■		■		■	B
S				■		■	Y
O	■	■				■	X
	T	O	R	U	I	B	

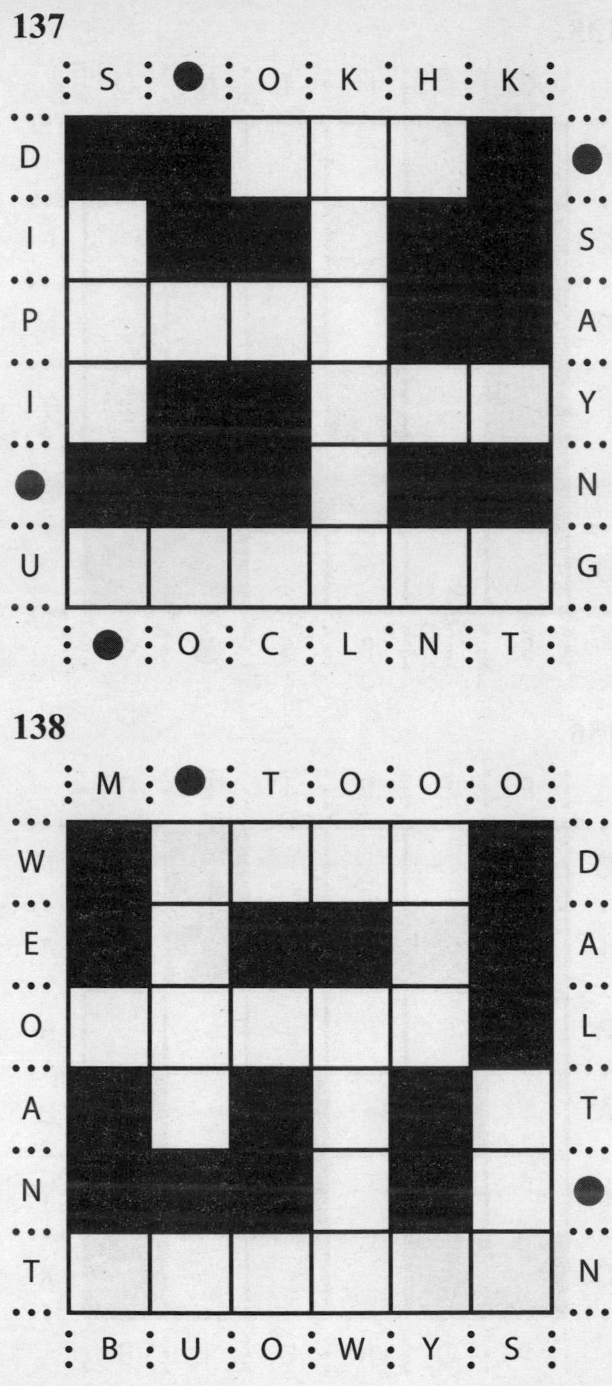
137
S O K H K
D I P I U
S A Y N G
O C L N T
138
M T O O O
W E O A N T
D A L T N
B U O W Y S

139

● P A E H L

A … U
T … N
● … ●
Z … H
A … C
R … E

E U L A E ●

140

C O M O I R

P … ●
I … S
T … B
O … H
E … I
● … T

A L R X A A

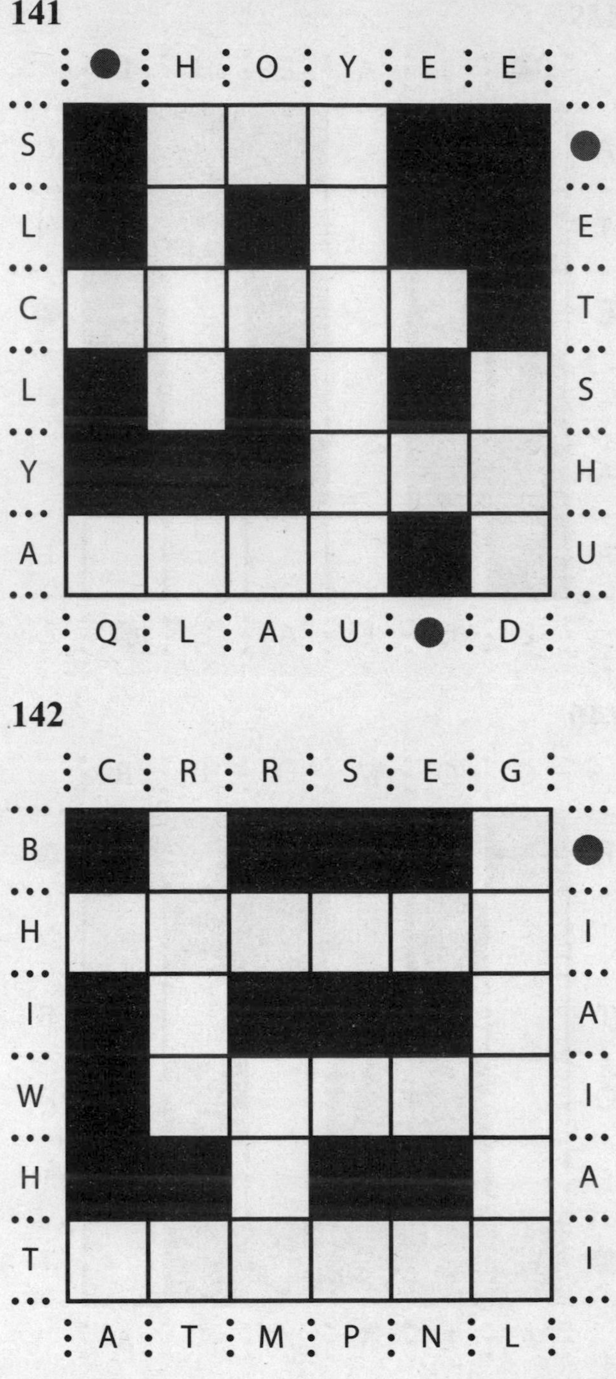
141
H O Y E E
S L C L Y A
E T S H U
Q L A U D
142
C R R S E G
B H I W H T
I A I A I
A T M P N L

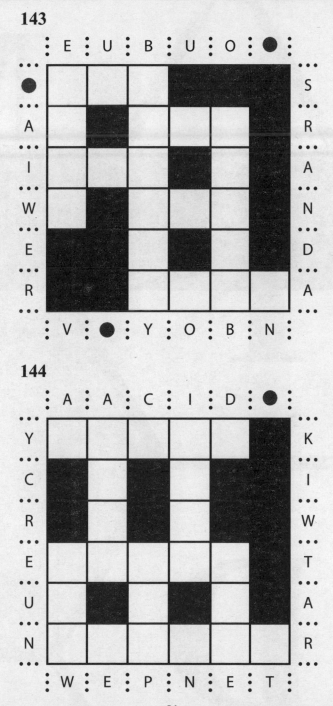

143

	E	U	B	U	O	●	
●							S
A							R
I							A
W							N
E							D
R							A
	V	●	Y	O	B	N	

144

	A	A	C	I	D	●	
Y							K
C							I
R							W
E							T
U							A
N							R
	W	E	P	N	E	T	

Polygon

How to Play

How to make words:

- All answer words must use the letter shown in the centre of the Polygon puzzle. For example, in the Polygon above, "noose" is allowed, but "moose" isn't.
- No answer word may use a letter more times than it appears in the Polygon. For example, "niece" is allowed (because two Es are given), but "concise" isn't, because there's only one C.
- Accented letters are allowed, and are considered identical to the same letters without the accent. For example, if the Polygon contains an E, words containing é, è or ê are allowed. C with a cedilla (ç) is considered the same as a plain C. If two words are the same apart from differences in accents, such as "pate" and "pâté", only one of them may be counted as an answer.
- The minimum word length varies. When the Polygon has a total of seven letters, the answer words must be at least three letters in length. When the total number of letters is eight, nine or ten, answers must be at least four letters long. The Polygon above has nine letters, so "con" is too short, but "icon" is allowed.

Acceptability of words:

- All answer words must be entries in the latest edition of the *Concise Oxford English Dictionary* (COED). The 12th edition was published in 2011.
- Answer words must be listed in COED without capital letters. For example, "Moonie" and "Miocene" aren't allowed.
- Answers must be listed in COED as single words, without hyphens or other punctuation such as apostrophes. For example, "come on" and "come-on" aren't allowed, and "amino" isn't allowed because COED has it only in the phrase "amino acid".
- Plural nouns aren't allowed, even if they're irregularly formed. For example, "coins", "monies" and "icemen" aren't allowed. However, if a plural noun is explicitly listed in COED as a different part of speech, it is allowed. For example, "forwards" (adverb) and "crumbs" (exclamation) are allowed.
- Only the base forms of verbs are allowed (the infinitive, without the word "to"), not any variations such as present tense, past tense or participles, even if they're irregularly formed. For example, "see" is allowed, but not "sees", "seeing" or "seen". However, if a verb form is explicitly listed in COED as a different part of speech, it is allowed. For example, "saw" (noun), "learned" (adjective) and "given" (adjective, preposition or noun) are allowed.
- Agent nouns ending in -er are allowed if they're listed in COED. For example, "mincer" is allowed, but "mooner" isn't.
- Basic forms of adjectives are allowed, but not comparatives (usually ending in -er) or superlatives (usually ending in -est). For example, "nice" is allowed, but "nicer" and "nicest" aren't. Irregular comparatives and superlatives such as "better", "best" and "worse" are disallowed as forms of adjectives, but many of them are also listed in COED as other parts of speech (eg "worst" = "get the better of"), and are therefore allowed on that basis.
- Adverbs ending in -ly aren't allowed.

  Any word in COED is allowed, even if it's marked as slang, archaic, US, etc.
- Occasionally, you may find words that fit all the above criteria but aren't listed among the printed answers. If you do, you can feel satisfied that you've outwitted the puzzle setter.

Hints for solving:

- Look for common beginnings, such as UN- or SUB-, and endings, such as -ER or -ISM. Look for pairs of letters that go well together, such as ST, PR or ND.
- Write out the letters in a different order, in case you spot something different.
- Don't forget to look for words that begin with a vowel.

  When you find a word, try reading it backwards, to see if it suggests another word.
- When you find a word, try to find all the rearrangements of its letters that also form words.
- When you find a word, try substituting the remaining letters into it.

Lexica | Polygon | Scrabble™ Challenge | Word Watch | Codeword

1

2

3

4

5

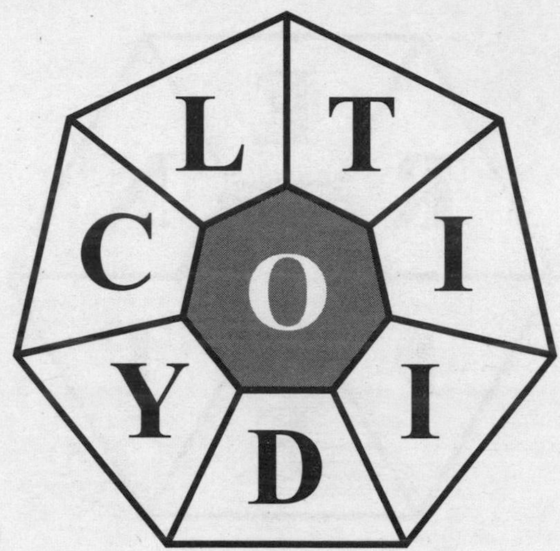

6

7

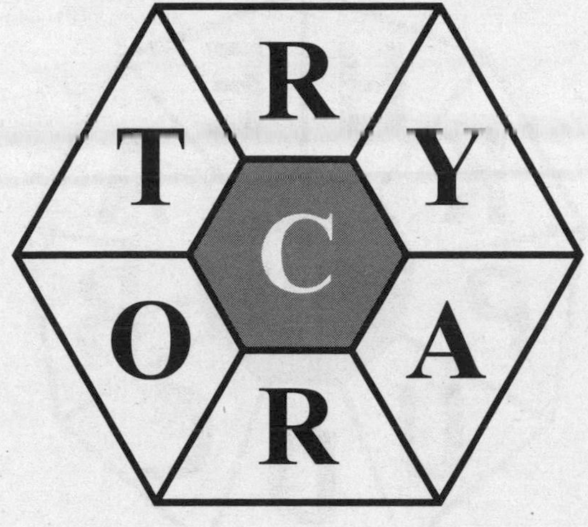

8

9

10

11

12

13

14

15

16

17

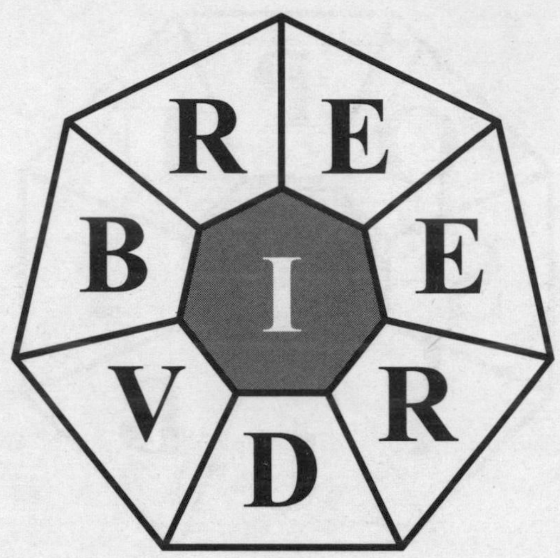

18

19

20

21

22

23

24

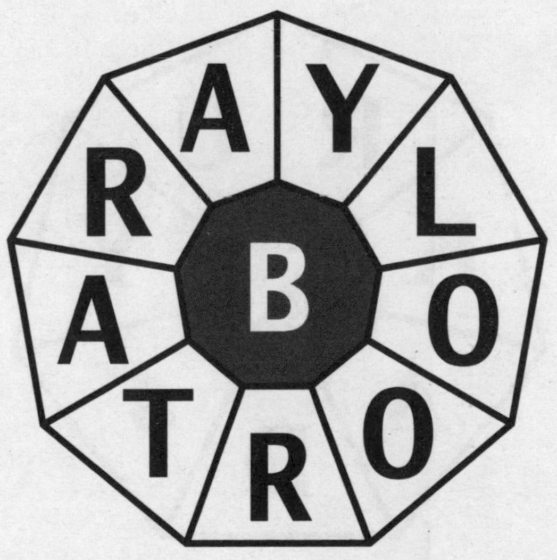

25

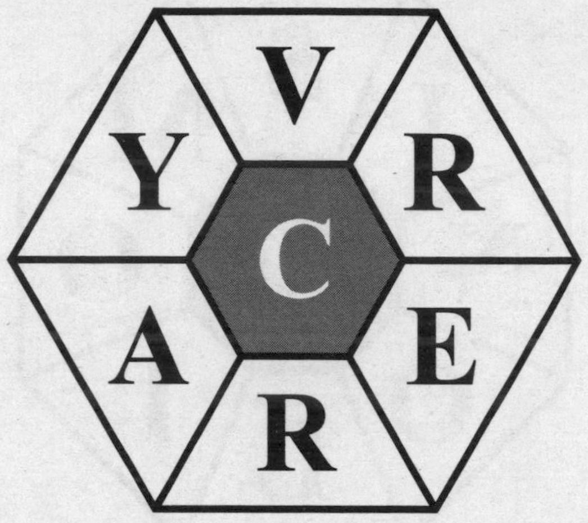

26

27

28

29

30

31

32

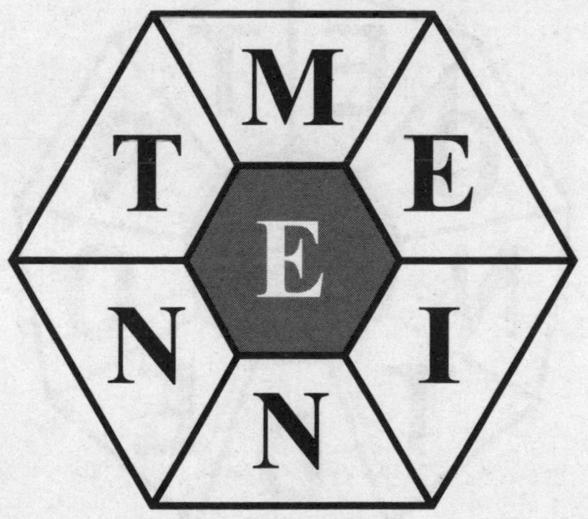

33

34

35

36

37

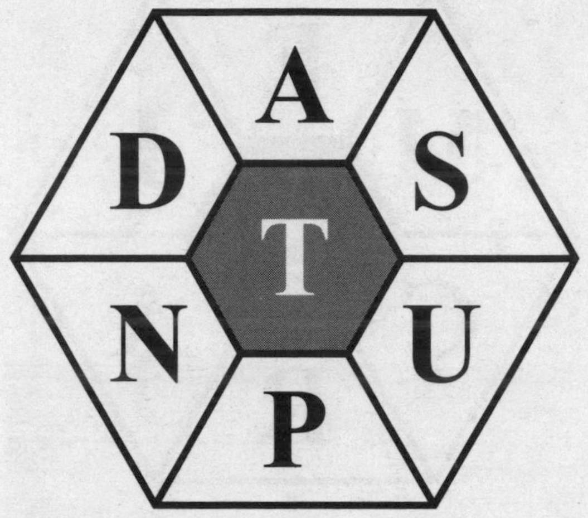

38

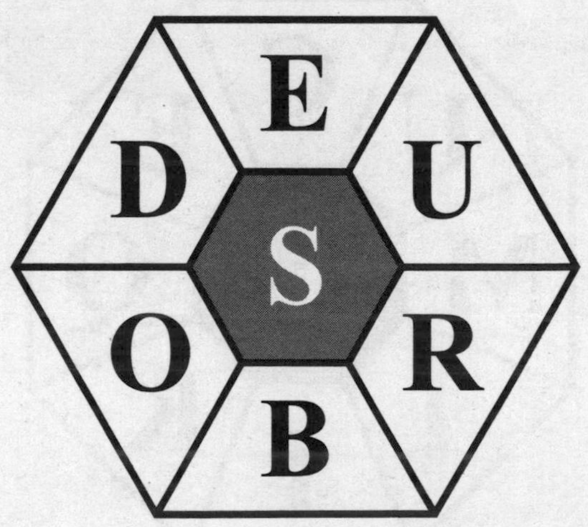

39

40

41

42

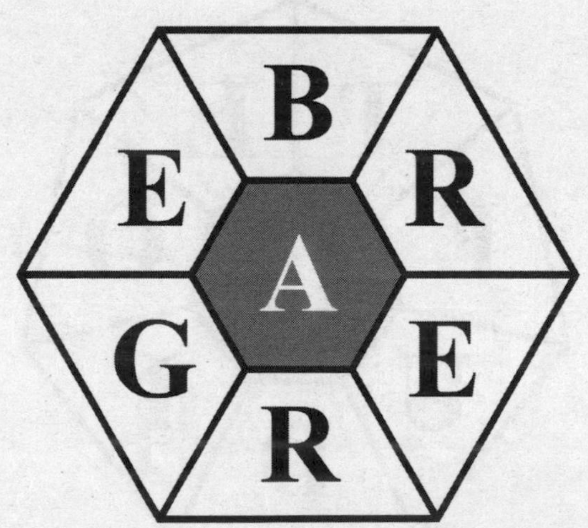

43

44

45

46

47

L A
I M U
O H
L

48

49

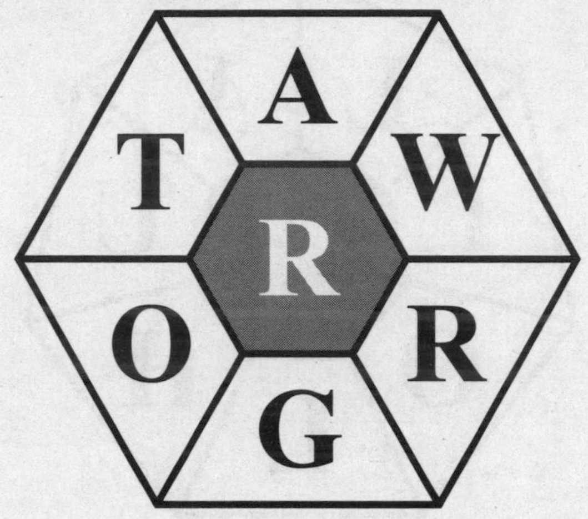

50

51

E
G A
T
L V
E

52

53

54

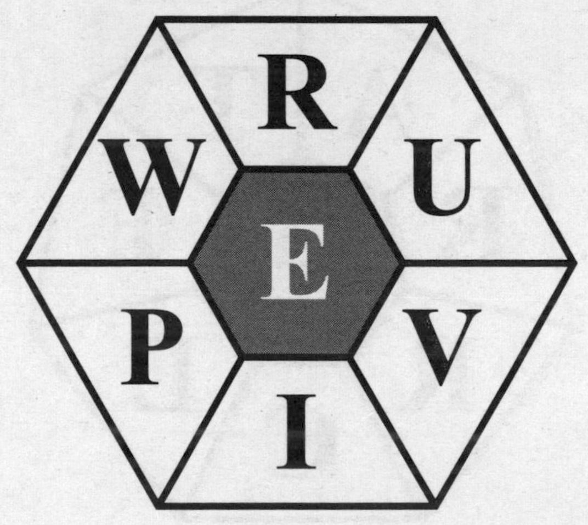

55

56

57

58

59

60

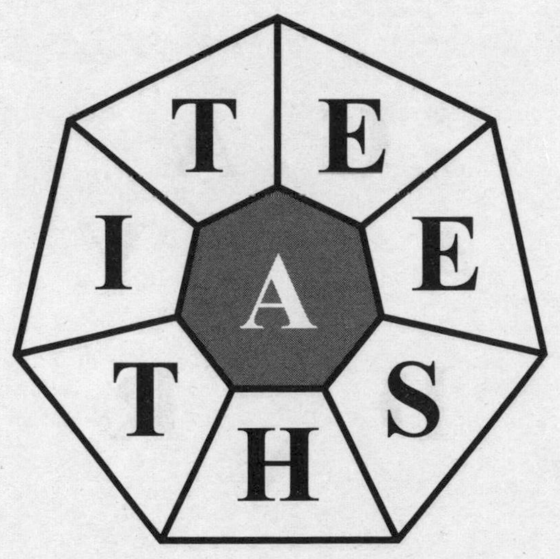

61

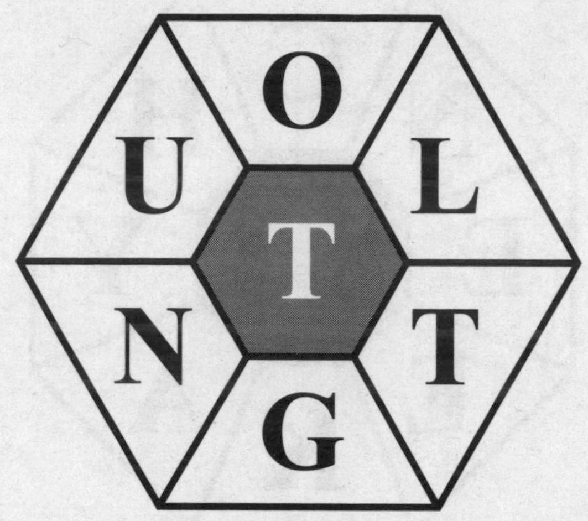

62

63

64

65

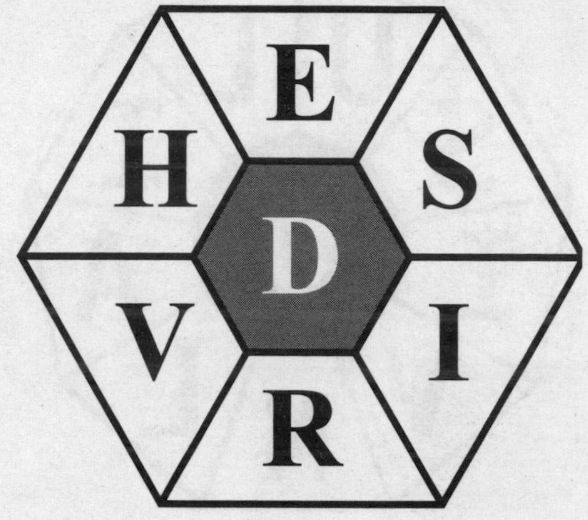

66

67

68

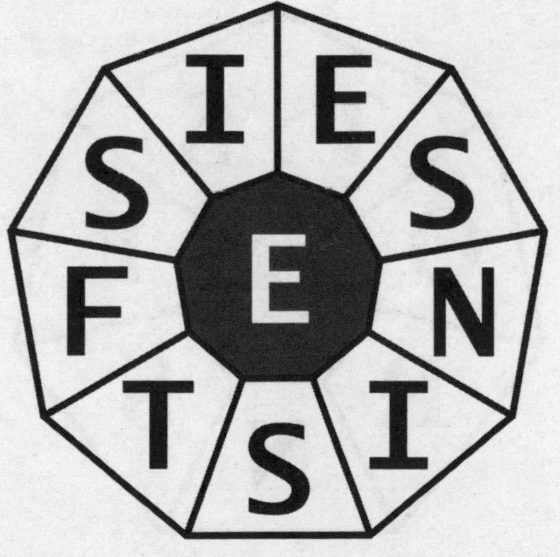

69

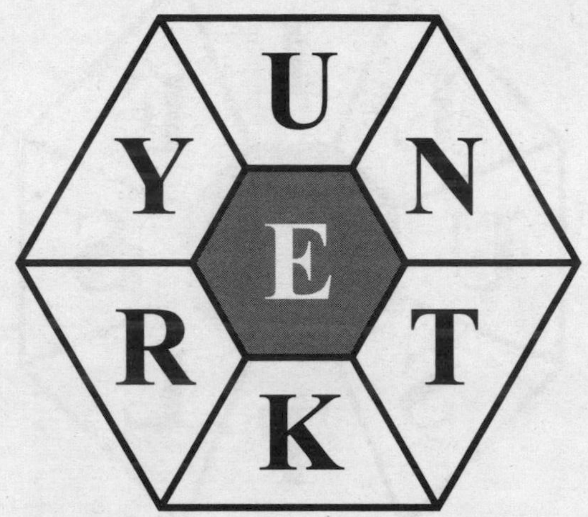

70

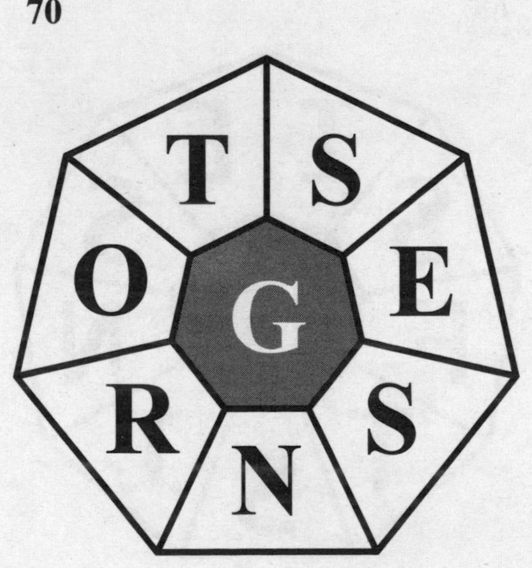

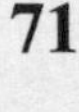

72

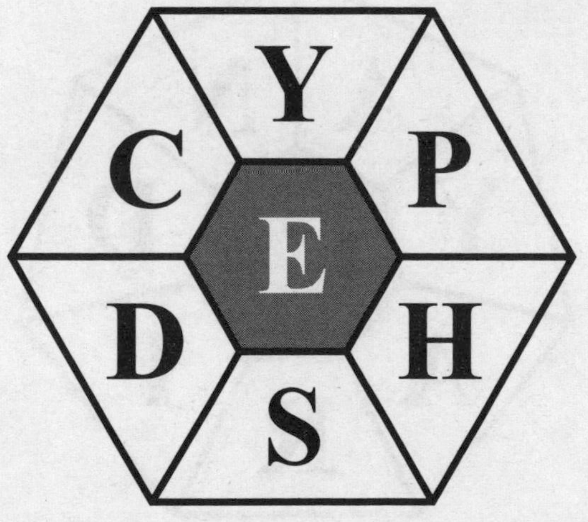

73

74

75

76

77

78

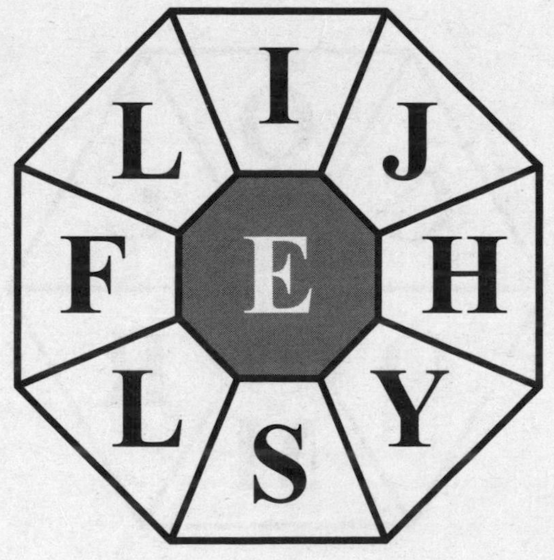

79

80

81

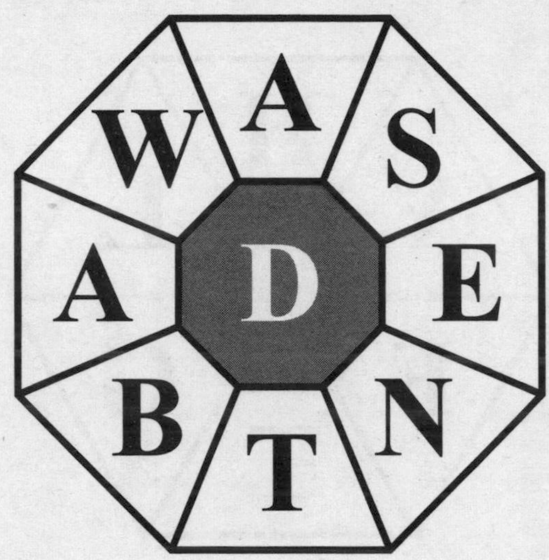

82

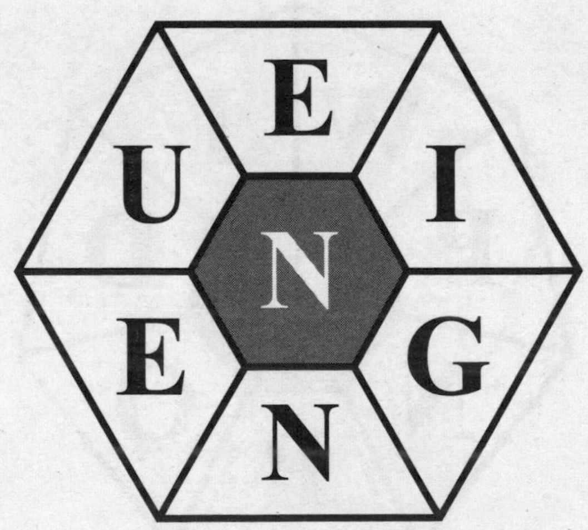

83

84

85

86

87

88

89

90

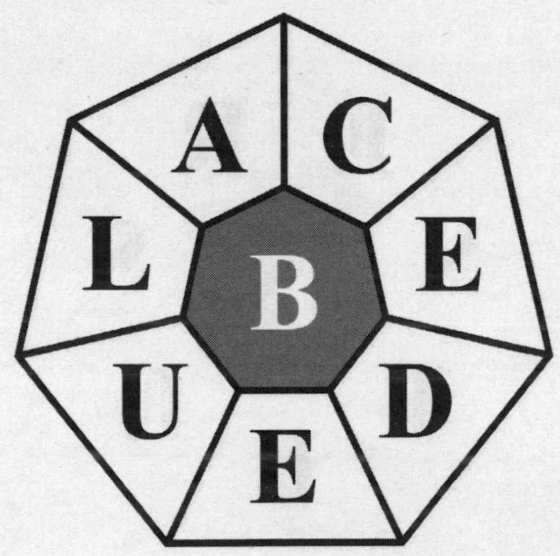

91

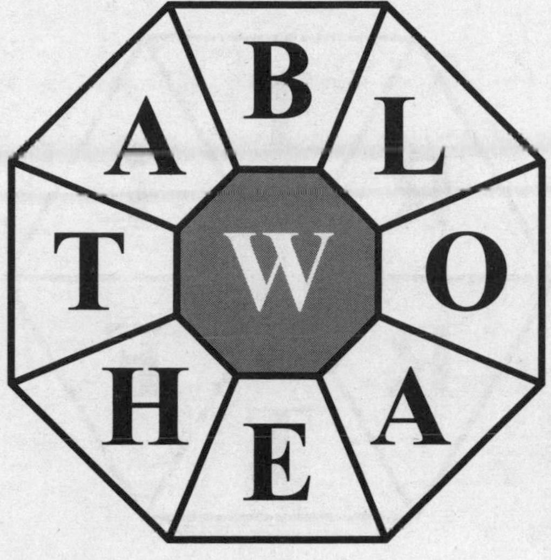

92

93

94

95

96

97

98

99

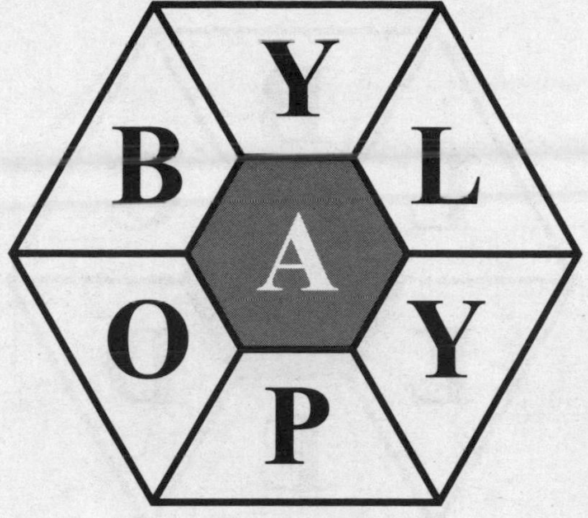

100

101

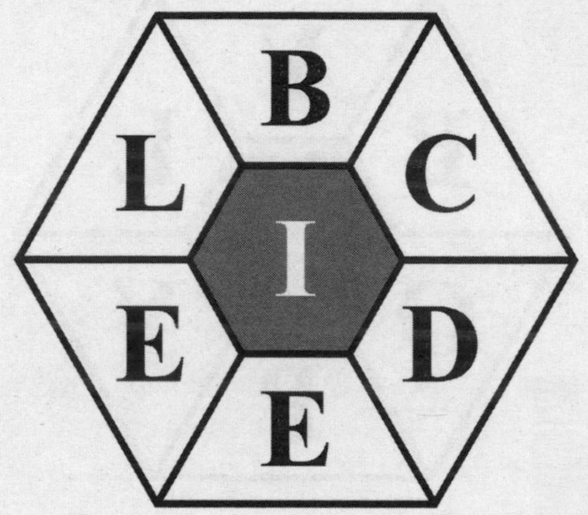

102

103

104

105

106

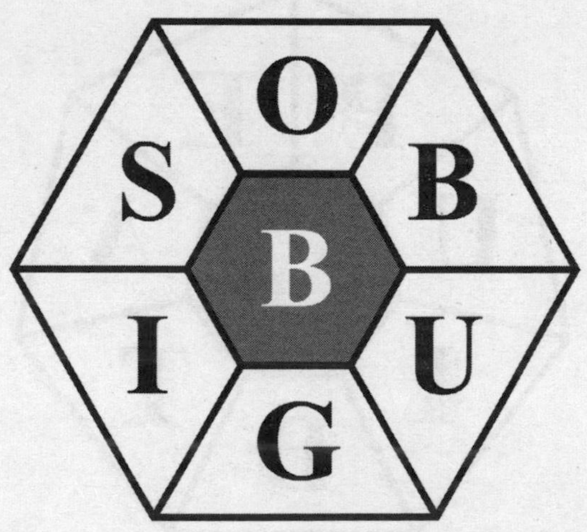

107

108

109

110

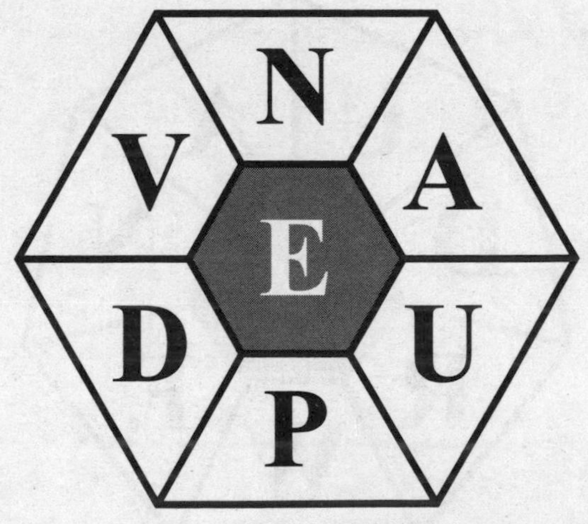

112

113

114

115

H
N M
A
N G
A

116

117

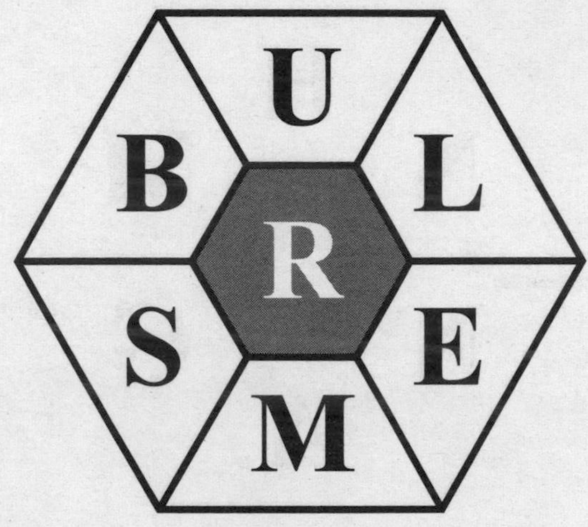

118

119

A L
G G
H
I N
N C E

120

121

122

123

124

125

126

127

128

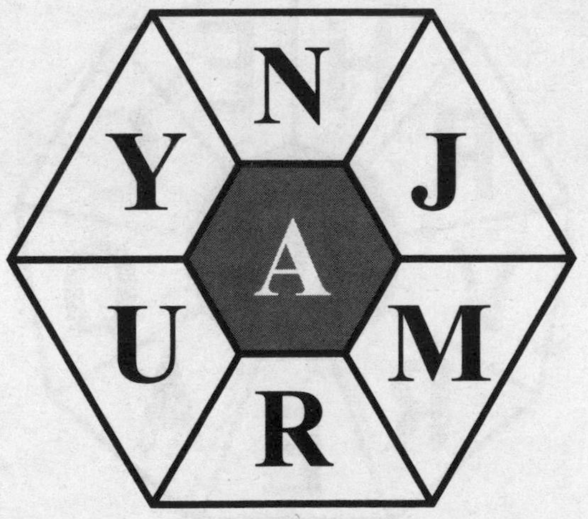

Lexica
Polygon
Scrabble™ Challenge
Word Watch
Codeword

129

130

131

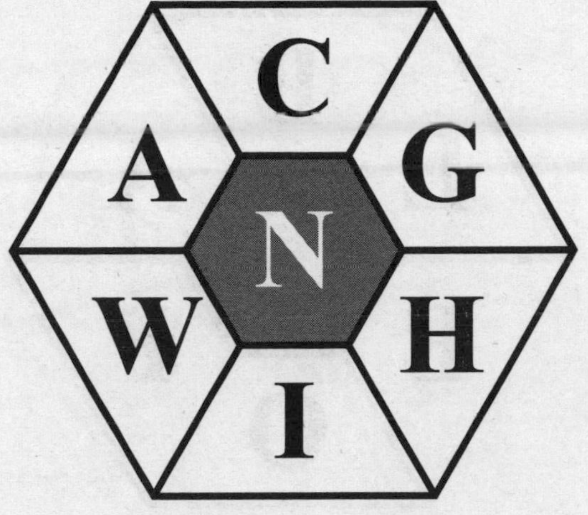

132

Lexica
Polygon
Scrabble™ Challenge
Word Watch
Codeword

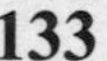
133

134

135

136

137

138

139

140

141

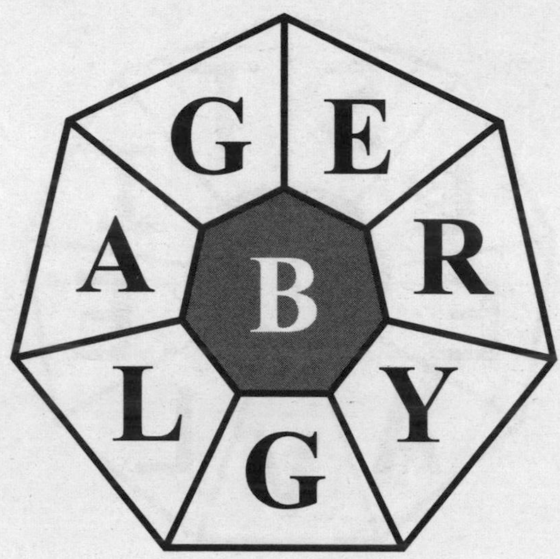

142

143

N
M
B
I
I
R
A

144

2L
A 1
L 1
2L
2L
A 1
P 3
E 1
R 1
2L
2L

Scrabble™ Challenge

How to Play

- Use only the board area shown.
- *Collins Official Scrabble™ Words* is the authority used, although the solutions are not unusual words.
- Standard Scrabble rules apply for making the word plays

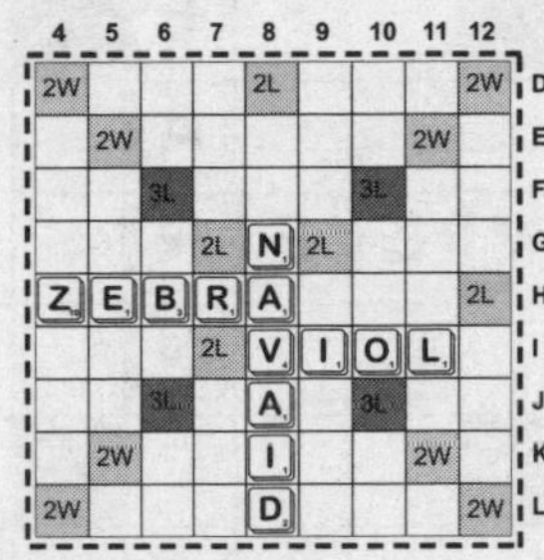

B A C O R U M

What play covers two double-word squares with this rack?

B O W S A G E

Can you score more than 34 points with this rack?

Key
2L = double letter
3L = triple letter
2W = double word
3W = triple word
Letter values
AEIOULNRST=1
DG=2 BCMP=3
FHVWY=4 K=5
JX=8 QZ=10

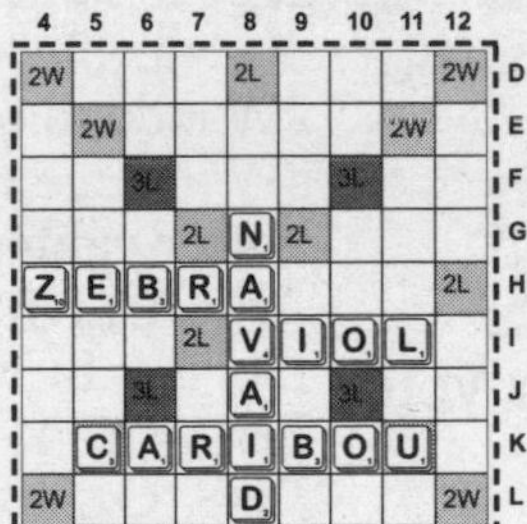

CARIBOU K5 across (44)

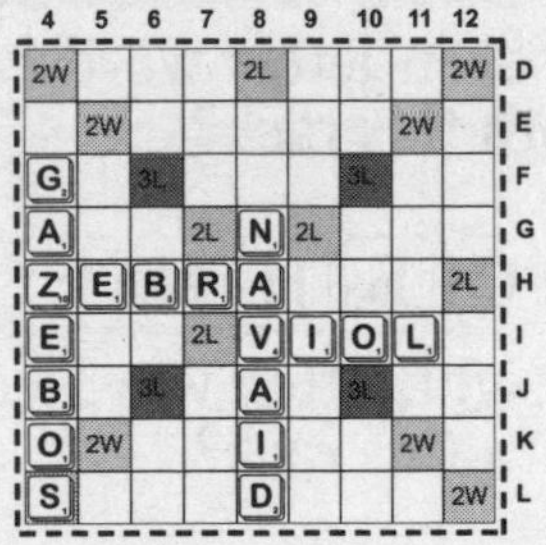

GAZEBOS F4 down (38)

1

	4	5	6	7	8	9	10	11	12
D	2W				2L				2W
E		2W			F	L	A	K	
F			3L			E	3L		
G				2L		A			
H	2L	E	M	B	E	R			2L
I				2L		N			
J			3L				3L		
K		2W						2W	
L	2W				2L				2W

R A Y L I F T

What seven-letter word can you play with this rack?

D O S H M E N

What eight-letter word can you play with this rack?

Key
2L = double letter
3L = triple letter
2W = double word
3W = triple word

Letter values
AEIOULNRST=1
DG=2 BCMP=3
FHVWY=4 K=5
JX=8 QZ=10

2

C H E F R E G

What play uses six of the letters from this rack?

T I G G E R Y

What play covers two triple-word squares using this rack?

Key
2L = double letter
3L = triple letter
2W = double word
3W = triple word

Letter values
AEIOULNRST=1
DG=2 BCMP=3
FHVWY=4 K=5
JX=8 QZ=10

3

	7	8	9	10	11	12	13	14	15
A		3W				2L			3W
B				U$_1$				2W	
C	2L		2L	M$_3$			2W		
D		2L		B$_3$		2W			2L
E				E$_1$	2W				
F			O$_1$	R$_1$	A$_1$			3L	
G	2L		R$_1$				2L		
H		W$_4$	E$_1$			2L			3W
I	2L		2L				2L		

E$_1$ E$_1$ I$_1$ J$_8$ L$_1$ Q$_{10}$ U$_1$

What's the highest score using one of the J or Q with this rack?

A$_1$ A$_1$ B$_3$ E$_1$ L$_1$ X$_8$ Z$_{10}$

What's the highest score using one of the X or Z with this rack?

Key
2L = double letter
3L = triple letter
2W = double word
3W = triple word

Letter values
AEIOULNRST=1
DG=2 BCMP=3
FHVWY=4 K=5
JX=8 QZ=10

4

	7	8	9	10	11	12	13	14	15
A		3W				2L			3W
B				3L		A	T	O	C
C	2L		2L			L	2W		
D		2L				I			2L
E		R			2W	G			
F		I	N	K	I	N	G	3L	
G	2L	G	2L	I			2L		
H		H	O	T		2L			3W
I	2L	T	2L				2L		

B O B Y O M P

What is the elusive triple word play with this rack?

N O T W Y F E

Can you score exactly 37 points with this rack?

Key
2L = double letter
3L = triple letter
2W = double word
3W = triple word

Letter values
AEIOULNRST=1
DG=2 BCMP=3
FHVWY=4 K=5
JX=8 QZ=10

5

	4	5	6	7	8	9	10	11	12
D	2W				2L				2W
E		2W						2W	
F			3L			L	3L		
G				2L		A			
H	K	I	D	D	E	R			2L
I				2L		G	R	O	W
J			3L			I	3L		
K		2W				S		2W	
L	2W				2L	H			2W

C L A P H E D

What play covers two double-word squares with this rack?

T H U M W I G

Can you score more than 26 points with this rack?

Key
2L = double letter
3L = triple letter
2W = double word
3W = triple word

Letter values
AEIOULNRST=1
DG=2 BCMP=3
FHVWY=4 K=5
JX=8 QZ=10

6

	4	5	6	7	8	9	10	11	12
D	2W				2L				2W
E		2W						2W	
F			3L		M	O	O	D	
G				2L	E	2L			
H	2L				N				2L
I				2L	D	2L			
J			3L		E		3L		
K		B	L	E	D			2W	
L	2W				2L				2W

I V Y T E A R

What seven-letter word can you play with this rack?

H A T E C U B

What eight-letter word can you play with this rack?

Key
2L = double letter
3L = triple letter
2W = double word
3W = triple word

Letter values
AEIOULNRST=1
DG=2 BCMP=3
FHVWY=4 K=5
JX=8 QZ=10

7

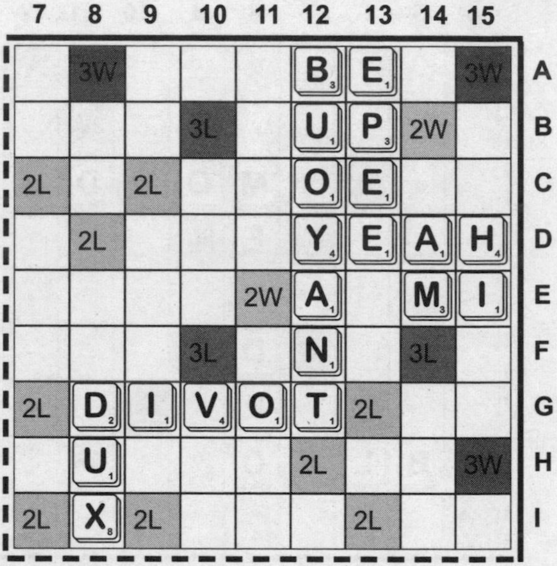

	7	8	9	10	11	12	13	14	15
A		3W				B	E		3W
B				3L		U	P	2W	
C	2L		2L			O	E		
D		2L				Y	E	A	H
E					2W	A		M	I
F				3L		N		3L	
G	2L	D	I	V	O	T	2L		
H		U				2L			3W
I	2L	X	2L				2L		

L I V E B A P

What play uses six of the letters from this rack?

What play covers two triple-word squares using this rack?

Key
2L = double letter
3L = triple letter
2W = double word
3W = triple word

Letter values
AEIOULNRST=1
DG=2 BCMP=3
FHVWY=4 K=5
JX=8 QZ=10

8

	7	8	9	10	11	12	13	14	15
A		3W				2L			3W
B				3L				2W	
C	2L		2L				2W		
D		2L				2W			2L
E		P	R	O	V	I	D	E	
F		U		3L				3L	
G	2L	R	2L				2L		
H		S				2L			3W
I	2L		2L				2L		

A D H J O Q U

What's the highest score using one of the J or Q with this rack?

B I O O R X Z

What's the highest score using one of the X or Z with this rack?

Key
2L = double letter
3L = triple letter
2W = double word
3W = triple word
Letter values
AEIOULNRST=1
DG=2 BCMP=3
FHVWY=4 K=5
JX=8 QZ=10

9

	7	8	9	10	11	12	13	14	15
A		3W				2L	O	U	R
B				3L			O	R	E
C	2L		2L				Z		
D		2L				N	Y		2L
E			A	L	L	Y			
F				I				3L	
G	2L		2L	A			2L		
H		P	E	R		2L			3W
I	2L		2L				2L		

F O R C L A N

What is the elusive triple word play with this rack?

Can you score exactly 23 points with this rack?

Key
2L = double letter
3L = triple letter
2W = double word
3W = triple word

Letter values
AEIOULNRST=1
DG=2 BCMP=3
FHVWY=4 K=5
JX=8 QZ=10

10

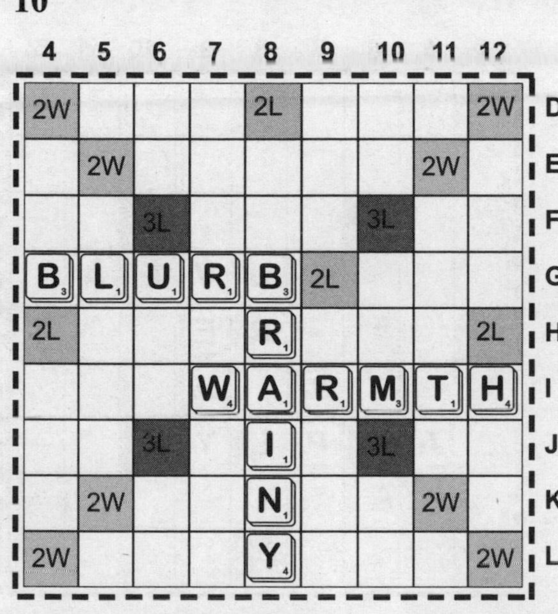

M I S P R E Y

What play covers two double-word squares with this rack?

D U V P E L F

Can you score more than 29 points with this rack?

Key
2L = double letter
3L = triple letter
2W = double word
3W = triple word

Letter values
AEIOULNRST=1
DG=2 BCMP=3
FHVWY=4 K=5
JX=8 QZ=10

11

	4	5	6	7	8	9	10	11	12
D	2W				2L				2W
E		2W						2W	
F			3L				3L		
G				2L	U	V	E	A	
H	2L				R	E			2L
I				2L		R			
J		A	M	P	L	Y	3L		
K		2W						2W	
L	2W				2L				2W

A C E H A R E

What seven-letter word can you play with this rack?

T A P L O I D

What eight-letter word can you play with this rack?

Key
2L = double letter
3L = triple letter
2W = double word
3W = triple word

Letter values
AEIOULNRST=1
DG=2 BCMP=3
FHVWY=4 K=5
JX=8 QZ=10

12

	7	8	9	10	11	12	13	14	15
A		3W				B	E		3W
B				3L		E	N	2W	
C	2L		2L			A	T		
D		E	L	E	C	T	I	O	N
E		M			2W		T	H	O
F		O		3L			Y	3L	
G	2L	V	2L				2L		
H		E				2L			3W
I	2L	D	2L				2L		

H A J W I G S

What play uses six of the letters from this rack?

G A D D I E S

What play covers two triple-word squares using this rack?

Key
2L = double letter
3L = triple letter
2W = double word
3W = triple word
Letter values
AEIOULNRST=1
DG=2 BCMP=3
FHVWY=4 K=5
JX=8 QZ=10

13

	7	8	9	10	11	12	13	14	15
A		3W				H	E	E	D
B				3L				2W	E
C	2L		2L				2W		F
D		2L				2W			R
E					2W		A		A
F				3L			B	3L	Y
G	M	O	W				L	A	S
H		R	E	M	O	V	E	D	3W
I	2L	B	2L				2L		

A E J L Q T U

What's the highest score using one of the J or Q with this rack?

A H O T W X Z

What's the highest score using one of the X or Z with this rack?

Key
2L = double letter
3L = triple letter
2W = double word
3W = triple word

Letter values
AEIOULNRST=1
DG=2 BCMP=3
FHVWY=4 K=5
JX=8 QZ=10

14

L U N A T O W

What is the elusive triple word play with this rack?

F A B M I S T

Can you score exactly 36 points with this rack?

Key
2L = double letter
3L = triple letter
2W = double word
3W = triple word

Letter values
AEIOULNRST=1
DG=2 BCMP=3
FHVWY=4 K=5
JX=8 QZ=10

15

	4	5	6	7	8	9	10	11	12
D	2W				2L				2W
E		2W						2W	
F			3L				3L		
G	G	R	O	W	E	R			
H	2L				M	A	R	S	H
I				2L		V			
J			3L			E	3L		
K		2W				N		2W	
L	2W				2L				2W

P O E M W I T

What play covers two double-word squares with this rack?

H I D Y K I N

Can you score more than 34 points with this rack?

Key
2L = double letter
3L = triple letter
2W = double word
3W = triple word

Letter values
AEIOULNRST=1
DG=2 BCMP=3
FHVWY=4 K=5
JX=8 QZ=10

16

	4	5	6	7	8	9	10	11	12
D	2W				2L				2W
E		2W					R	2W	
F			3L				E		
G				2L		2L	E		
H	2L		R	O	U	N	D		2L
I			U	2L		2L			
J			I				3L		
K		2W	N					2W	
L	2W				2L				2W

E A R L U N G

What seven-letter word can you play with this rack?

I V Y D A R E

What eight-letter word can you play with this rack?

Key
2L = double letter
3L = triple letter
2W = double word
3W = triple word

Letter values
AEIOULNRST=1
DG=2 BCMP=3
FHVWY=4 K=5
JX=8 QZ=10

17

	7	8	9	10	11	12	13	14	15
A		3W			A	M			3W
B				3L	X	I		2W	
C	2L		2L			T	H	O	U
D		2L				T	E	M	P
E					2W	E			
F				3L		N		3L	
G	2L		2L	W	A	S	H		
H		O	B	E	Y	2L			3W
I	2L		2L				2L		

P E T E K E Y

What play uses six of the letters from this rack?

C O N O S E S

What play covers two triple-word squares using this rack?

Key
2L = double letter
3L = triple letter
2W = double word
3W = triple word

Letter values
AEIOULNRST=1
DG=2 BCMP=3
FHVWY=4 K=5
JX=8 QZ=10

18

	7	8	9	10	11	12	13	14	15
A		3W				2L			3W
B				3L				2W	
C	2L		2L				2W		
D		2L		E	M	B	E	D	2L
E				R	2W				
F			A	R	K			3L	
G	2L	P	A				2L		
H		O	H			2L			3W
I	2L	T	2L				2L		

A E J M Q U Y

What's the highest score using one of the J or Q with this rack?

A A G T U X Z

What's the highest score using one of the X or Z with this rack?

Key
2L = double letter
3L = triple letter
2W = double word
3W = triple word

Letter values
AEIOULNRST=1
DG=2 BCMP=3
FHVWY=4 K=5
JX=8 QZ=10

19

	7	8	9	10	11	12	13	14	15	
		3W				2L	T	E	D	A
				3L			O	2W		B
	2L		2L				W			C
		2L	R	O	T	U	N	D	2L	D
				U	2W					E
				T				3L		F
	2L		2L	D			2L			G
		P	R	O		2L			3W	H
	2L		2L				2L			I

I C Y H E A P

What is the elusive triple word play with this rack?

B I O W O R P

Can you score exactly 31 points with this rack?

Key
2L = double letter
3L = triple letter
2W = double word
3W = triple word

Letter values
AEIOULNRST=1
DG=2 BCMP=3
FHVWY=4 K=5
JX=8 QZ=10

20

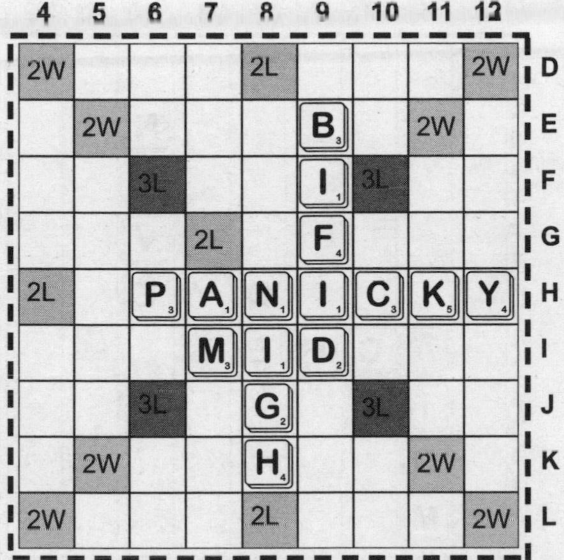

I M P O L E S

What play covers two double-word squares with this rack?

B O T H G A Y

Can you score more than 30 points with this rack?

Key
2L = double letter
3L = triple letter
2W = double word
3W = triple word

Letter values
AEIOULNRST=1
DG=2 BCMP=3
FHVWY=4 K=5
JX=8 QZ=10

21

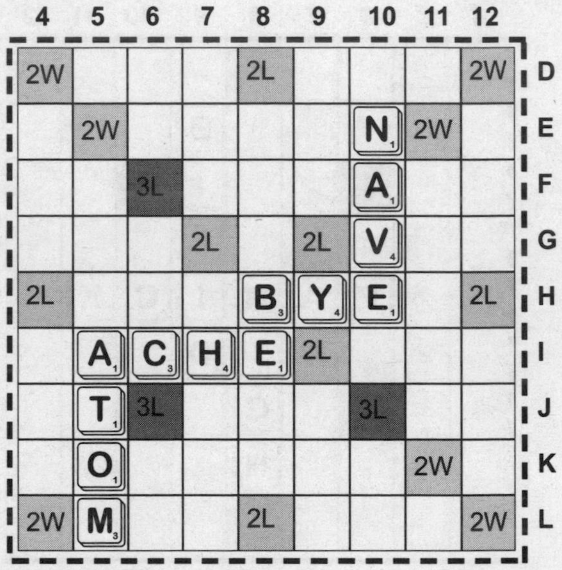

N E C K P E A

What seven-letter word can you play with this rack?

B I P U N A L

What eight-letter word can you play with this rack?

Key
2L = double letter
3L = triple letter
2W = double word
3W = triple word

Letter values
AEIOULNRST=1
DG=2 BCMP=3
FHVWY=4 K=5
JX=8 QZ=10

22

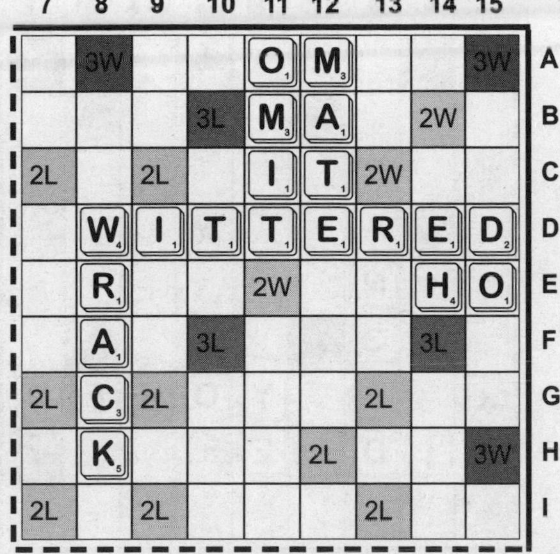

E Y E L U L U

What play uses six of the letters from this rack?

S H U N I C E

What play covers two triple-word squares using this rack?

Key
2L = double letter
3L = triple letter
2W = double word
3W = triple word

Letter values
AEIOULNRST=1
DG=2 BCMP=3
FHVWY=4 K=5
JX=8 QZ=10

23

	7	8	9	10	11	12	13	14	15
A		3W				2L			3W
B				3L				2W	
C	2L		R				2W		
D		2L	A			2W			2L
E			N		2W				
F			G	3L				3L	
G	2L		E		Y	O	K	E	D
H		I	D	L	E	2L			3W
I	2L		2L				2L		

A J L M O Q U

What's the highest score using one of the J or Q with this rack?

F N O R U X Z

What's the highest score using one of the X or Z with this rack?

Key
2L = double letter
3L = triple letter
2W = double word
3W = triple word

Letter values
AEIOULNRST=1
DG=2 BCMP=3
FHVWY=4 K=5
JX=8 QZ=10

24

N E W D U S K

What is the elusive triple word play with this rack?

B E W H I L E

Can you score exactly 35 points with this rack?

Key
2L = double letter
3L = triple letter
2W = double word
3W = triple word

Letter values
AEIOULNRST=1
DG=2 BCMP=3
FHVWY=4 K=5
JX=8 QZ=10

25

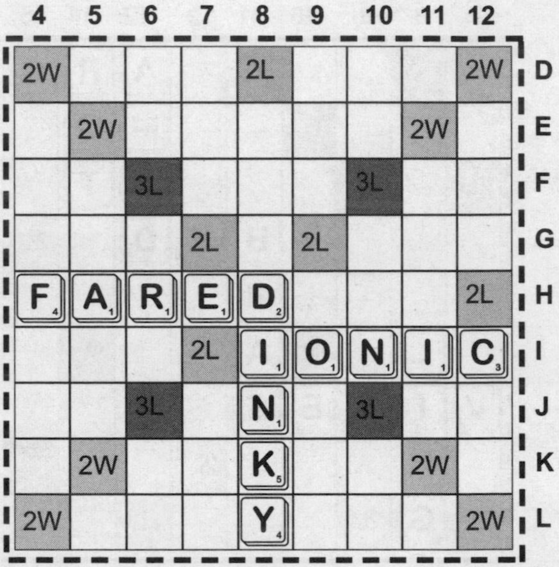

G₂ R₁ O₁ W₄ C₃ E₁ L₁

What play covers two double-word squares with this rack?

B₃ O₁ Z₁₀ W₄ A₁ G₂ O₁

Can you score more than 40 points with this rack?

Key
2L = double letter
3L = triple letter
2W = double word
3W = triple word

Letter values
AEIOULNRST=1
DG=2 BCMP=3
FHVWY=4 K=5
JX=8 QZ=10

26

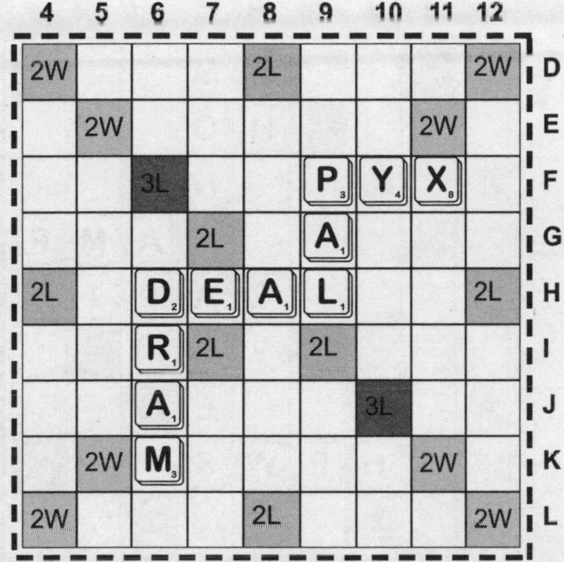

I M P L O A D

What seven-letter word can you play with this rack?

L A C T I S M

What eight-letter word can you play with this rack?

Key
2L = double letter
3L = triple letter
2W = double word
3W = triple word

Letter values
AEIOULNRST=1
DG=2 BCMP=3
FHVWY=4 K=5
JX=8 QZ=10

27

	7	8	9	10	11	12	13	14	15	
		3W			A	M			3W	A
				3L	H	O		2W		B
	2L		2L			N	2W			C
		2L				T	A	M	P	D
					R	A	D	I	I	E
				3L		G		3L		F
	2L		2L			E	2L			G
		C	H	E	W	S			3W	H
	2L		2L				2L			I

B O L D L A W

What play uses six of the letters from this rack?

What play covers two triple-word squares using this rack?

Key
2L = double letter
3L = triple letter
2W = double word
3W = triple word

Letter values
AEIOULNRST=1
DG=2 BCMP=3
FHVWY=4 K=5
JX=8 QZ=10

28

	7	8	9	10	11	12	13	14	15
A		3W				W			3W
B				3L		E		2W	
C	2L		2L		T	A	2W		
D		2L			O	R			2L
E					N				
F		L		3L	E			3L	
G	2L	E	Y	E	D		2L		
H		D				2L			3W
I	2L		2L				2L		

A F I J Q S U

What's the highest score using one of the J or Q with this rack?

E F N N O X Z

What's the highest score using one of the X or Z with this rack?

Key
2L = double letter
3L = triple letter
2W = double word
3W = triple word

Letter values
AEIOULNRST=1
DG=2 BCMP=3
FHVWY=4 K=5
JX=8 QZ=10

29

	7	8	9	10	11	12	13	14	15
A		3W				2L	I	D	E
B				3L			M	2W	
C	2L		2L				A		
D		2L		B	O	U	G	H	2L
E			W	E	2W		E		
F			A	3L				3L	
G	2L		R				2L		
H		A	N	T	I	2L			3W
I	2L		2L				2L		

G U N C Y T E

What is the elusive triple word play with this rack?

B R O W F C T

Can you score exactly 38 points with this rack?

Key
2L = double letter
3L = triple letter
2W = double word
3W = triple word

Letter values
AEIOULNRST=1
DG=2 BCMP=3
FHVWY=4 K=5
JX=8 QZ=10

30

	4	5	6	7	8	9	10	11	12
D	2W				F				2W
E		2W			O			2W	
F			3L		L		3L		
G				2L	L	2L			
H	2L			M	Y	S	T	I	C
I	W	E	R	E		2L			
J			3L				3L		
K		2W						2W	
L	2W				2L				2W

P A N T G U M

What play covers two double-word squares with this rack?

R I Z E P I P

Can you score more than 40 points with this rack?

Key
2L = double letter
3L = triple letter
2W = double word
3W = triple word

Letter values
AEIOULNRST=1
DG=2 BCMP=3
FHVWY=4 K=5
JX=8 QZ=10

31

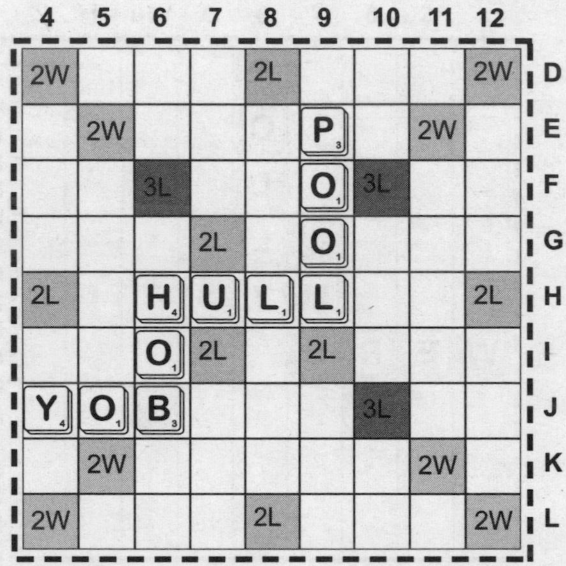

M O R E G A F

What seven-letter word can you play with this rack?

What eight-letter word can you play with this rack?

Key
2L = double letter
3L = triple letter
2W = double word
3W = triple word

Letter values
AEIOULNRST=1
DG=2 BCMP=3
FHVWY=4 K=5
JX=8 QZ=10

32

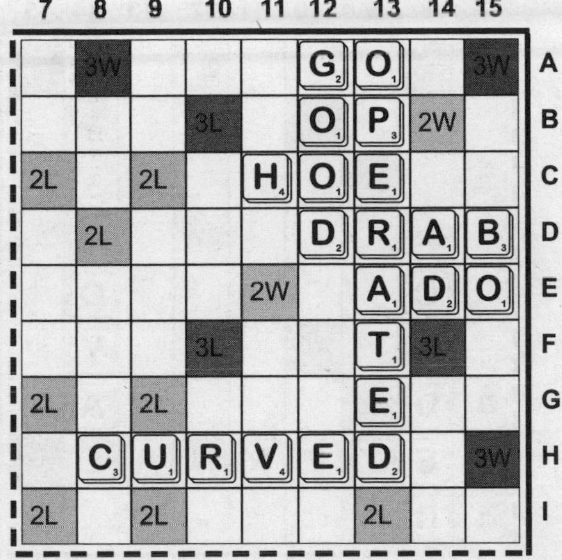

W A C K S Y D

What play uses six of the letters from this rack?

D I M E R A L

What play covers two triple-word squares using this rack?

Key
2L = double letter
3L = triple letter
2W = double word
3W = triple word

Letter values
AEIOULNRST=1
DG=2 BCMP=3
FHVWY=4 K=5
JX=8 QZ=10

33

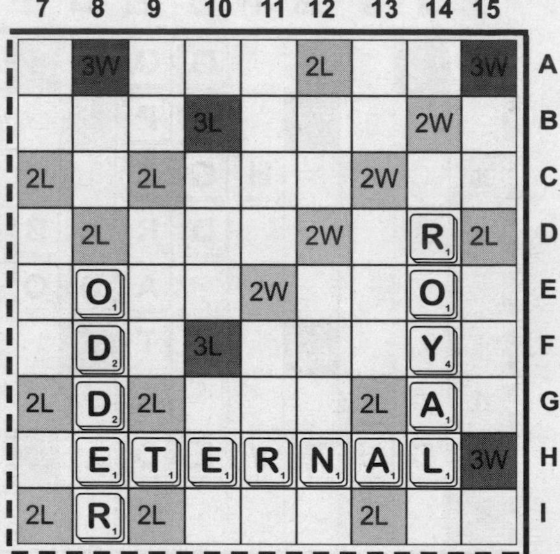

A A C E J Q U

What's the highest score using one of the J or Q with this rack?

E E I L T X Z

What's the highest score using one of the X or Z with this rack?

Key
2L = double letter
3L = triple letter
2W = double word
3W = triple word

Letter values
AEIOULNRST=1
DG=2 BCMP=3
FHVWY=4 K=5
JX=8 QZ=10

34

	7	8	9	10	11	12	13	14	15
A		3W				2L	W	E	D
B				3L			A	2W	
C	2L		2L		G	O	N	E	
D		2L			I	2W			2L
E					V				
F		W	A	G	E			3L	
G	2L	A	X				2L		
H		R	E			2L			3W
I	2L		2L				2L		

H A R D P E T

What is the elusive triple word play with this rack?

D A N M O N K

Can you score exactly 42 points with this rack?

Key
2L = double letter
3L = triple letter
2W = double word
3W = triple word

Letter values
AEIOULNRST=1
DG=2 BCMP=3
FHVWY=4 K=5
JX=8 QZ=10

35

4	5	6	7	8	9	10	11	12	
2W				W				2W	D
	2W			I			2W		E
		3L		N		3L			F
			2L	D	2L				G
2L				I				2L	H
V	E	T	O	E	D				I
		3L	B	R	A	W	L		J
	2W						2W		K
2W				2L				2W	L

H O Y D A M P

What play covers two double-word squares with this rack?

O V A L F A P

Can you score more than 27 points with this rack?

Key
2L = double letter
3L = triple letter
2W = double word
3W = triple word

Letter values
AEIOULNRST=1
DG=2 BCMP=3
FHVWY=4 K=5
JX=8 QZ=10

36

O P T I C L E

What seven-letter word can you play with this rack?

S O C K H A M

What eight-letter word can you play with this rack?

Key
2L = double letter
3L = triple letter
2W = double word
3W = triple word

Letter values
AEIOULNRST=1
DG=2 BCMP=3
FHVWY=4 K=5
JX=8 QZ=10

37

	7	8	9	10	11	12	13	14	15
A		3W			A	M			3W
B				3L	L	A		2W	
C	2L		2L		O	R	2W		
D		2L			O	B	E	A	H
E					2W	L		X	I
F				3L		I		3L	
G	2L		2L			N	2L		
H		A	M	O	N	G			3W
I	2L		2L				2L		

R U K U N I A

What play uses six of the letters from this rack?

R I B P O E T

What play covers two triple-word squares using this rack?

Key
2L = double letter
3L = triple letter
2W = double word
3W = triple word

Letter values
AEIOULNRST=1
DG=2 BCMP=3
FHVWY=4 K=5
JX=8 QZ=10

38

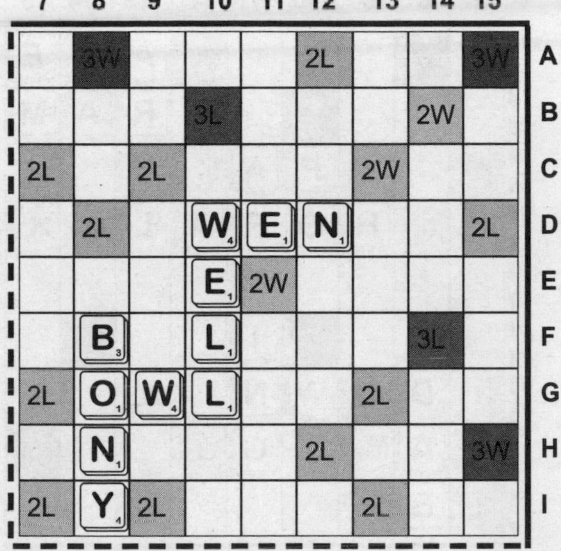

D E E J Q T U

What's the highest score using one of the J or Q with this rack?

C I O T X Y Z

What's the highest score using one of the X or Z with this rack?

Key
2L = double letter
3L = triple letter
2W = double word
3W = triple word

Letter values
AEIOULNRST=1
DG=2 BCMP=3
FHVWY=4 K=5
JX=8 QZ=10

39

C H U G P Y E

What is the elusive triple word play with this rack?

N O W D A Y S

Can you score exactly 44 points with this rack?

Key
2L = double letter
3L = triple letter
2W = double word
3W = triple word

Letter values
AEIOULNRST=1
DG=2 BCMP=3
FHVWY=4 K=5
JX=8 QZ=10

40

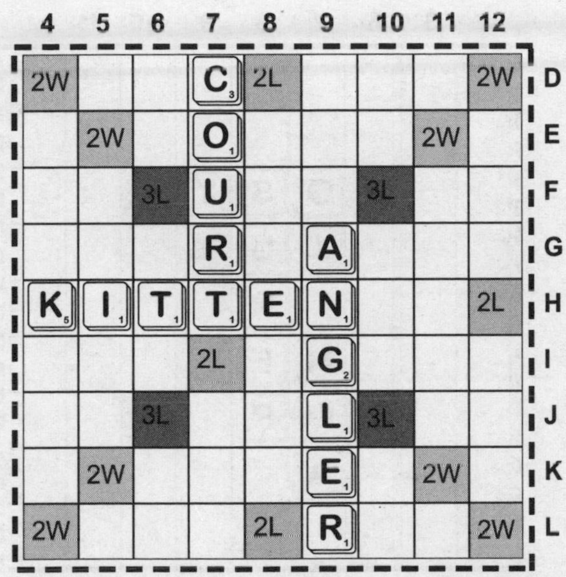

C R Y P L A N

What play covers two double-word squares with this rack?

I C Y D I M M

Can you score more than 35 points with this rack?

Key
2L = double letter
3L = triple letter
2W = double word
3W = triple word

Letter values
AEIOULNRST=1
DG=2 BCMP=3
FHVWY=4 K=5
JX=8 QZ=10

41

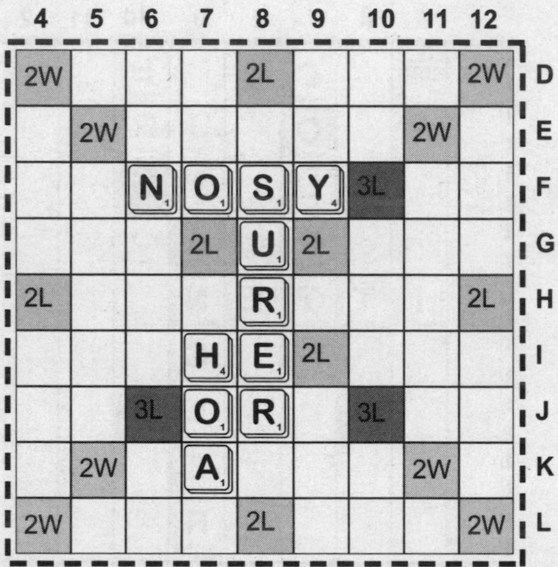

T I M E B U N

What seven-letter word can you play with this rack?

W I S E M O T

What eight-letter word can you play with this rack?

Key
2L = double letter
3L = triple letter
2W = double word
3W = triple word

Letter values
AEIOULNRST=1
DG=2 BCMP=3
FHVWY=4 K=5
JX=8 QZ=10

42

L U K S W I M

What play uses six of the letters from this rack?

S P A R R E E

What play covers two triple-word squares using this rack?

Key
2L = double letter
3L = triple letter
2W = double word
3W = triple word

Letter values
AEIOULNRST=1
DG=2 BCMP=3
FHVWY=4 K=5

43

B D E J I Q U

What's the highest score using one of the J or Q with this rack?

A N S T X Y Z

What's the highest score using one of the X or Z with this rack?

Key
2L = double letter
3L = triple letter
2W = double word
3W = triple word

Letter values
AEIOULNRST=1
DG=2 BCMP=3
FHVWY=4 K=5
JX=8 QZ=10

44

P I F F E L O

What is the elusive triple word play with this rack?

W A F O F U G

Can you score exactly 37 points with this rack?

Key
2L = double letter
3L = triple letter
2W = double word
3W = triple word
Letter values
AEIOULNRST=1
DG=2 BCMP=3
FHVWY=4 K=5
JX=8 QZ=10

45

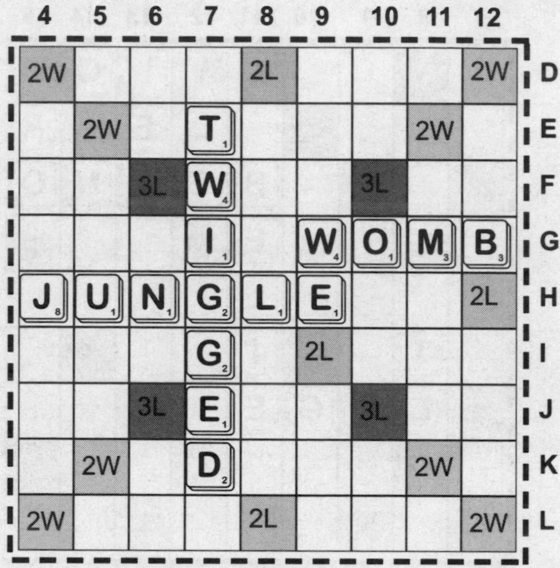

H A S G I R O

What play covers two double-word squares with this rack?

P O O R T I E

Can you score more than 36 points with this rack?

Key
2L = double letter
3L = triple letter
2W = double word
3W = triple word

Letter values
AEIOULNRST=1
DG=2 BCMP=3
FHVWY=4 K=5
JX=8 QZ=10

46

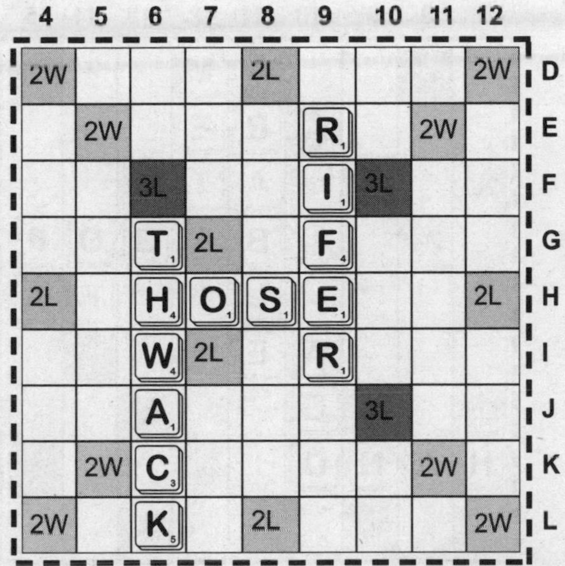

T O I L B A R

What seven-letter word can you play with this rack?

U N B O D I E

What eight-letter word can you play with this rack?

Key
2L = double letter
3L = triple letter
2W = double word
3W = triple word

Letter values
AEIOULNRST=1
DG=2 BCMP=3
FHVWY=4 K=5
JX=8 QZ=10

47

	7	8	9	10	11	12	13	14	15
A		3W			A	M			3W
B				3L	R	E		2W	
C	2L		2L		A	T	2W		
D		2L			B	E	B	O	P
E					L			F	A
F				W	E			3L	
G	2L		2L	E			2L		
H	H	A	N	D		2L			3W
I	2L		2L				2L		

W O O D H U E

What play uses six of the letters from this rack?

C O N D I S Y

What play covers two triple-word squares using this rack?

Key
2L = double letter
3L = triple letter
2W = double word
3W = triple word

Letter values
AEIOULNRST=1
DG=2 BCMP=3
FHVWY=4 K=5
JX=8 QZ=10

48

A I J L O Q U

What's the highest score using one of the J or Q with this rack?

E M O R T X Z

What's the highest score using one of the X or Z with this rack?

Key
2L = double letter
3L = triple letter
2W = double word
3W = triple word
Letter values
AEIOULNRST=1
DG=2 BCMP=3
FHVWY=4 K=5
JX=8 QZ=10

49

	7	8	9	10	11	12	13	14	15
A		3W				W	E	E	D
B				3L				M	
C	2L		2L				2W	U	
D		2L			C	O	P	S	2L
E					2W	L			
F		R	A	D	I	I		3L	
G	N	I	T			V	2L		
H		V	E	R	S	E			3W
I	2L	E	2L				2L		

B A D O W E R

What is the elusive triple word play with this rack?

B E N D P E C

Can you score exactly 29 points with this rack?

Key
2L = double letter
3L = triple letter
2W = double word
3W = triple word

Letter values
AEIOULNRST=1
DG=2 BCMP=3
FHVWY=4 K=5
JX=8 QZ=10

50

H U M A T E D

What play covers two double-word squares with this rack?

C O M I F E X

Can you score more than 38 points with this rack?

Key
2L = double letter
3L = triple letter
2W = double word
3W = triple word

Letter values
AEIOULNRST=1
DG=2 BCMP=3
FHVWY=4 K=5
JX=8 QZ=10

51

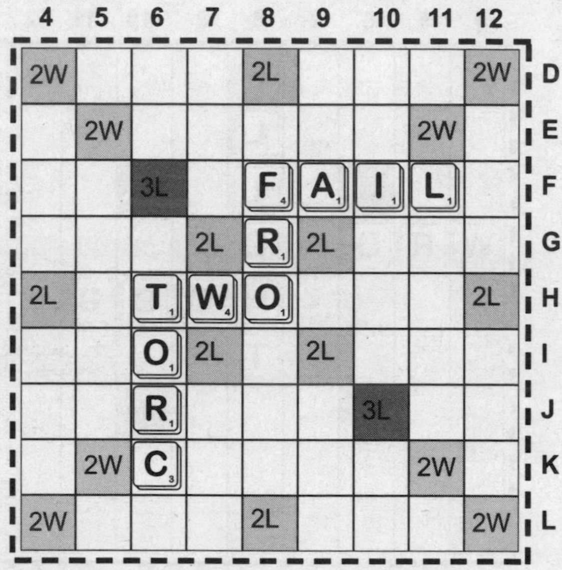

H E N B A T E

What seven-letter word can you play with this rack?

D O U R C O Y

What eight-letter word can you play with this rack?

Key
2L = double letter
3L = triple letter
2W = double word
3W = triple word

Letter values
AEIOULNRST=1
DG=2 BCMP=3
FHVWY=4 K=5
JX=8 QZ=10

52

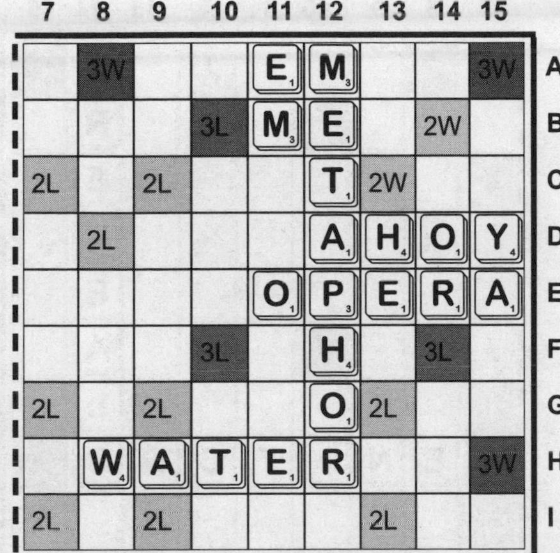

T O Y P A R K

What play uses six of the letters from this rack?

C O R Y B U N

What play covers two triple-word squares using this rack?

Key
2L = double letter
3L = triple letter
2W = double word
3W = triple word

Letter values
AEIOULNRST=1
DG=2 BCMP=3
FHVWY=4 K=5
JX=8 QZ=10

53

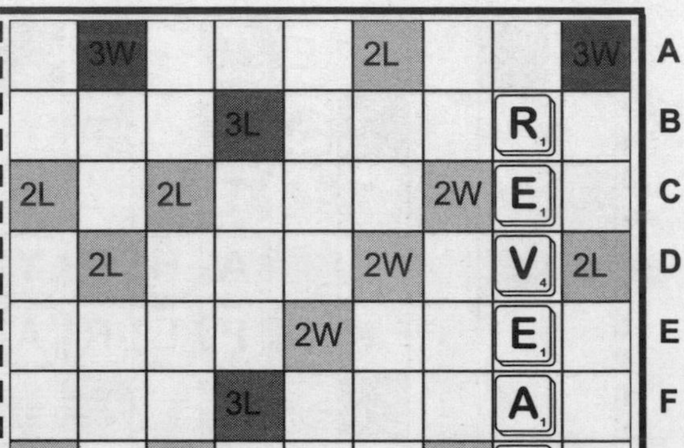

What's the highest score using one of the J or Q with this rack?

What's the highest score using one of the X or Z with this rack?

Key
2L = double letter
3L = triple letter
2W = double word
3W = triple word

Letter values
AEIOULNRST=1
DG=2 BCMP=3
FHVWY=4 K=5
JX=8 QZ=10

54

Y A N K P O D

What is the elusive triple word play with this rack?

F E R N P E G

Can you score exactly 36 points with this rack?

Key
2L = double letter
3L = triple letter
2W = double word
3W = triple word

Letter values
AEIOULNRST=1
DG=2 BCMP=3
FHVWY=4 K=5
JX=8 QZ=10

55

	4	5	6	7	8	9	10	11	12
D	2W				2L				2W
E		2W		C				2W	
F			3L	R			3L		
G				E		B			
H	2L			S	T	E	A	M	Y
I	S	T	A	T	I	C			
J			3L			A	3L		
K		2W				L		2W	
L	2W				2L	M			2W

A E R O B I P

What play covers two double-word squares with this rack?

H O B T H R Y

Can you score more than 39 points with this rack?

Key
2L = double letter
3L = triple letter
2W = double word
3W = triple word
Letter values
AEIOULNRST=1
DG=2 BCMP=3
FHVWY=4 K=5
JX=8 QZ=10

56

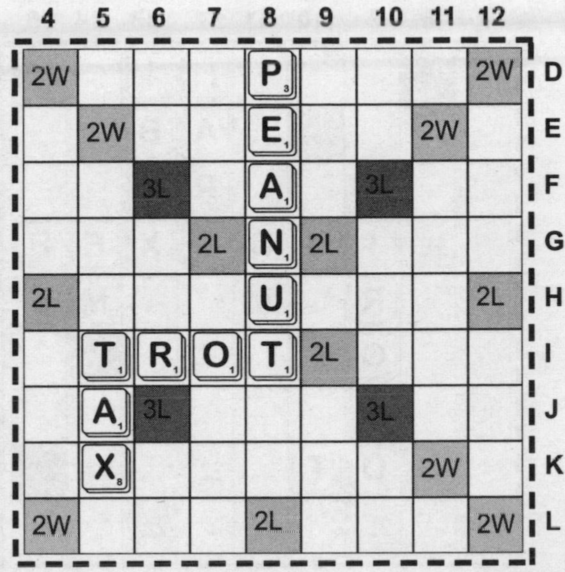

A M P H O D E

What seven-letter word can you play with this rack?

P I G B A S E

What eight-letter word can you play with this rack?

Key
2L = double letter
3L = triple letter
2W = double word
3W = triple word

Letter values
AEIOULNRST=1
DG=2 BCMP=3
FHVWY=4 K=5
JX=8 QZ=10

57

	7	8	9	10	11	12	13	14	15
A		3W				H	I		3W
B				3L		A	B	2W	
C	2L		2L			R	E		
D		2L	I	N	D	E	X	E	R
E			R		2W			M	E
F			O	3L				3L	
G	2L		K				2L		
H		N	O	T		2L			3W
I	2L		2L				2L		

O V I B U S H

What play uses six of the letters from this rack?

S P U N G A S

What play covers two triple-word squares using this rack?

Key
2L = double letter
3L = triple letter
2W = double word
3W = triple word

Letter values
AEIOULNRST=1
DG=2 BCMP=3
FHVWY=4 K=5
JX=8 QZ=10

58

	7	8	9	10	11	12	13	14	15
A		3W				A			3W
B				3L		L		2W	
C	2L		2L			T	2W		
D		2L			H	O			2L
E					O				
F		D		3L	M			3L	
G	2L	R	A	Y	E	D	2L		
H		Y				2L			3W
I	2L		2L				2L		

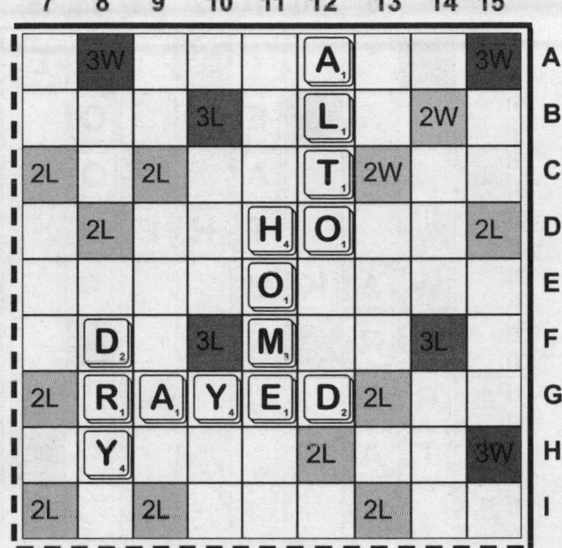

E E J Q R S U

What's the highest score using one of the J or Q with this rack?

A F I R W X Z

What's the highest score using one of the X or Z with this rack?

Key
2L = double letter
3L = triple letter
2W = double word
3W = triple word

Letter values
AEIOULNRST=1
DG=2 BCMP=3
FHVWY=4 K=5
JX=8 QZ=10

59

B Y E J O S H

What is the elusive triple word play with this rack?

H O P F E S T

Can you score exactly 41 points with this rack?

Key
2L = double letter
3L = triple letter
2W = double word
3W = triple word

Letter values
AEIOULNRST=1
DG=2 BCMP=3
FHVWY=4 K=5
JX=8 QZ=10

60

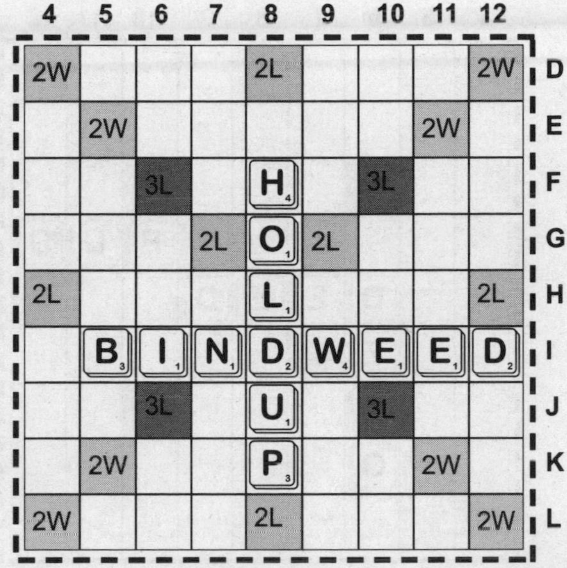

A T H O L I C

What play covers two double-word squares with this rack?

U N B A R O W

Can you score more than 28 points with this rack?

Key
2L = double letter
3L = triple letter
2W = double word
3W = triple word

Letter values
AEIOULNRST=1
DG=2 BCMP=3
FHVWY=4 K=5
JX=8 QZ=10

61

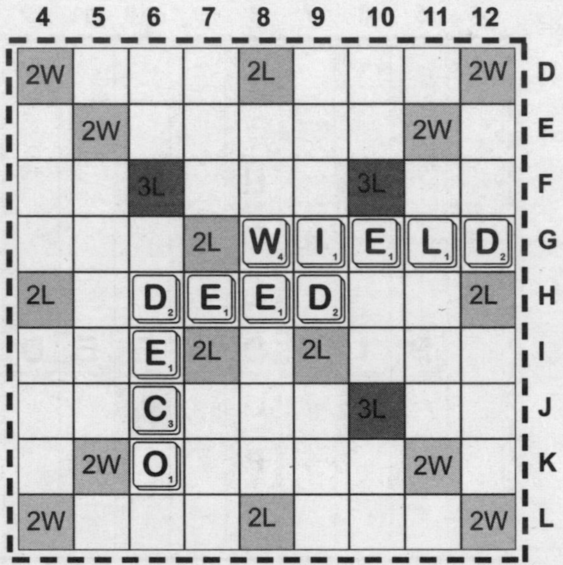

A B B R U G E

What seven-letter word can you play with this rack?

What eight-letter word can you play with this rack?

Key
2L = double letter
3L = triple letter
2W = double word
3W = triple word

Letter values
AEIOULNRST=1
DG=2 BCMP=3
FHVWY=4 K=5
JX=8 QZ=10

62

F I N D C A T

What play uses six of the letters from this rack?

I C Y H E E T

What play covers two triple-word squares using this rack?

Key
2L = double letter
3L = triple letter
2W = double word
3W = triple word

Letter values
AEIOULNRST=1
DG=2 BCMP=3
FHVWY=4 K=5
JX=8 QZ=10

63

	7	8	9	10	11	12	13	14	15
A		3W				2L			3W
B				3L				2W	
C	2L		2L		T	R	I	C	E
D		2L				E			2L
E					2W	N			
F		B	O	U	N	D		3L	
G	2L	E	F				2L		
H		D				2L			3W
I	2L		2L				2L		

A E E H J Q U

What's the highest score using one of the J or Q with this rack?

A H O T W X Z

What's the highest score using one of the X or Z with this rack?

Key
2L = double letter
3L = triple letter
2W = double word
3W = triple word

Letter values
AEIOULNRST=1
DG=2 BCMP=3
FHVWY=4 K=5
JX=8 QZ=10

64

What is the elusive triple word play with this rack?

Can you score exactly 41 points with this rack?

Key
2L = double letter
3L = triple letter
2W = double word
3W = triple word

Letter values
AEIOULNRST=1
DG=2 BCMP=3
FHVWY=4 K=5
JX=8 QZ=10

9 TALEA

a. A counting stick

b. Rhythm

c. A grass

11 TAOVALA

a. Semolina liquor

b. A board game

c. A sporran

b. To bluster

c. A sea-fis

16 BRETELLE

a. A shoulder-strap

b. A female Breton

c. Fermented black currant liquor

10 COLOPHONY

a. Part singing

b. Abdominal surgery

12 COMICES

a. An assembly

How to Play

Select the correct answer that defines the head word.

DEADOH
a. Drunk
b. Asleep
c. Driedt flowers

DRAMBUIE
a. A breed of terrier
b. A whisky liqueur
c. A Highland plaid

WEATHERGALL
a. An imperfect rainbow
b. A storm-sail
c. A jelly-fish

VANDEMONIAN
a. A din of devils
b. Tasmanian
c. Sale by barter

1 TERENA

a. Earthenware

b. Amerindians

c. A song-bird

2 BARRELET

a. A Baronet

b. A small barrel

c. A sawn-off shot-gun

3 SOBRANYE

a. An expensive brand of cigarette

b. A parliament

c. A soporific

4 BRACKMARD

a. A sword

b. A breed of duck

c. Clay and wattle

5 NIN

a. A fish

b. A wish

c. A grandmother

6 PARIETINES

a. Ruins

b. Renewings

c. Sewings

7 ICONIAN

a. Iconic

b. Conical

c. Of a town in Asia Minor

8 PEPLOS

a. The people

b. A voting pebble

c. A robe

9 **TALEA**
a. A counting stick
b. Rhythm
c. A grass

10 **COLOPHONY**
a. Part singing
b. Abdominal surgery
c. Resin

11 **TAOVALA**
a. Semolina liquor
b. A board game
c. A sporran

12 **COMICES**
a. An assembly
b. A nest of mice
c. Roman clowns

13 **BLUDGER**
a. A pimp
b. To bluster
c. A sea-fis

14 **WARPISS**
a. Equine urine
b. A harpist
c. To throw away

15 **BRETELLE**
a. A shoulder-strap
b. A female Breton
c. Fermented black currant liquor

16 **ZEPHYR**
a. A games shirt
b. A moth
c. The Phoeniciant digraph ZR

17 LAMA

a. A camel

b. Gold cloth

c. A mother-in-law

18 SPES

a. Pebbles

b. Guesses

c. Hope

19 MORGANATIC

a. Of Welsh Nationalism

b. An organ

c. Male chauvinist marriage

20 SULLAN

a. Sulky

b. Of an aristo dictator

c. A junior officer

21 IARFINE

a. A fine in chattels

b. An Irish clan

c. OK!

22 SEMINIUM

a. A Roman coin

b. A first principle

c. A school

23 LATOUR

a. A style of painting

b. A turret

c. A wine

24 SIPE

a. To percolate

b. A bird

c. If possible

25 RATAFIA
a. Basket fibre
b. Rats' bane
c. A drink

26 CATSO
a. A conspirator
b. Crumbs
c. The mint catnip

27 PROSOPAGNOSIA
a. Sinusitis
b. Lack of recognition
c. A soporific herb

28 CROCKARD
a. Money
b. An old crock
c. Sherds of pottery

29 CULPON
a. A culprit
b. A piece cut off
c. A banneret

30 WHIPPOORWILL
a. A flogging bench
b. A bird
c. A tree

31 CENATION
a. A Central European Nation
b. Celebration
c. Dinner

32 TOCHUS
a. The Greek digraph TCH
b. The bottom
c. A crane

33 SWENG
a. A blow
b. A sword
c. To cheat

34 LOGIAN
a. Logical
b. Sacred quotations
c. The Librarian at New Hall

35 SURICATE
a. A surrogate
b. A meerkat
c. A Carthaginian priest

36 MANCALA
a. Hand-cuffs
b. A magic circle
c. A board game

37 BADINEUR
a. A skater
b. A pater
c. A japer

38 YALI
a. A bird
b. A house
c. A manservant

39 AGBA
a. The Persian alphabet
b. A tree
c. A cooker

40 AURICLE
a. The ear
b. Golden
c. An ear-trumpet

41 POLISSON

a. A Glasgow police van

b. A rascal

c. A young urban citizen

42 CHONDRE

a. To vomit

b. A grain

c. A Greek unit of weight

43 RAVINEMENT

a. Extreme hunger

b. Uneven sediment

c. Fear of narrows

44 CATHETUS

a. A bladder tube

b. Enthroned

c. A perpendicular

45 CLUSTERFIST

a. A bouquet

b. An uppercut

c. An oaf

46 PUKATEA

a. Green tea

b. A tree

c. A club

47 CISSOID

a. Rather timorous

b. A curve

c. A scythe

48 POUSADA

a. An inn

b. A pastry

c. The woodlouse

49 PENTATONIC

a. A health drink

b. Five times

c. A scale

50 GRANDEE

a. A Spanish nobleman

b. Capital letter E

c. A great-grandmother

51 RAMBLAGE

a. The right to ramble

b. Senility

c. Rough pasture

52 FLAUGHTBRED

a. A mongrel

b. Mocked

c. With arms spread

53 DOWF

a. Dull

b. A game played with knucklebones

c. To undress

54 DEADOH

a. Drunk

b. Asleep

c. Dried flowers

55 EURAQUILO

a. An eagle

b. A wind

c. Eurasian

56 PUBBY

a. Pubescent

b. A bull terrier

c. To do with pubs

57 CHANNER
a. To mutter
b. A bell ringer
c. A half-crown coin

58 JISM
a. A Muslim sect
b. Energy
c. Chauvinism

59 COLOBIN
a. The rectum
b. A monkey
c. A wastepaper basket

60 LUES BOSWELLIANA
a. Gout
b. Hyper admiration
c. Early shorthand

61 BASHLIK
a. To whip
b. A hood
c. An indentured serf

62 VIEWY
a. Picturesque
b. Opinionated
c. A kaleidoscope

63 BARKLE
a. To sparkle
b. A little boat
c. To cake

64 WHOPSTRAW
a. A country bumpkin
b. Greedy
c. A thresher

65 TIRRA-LIRRA

a. The song of the skylark

b. Odds and ends

c. Trivial chat

66 JOCKER

a. A Highlander

b. A punster

c. A tramp

67 TOWAI

a. Charge for towing a vessel

b. A tree

c. Maori farewell

68 HOMEY

a. An immigrant

b. Comfortable

c. A pigeon

69 SLOYD

a. Drunk

b. Dirty

c. Carpentry

70 ASIGMATIC

a. Long-sighted

b. Meaningless

c. Without S

71 SIDEWINDER

a. A wing at the Eton Field Game

b. A snake

c. A stitch

72 BARRETTE

a. A barmaid

b. A hilt

c. A bird

73 VESTIARY

a. To do with beasts
b. To do with clothes
c. To do with servants

74 AUBUSSON

a. Tapestry
b. Almond flavoured drink
c. Thorny undergrowth

75 VIVERRINE

a. Beside the River Rhine
b. Related to civets
c. Alive

76 DEANESS

a. A female Dean
b. To disinfect
c. The descent of a mountain

77 VALGUS

a. The common herd
b. A club-foot
c. A lyric metre

78 JIVA

a. Life
b. A dance
c. An ancestor

79 VOUTRY

a. Adultery
b. A wish
c. An election

80 INCHE

a. A fly
b. A chieftain
c. Mr

81 ROUGHBACK

a. A rugby-player

b. A fish

c. A breed of dog

82 FLATION

a. Price rise

b. Breathing

c. An uncharged atomic particle

83 RATOON

a. A colony of rats

b. An okra stew

c. To prune

84 FRACEDO

a. Putrid heat

b. Neutered meat

c. A lucid beat

85 NAVICULA

a. A mosquito

b. the navel

c. An incense-holder

86 ERIA

a. Yesterday (Sunday)

b. A silk-worm

c. A liquid measure

87 ONDE

a. To breathe

b. A wave

b. Whence

88 CHEESA

a. Cheddar

b. An explosive

c. The Phoenician digraph CSH

89 FLOSCULATION
a. Sweating
b. Blushing
c. A figure of speech

90 SPHAIRISTIKE
a. An insect
b. A two handled Attic bowl
c. Tennis

91 FRITHSTOOL
a. Sanctuary
b. Constipation
c. A poisonous red toadstool

92 TELEDU
a. A kind of badger
b. An Indian language
c. A couch-potato for television

93 ZAMANG
a. A scimitar
a. A chief
c. A tree

94 CREPIS
a. Sandals
b. A herb
c. A pancake

95 VORAX
a. A whirlpool
b. Hungry
c. A bird

96 BURKE
a. A traitor
b. To evade
c. A cloak

2 4
22 4 5 21
14
21 18 4 22
23
25 12 21

17
12
6
9
12
17 N
1
23
23
4 A
2
12
22
4
21
17
1
14
13
6
2
4
Codeword

How to Play

- Numbers are substituted for letters in the crossword grid.
- Below the grid is the key. Some letters are solved.
- When you have completed your first word or phrase you will have the clues to more letters. Enter them in the key grid and the main grid and check the letters on the alphabet list as you complete them.

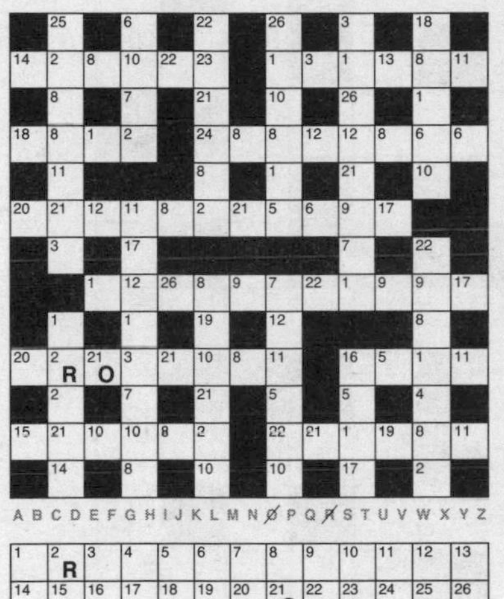

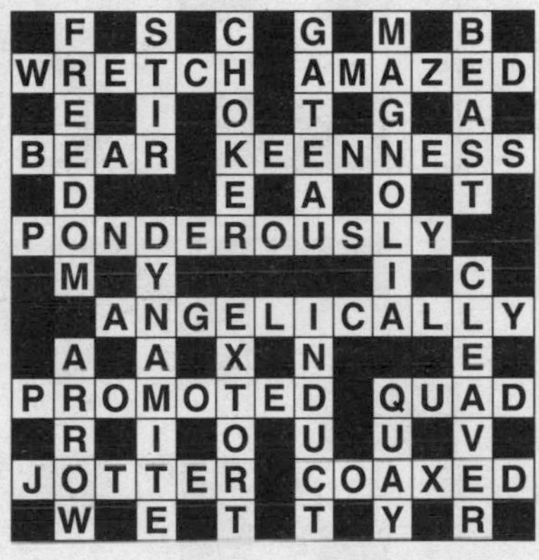

1

25		9		6	9	21	1	19		19		7
16	8	22	19	9		9		1	17	1	19	24
9		14		7	21	19	9	6		18		16
7	11	1	9	24		12		9		16	19	20
10				1		14	12	4	9	14		
23	20	26	9	3	1	7		7		9	19	21
20		12								19		12
18	16	4		13		22	14	12	16	7	12	20
		9	19	12	8	9		19				2 F
5	12	18		20		15		9	14	23	22	23 I
12		23		23	3	1	9	14		24		19 R
24	1	20	12	20		19		14	12	21	16	8
7		18		18	16	7	10	4		10		7

A B C D E ~~F~~ G H ~~I~~ J K L M N O P Q ~~R~~ S T U V W X Y Z

1	2 F	3	4	5	6	7	8	9	10	11	12	13
14	15	16	17	18	19 R	20	21	22	23 I	24	25	26

2

11	23	17	12	■	11	23	23	16	11	25	13	■
■	26	■	12	■	1	■	18	■	25	■	15	■
22	16	19	17	21	18	■	15	16	20	17	21	3
■	12	■	■	■	12	■	16	■	12	■	10	■
10	12	23	24 C	21 A	17 L	12	23	■	19	11	23	6
■	9	■	7	■	■	■	12	■	14	■	■	■
10	12	20	21	24	7	■	23	8	12	12	18	23
■	■	■	1	■	12	■	■	■	24	■	19	■
10	15	2	2	■	24	11	24	21	20	19	11	4
■	22	■	12	■	6	■	19	■	■	■	5	■
25	12	16	19	21	17	■	11	25	19	15	21	10
■	3	■	12	■	12	■	22	■	15	■	20	■
■	23	21	10	11	23	20	23	■	10	19	12	3

~~A~~ B ~~C~~ D E F G H I J K ~~L~~ M N O P Q R S T U V W X Y Z

1	2	3	4	5	6	7	8	9	10	11	12	13

14	15	16	17	18	19	20	21	22	23	24	25	26
			L				A			C		

3

4	22	13	12	■	18	6	23	7	14	2	11	■
■	2	■	2	■	4	■	17	■	12	■	6	■
15	4	22	4	5	21	■	9	12	17 N	1	23	21
■	10	■	■	■	14	■	23	■	4 A	■	2	■
4	1	2	21	18	4	22	12	■	22	4	21	3
■	12	■	23	■	■	■	17	■	1	■	■	■
14	2	1	25	12	21	■	14	13	6	2	4	16
■	■	■	8	■	26	■	■	■	23	■	19	■
4	18	21	12	■	23	17	7	1	21	14	12	24
■	2	■	22	■	1	■	23	■	■	■	2	■
20	1	7	14	12	2	■	21	5	1	20	14	21
■	21	■	12	■	12	■	14	■	2	■	12	■
■	15	6	24	12	21	14	11	■	3	1	24	21

~~A~~ B C D E F G H I J K L M ~~N~~ O P Q R S T U V W X Y Z

1	2	3	4	5	6	7	8	9	10	11	12	13
			A									
14	15	16	17	18	19	20	21	22	23	24	25	26
			N									

4

	22		25		5		22		10		11	
14	7 H	26 I	2 L	1	22		1	15	2	5	26	6
	21		21		19		13		5		1	
23	1	22	9		1	15	9	21	16	1	6	8
	25				15		1		26		3	
14	21	6	24	22	9	5	9	26	21	4		
	13		4						2		26	
		15	21	4	15	2	18	22	26	21	4	22
	20		15		18		4				12	
19	18	15	24	1	6	1	16		17	21	1	3
	26		21		9		18		21		4	
11	2	21	18	9	22		2	26	10	7	9	22
	2		9		3		3		22		22	

A B C D E F G ~~H~~ ~~I~~ J K ~~L~~ M N O P Q R S T U V W X Y Z

1	2	3	4	5	6	7	8	9	10	11	12	13
	L					H						
14	**15**	**16**	**17**	**18**	**19**	**20**	**21**	**22**	**23**	**24**	**25**	**26**
												I

5

6	1	4	7	23	■	8	4	4	13	20	24	24
■	13	■	12	■	4	■	13	■	7	■	15	■
24	20	1	19 B	8 O	13 R	16	20	■	8	4	9	24
■	16	■	7	■	8	■	24	■	2	■	20	■
3	1	19	19	20	23	■	20	16	24	9	20	■
■	■	■	20	■	9	■	16	■	■	■	18	■
8	26	20	23	■	14	1	2	■	2	8	5	24
■	1	■	■	■	2	■	1	■	17	■	■	■
■	21	9	16	25	7	■	2	8	26	20	11	24
■	21	■	20	■	6	■	7	■	1	■	8	■
21	11	8	26	■	20	22	8	13	14	7	24	2
■	20	■	20	■	11	■	16	■	10	■	20	■
8	24	4	13	20	5	24	■	9	24	9	13	4

A ~~B~~ C D E F G H I J K L M N ~~O~~ P Q ~~R~~ S T U V W X Y Z

1	2	3	4	5	6	7	8	9	10	11	12	13
							O					R
14	15	16	17	18	19	20	21	22	23	24	25	26
					B							

6

6	■	25	■	6	■	20	■	25	■	3	■	15
11	8	19 U	10 L	16	12	11	■	16	26	19	15	11
15	■	7	■	7	■	25	■	10	■	8	■	3
11	6	6	11	21	■	12	15	16	17	16	2	10
12	■	19	■	2	■	■	■	8	■	■	■	16
■	22	15	16	12	2	13	23	2	7	22	10	23
16	■	7	■	■	■	16	■	■	■	10	■	25
21	2	25	25	11	15	12	16	12	2	24	7	■
11	■	■	■	17	■	■	■	2	■	15	■	13
3	11	16	13	24	1	10	■	16	14	2	16	10
12	■	18	■	4	■	24	■	15	■	24	■	16
10	16	12	9	11	■	3	10	16	5	19	11	25
23	■	25	■	25	■	11	■	25	■	25	■	4

A B C D E F G H I J K ~~L~~ M N O P Q R S T ~~U~~ V W X Y Z

1	2	3	4	5	6	7	8	9	10	11	12	13
									L			
14	15	16	17	18	19	20	21	22	23	24	25	26
					U							

7

25	21	23	4	7	8	13	■	4	7	24	23	15
7	■	3	■	24	■	8	■	15	■	2	■	3
19 R	8	15	3	25	■	4	6	3	19	24	15	4
21 O	■	11	■	5	■	3	■	25	■	16	■	6
14 N	8	4	11	15	8	4	■	8	20	3	15	4
3	■	■	■	8	■	11	■	■	■	14	■	■
25	21	24	19	4	8	■	22	24	9	9	8	13
■	■	2	■	■	■	6	■	18	■	■	■	3
9	15	3	14	11	■	21	6	12	15	8	14	11
12	■	24	■	7	■	8	■	24	■	10	■	7
4	12	26	22	8	25	11	■	19	24	3	4	8
11	■	15	■	1	■	3	■	3	■	11	■	19
21	20	8	19	11	■	25	19	24	4	4	15	17

A B C D E F G H I J K L M ~~N~~ ~~O~~ P Q ~~R~~ S T U V W X Y Z

1	2	3	4	5	6	7	8	9	10	11	12	13
14 N	15	16	17	18	19 R	20	21 O	22	23	24	25	26

8

11	26	20	3	24	11		23	19	25	25	10	26
5		11		20		24		25		6		18
19	11	2	6	25		13	6	17	19	3	6	11
20				11		20		6		20		7
11	24	13	6	4	7	18	7		15	25	18	10
2		20		18		4		14		25		3
	11	9	3	24 P	20 A	15 T	2	6	15	18	8	
11		20		11		18		25		6		20
15	20	1	11		10	22	6	25	19	11	6	7
20		10		20		6		9				7
8	10	19	4	8	18	13		8	25	20	16	6
12		15		25		9		20		21		25
11	9	11	15	6	3		12	4	6	6	13	11

~~A~~ B C D E F G H I J K L M N O ~~P~~ Q R S ~~T~~ U V W X Y Z

1	2	3	4	5	6	7	8	9	10	11	12	13
14	15 T	16	17	18	19	20 A	21	22	23	24 P	25	26

9

	24		22		18		7		1		22	
23	7	12	3	3	26		26	4	25 B	21 I	3	22
	26		10		4	12	17		12		10	
2	4	1	25		23		12		3	1	24	8
	12			20	26	10	11	2			24	
1	22	3	12	4		22		1	9	21	26	13
		12		21	24	21	12	4		4		
14	10	1	4	3		5		12	19	12	24	3
	16			12	2	23	12	2			7	
24	7	10	13		1		13		19	1	21	11
	12		26		21	13	16		1		5	
24	11	26	24	8	22		3	12	13	16	3	22
	2		8		15		15		22		6	

A ~~B~~ C D E F G H ~~I~~ J K L M N O P Q R S T U V W X Y Z

1	2	3	4	5	6	7	8	9	10	11	12	13
14	**15**	**16**	**17**	**18**	**19**	**20**	**21**	**22**	**23**	**24**	**25**	**26**
							I				B	

10

22	14	6	11	19	24	23	11	■	4	24	3	6
19	■	3	■	14	■	14	■	11	■	2	■	24
24	7	17	23	21	■	3	13	21	15	17	22	21
22	■	19	■	25	■	21	■	17	■	9	■	21
18	24	21	11	■	10	15	14	22	22	14	19	24
■	■	25	■	24	■	16	■	18	■	■	■	3
1	14	16	3	7	11	■	9	3	16	11	3	15
3	■	■	■	11	■	3	■	1	■	21	■	■
12	15	3	8	20	3	7	21	■	5	24	7	22
20	■	1	■	19	■	24	■	10	■	2	■	19
11	3	24	5	24	7	9	■	20	4	20	19	17
3	■	12	■	7	■	2	■	7	■	19	■	7
1	17	16	11	■	26	17	7	9	19 L	24 I	7 N	9

A B C D E F G H ~~I~~ J K ~~L~~ M ~~N~~ O P Q R S T U V W X Y Z

1	2	3	4	5	6	7	8	9	10	11	12	13
						N						
14	**15**	**16**	**17**	**18**	**19**	**20**	**21**	**22**	**23**	**24**	**25**	**26**
					L					I		

Lexica | Polygon | Scrabble™ Challenge | Word Watch | Codeword

11

■	■	12	1	2	3	25	25	23	5	18	13	■
6	■	2	■	12	■	18	■	22	■	2	■	1
25	15	25	3	11	2	1	■	18	25	1	16	25
25	■	26	■	25	■	22	■	3	■	26	■	22
18	2	17	25	23	■	13	■	25	22	17	25	23
■	14	■	16	■	10	25	5	■	23	■	■	25
20	1	25	25	21	25	■	3	2	14	13	22	1
5	■	■	18	■	23	22	7	■	10	■	8	■
17	10	2	11	17	■	10	■	2	11	19	25	1
9	■	4	■	22	■	20	■	20	■	22	■	25
14	18	10	25	11	■	5	23	2	10	5	17	25
25	■	5	■	7	■	18	■	25	■	1	■	24
■	17	12 P	14 U	1 R	5	2	14	17	10	7	■	■

A B C D E F G H I J K L M N O ~~P~~ Q ~~R~~ S T ~~U~~ V W X Y Z

1 R	2	3	4	5	6	7	8	9	10	11	12 P	13
14 U	15	16	17	18	19	20	21	22	23	24	25	26

12

16	26	6	1	■	4	■	1	■	18	16	26	23
21	■	7	■	23	11	17	20	12	■	21	■	21
19	26	11	7	■	20	■	1	■	22	11	17	8
2	■	22	11	21	8	■	26	14	20	12	■	26
■	1	■	21	■	15	20	12	■	13	■	3	■
23	21	17 U	15 L	12 T	2	■	2	26	21	11	15	2
■	13	■	■	7	■	■	■	2	■	■	26	■
25	21	20	15	26	22	■	8	26	21	1	26	11
■	15	■	20	■	26	5	7	■	17	■	22	■
10	■	24	26	11	3	■	10	7	11	26	■	8
16	21	1	22	■	21	■	9	■	21	15	15	2
26	■	20	■	20	10	10	17	26	■	10	■	12
22	17	12	2	■	26	■	26	■	8	26	10	16

A B C D E F G H I J K ~~L~~ M N O P Q R S ~~T~~ ~~U~~ V W X Y Z

1	2	3	4	5	6	7	8	9	10	11	12 T	13
14	15 L	16	17 U	18	19	20	21	22	23	24	25	26

13

■	19	■	2	■	13	■	■	■	14	■	17	■
19	18	2 P	9 O	7	19	4	■	20	9	6	23	24
■	24	■	7	■	7	■	24	■	23	■	9	■
17	23	8	24	■	24	25	3	21	5	3	21	15
■	8	■	6	■	■	■	16	■	■	■	22	■
■	■	2	23	9	1	3	24	■	17	16	19	14
■	7	■	19	■	9	■	19	■	9	■	4	■
26	6	8	4	■	23	19	4	3	8	16	■	■
■	23	■	■	■	8	■	■	■	23	■	13	■
3	21	4	6	16	15	19	4	■	4	23	3	2
■	8	■	15	■	19	■	9	■	3	■	16	■
7	10	3	16	19	■	12	9	3	21	24	16	11
■	19	■	11	■	■	■	10	■	15	■	8	■

A B C D E F G H I J K L M N Ø P̸ Q R S T U V W X Y Z

1	2 P	3	4	5	6	7	8	9 O	10	11	12	13
14	15	16	17	18	19	20	21	22	23	24	25	26

14

■	26	■	1	■	14	■	26	■	5	■	6	■
21	12	20	3	1	8	■	4	8	20	25	4	1
■	13	■	1	■	2	■	2	■	13	■	16	■
2	15	14	8	10	20	8	16	■	24	20	16	15
■	14	■	24	■	■	■	12	■	■	■	23	■
4	8	21	26	■	20	21	26	23	20	24	1	24
■	■	■	8	■	8	■	18	■	8	■	■	■
23	1	8	16	2	15	1	8	■	17	20	2	24
■	7	■	■	■	14	■	■	■	23	■	20	■
24	13	12	19	■	11	14	13	2 T	20 I	24 S	22	24
■	1	■	26	■	20	■	14	■	9	■	1	■
17	23	14	4	8	2	■	3	26	2	1	12	24
■	24	■	12	■	24	■	1	■	24	■	24	■

A B C D E F G H ~~I~~ J K L M N O P Q R ~~S~~ ~~T~~ U V W X Y Z

1	2	3	4	5	6	7	8	9	10	11	12	13
	T											

14	15	16	17	18	19	20	21	22	23	24	25	26
						I				S		

15

8	21	15	12	23	25		20	5	2	23	25	16
	20		26		14		25		11		7	
14	2	23	10	26	23	9	25		1	20	11	12
	8		15		19		23		23		23	
12	23	20	11		26	6	3	23	2	10	20	21
			20		20						17	
	23	22	19	23	21	21	23	6	3	21	18	
	6						24		2			
20	1	1	26	3	26	10	23		20	25	17	25
	26		1		1		19		14		6	
23	6	10	18		23	22	3	2	23	13	23	25
	8		21		20		23		4		23	
14	25	20 A	21 L	13	25		1	9	23	21	21	25

~~A~~ B C D E F G H I J K ~~L~~ M N O P Q R S T U V W X Y Z

1	2	3	4	5	6	7	8	9	10	11	12	13
14	15	16	17	18	19	20	21	22	23	24	25	26
						A	L					

16

■	12	■	9	■	26	■	25	■	2	■	12	■
24	2 H	18 I	16 M	11	7	9	4	■	25	17	25	15
■	9	■	18	■	25	■	7	■	7	■	7	■
20	9	15	4	21	14	■	9	7	10	18	14	■
■	13	■	4	■	6	■	9	■	■	■	22	■
4	9	16	18	■	9	1	20	7	21	18	24	4
■	■	■	21	■	■	■	■	■	3	■	■	■
12	2	9	14	9	3	9	15	■	9	22	15	21
■	21	■	■	■	18	■	9	■	15	■	21	■
■	22	4	22	25	7	■	6	7	9	14	6	2
■	15	■	20	■	9	■	21	■	25	■	19	■
25	7	24	21	■	4	5	22	25	24	24	9	23
■	8	■	14	■	24	■	20	■	4	■	24	■

A B C D E F G H I J K L M N O P Q R S T U V W X Y Z

1	2	3	4	5	6	7	8	9	10	11	12	13
	H											

14	15	16	17	18	19	20	21	22	23	24	25	26
		M		I								

17

13	21	3	25	5	6	7	5			16	20	5
25 I		21		18		10		2				18
9 N	21	15	6	25	9	17		22		15		25
24 C			7			11		5	21	16	7	10
6			20	24	15		26			7		5
7	14	7	4		22		22		6	7	1	
5			15	7	4	1	25	9	25			1
	24	21	5		9		15		15	21	17	20
2		20			5		7	23	15			19
3	25	23	15	5		7			7			7
20		5		25		2	7	20	4	7	4	5
8				12		2		3		16		15
7	14	7			13	5	20	3	15	7	4	11

A B ~~C~~ D E F G H ~~I~~ J K L M ~~N~~ O P Q R S T U V W X Y Z

1	2	3	4	5	6	7	8	9	10	11	12	13
								N				
14	**15**	**16**	**17**	**18**	**19**	**20**	**21**	**22**	**23**	**24**	**25**	**26**
										C	I	

18

6	2	10	5	11	18	■	5	2	23	10	4	20
2	■	8	■	14	■	4	■	21	■	6	■	10
25	5	3	10	6	16	10	■	13	14	3	10	5
6	■	8	■	15	■	5	■	2	■	2	■	11
■	10	5	13	26	■	13	7	2	2	5	14	25
19	■	2	■	■	■	7	■	15	■	■	■	14
8	6	15	14	2	26	■	8	26	2	12	8	9
4	■	■	■	1	■	10	■	■	■	25	■	26
11	2	15	11	8	3	26	■	4	10	5	17	■
9	■	5	■	10	■	14	■	8	■	22	■	2
14	15	14	25	24	■	15	2	12	5 R	10 A	18	26
6	■	23	■	2	■	2	■	24	■	5	■	20
3	5	2	2	15	18	■	22	14	9	15	9	18

~~A~~ B C D E F G H I J K L M N O P Q ~~R~~ S T U V W X Y Z

1	2	3	4	5 R	6	7	8	9	10 A	11	12	13
14	15	16	17	18	19	20	21	22	23	24	25	26

19

8	3	23	5	■	4	21	19	20	9	3	20	7
15	■	21	■	16	■	5	■	1	■	10	■	5
24	22	15	10	8	5	10	■	17	15	1	14	5
11	■	23	■	15	■	7	■	13	■	8	■	23
19	20	3	16	1	■	5	2	21	15	8	5	■
5	■	■	■	5	■	4	■	■	■	3	■	26
22	5	24	5	10	5	■	16	15	4	24	3	15
4	■	15	■	■	■	18	■	4	■	■	■	8
■	4	8	5	15	25	5	■	4	13	8	3	9
4	■	1	■	6	■	4	■	19	■	5	■	25
20	15	13	13	15	■	9	3	17	13	15	20	3
15	■	4	■	3	■	5	■	5	■	4	■	20
13	22 R	12 O	26 W	8	5	22	4	■	24	21	19	7

A B C D E F G H I J K L M N ~~O~~ P Q ~~R~~ S T U V ~~W~~ X Y Z

1	2	3	4	5	6	7	8	9	10	11	12 O	13
14	15	16	17	18	19	20	21	22 R	23	24	25	26 W

20

	4		4		11		15		4		11	
4	18	8	18	11	22		1	7	13	8	20	14
	12		24		8	11	14		24		24	
18	20	24	17	8	11		4		7	12	3	14
	14				5	8	18				24	
24	21	24	13	18		17		16	12	12	18	2
		17		8	6	25	24	2		24		
10	20	12	26	14		12		14	14	20	8	14
	14				10	12	16				20	
7	24	25	18		9		12	20 R	24 A	18 T	12	20
	25		12		12	23	6		3		6	
17	25	12	23	14	20		14	25	8	19	8	20
	2		6		21		21		21		11	

~~A~~ B C D E F G H I J K L M N O P Q ~~R~~ S ~~T~~ U V W X Y Z

1	2	3	4	5	6	7	8	9	10	11	12	13
14	15	16	17	18 T	19	20 R	21	22	23	24 A	25	26

21

■	15	■	23	■	18	■	1	■	7	■	11	■
14	11	21	21	7	2	■	9	1	4	18	16	8
■	1	■	1	■	18	5	12	■	18	■	22	■
9	12	18	10	■	3	■	7	■	21	3	11	19
■	7	■	■	■	10	1	2	■	■	■	9	■
1	2	3	17	19	■	13	■	13	1	21	19	24
■	■	5	■	3	25	25	7	5	■	1	■	■
1	6	6	3	19	■	11	■	26	3	2	7	21
■	1 A	■	■	■	18	21	12	■	■	■	20	■
2	5 R	1	13	■	23	■	18	■	13	14	18	17
■	7	■	1	■	18	3	16	■	1	■	19	■
25	21	1	8	3	16	■	12	18	2	16	7	26
■	26	■	7	■	8	■	26	■	7	■	2	■

~~A~~ B C D E F G H I J K L M N O P Q ~~R~~ S T U V W X Y Z

1	2	3	4	5	6	7	8	9	10	11	12	13
A				R								
14	15	16	17	18	19	20	21	22	23	24	25	26

22

4	25	7	8	9	23	■	1	4	8	1	3	9
15	■	24	■	15	■	19	■	13	■	23	■	15
17	7	7	■	23	15	1	11	14	1	12	15	23
15	■	5	■	6	■	8	■	■	■	1	■	12
23	17	15	1	8	■	19	16	10	7	5	15	23
26	■	■	■	3	■	3	■	13	■	6	■	■
■	18	8	7	19 B	1 A	26 T	3	7	5	15	8	■
■	■	15	■	15	■	14	■	8	■	■	■	15
1	9	20	3	23	15	8	■	3	26	15	2	23
18	■	15	■	■	■	1	■	4	■	22	■	26
23	18	1	10	21	15	26	26	3	■	6	14	15
15	■	13	■	14	■	15	■	15	■	15	■	15
23	1	23	21	15	23	■	1	23	16	13	14	2

~~A~~ ~~B~~ C D E F G H I J K L M N O P Q R S ~~T~~ U V W X Y Z

1	2	3	4	5	6	7	8	9	10	11	12	13
A												
14	**15**	**16**	**17**	**18**	**19**	**20**	**21**	**22**	**23**	**24**	**25**	**26**
					B							T

23

	10		10		5		12		12		21	
10	20	23	2	3	23		8	22	19	2	11	5
	8		19		15		15		7		24	
10	18	23	4		1	7	19	26	20	19	2	10
	22				23		7		24		9	
16	19	26	15	10	22	8	23	14	8	7		
	20		23						20		24	
		19	26	20	18	8	24	9	17	24	2	9
	24		4 B		24		2				6	
26	2	17	24 I	2	9	8	15		12	16	8	13
	1		2 N		9		8		16		1	
1	26	15	9	8	16		8	25	26	24	20	11
	7		10		11		15		13		10	

A ~~B~~ C D E F G H ~~I~~ J K L M ~~N~~ O P Q R S T U V W X Y Z

1	2	3	4	5	6	7	8	9	10	11	12	13
	N		B									
14	**15**	**16**	**17**	**18**	**19**	**20**	**21**	**22**	**23**	**24**	**25**	**26**
										I		

24

15	7	12	20	10	4	3	22		16	2	14	9
7		13		25		20		19		3		14
12	19	25	10	26		21	7	25	19	19	26	7
19		12		21		14		4		3		23
8	12	15	26		18	14	20	4	26	15	15	3
		3		21		7		2				20
2	12	18	23	26	21		16	26	2	14	20	6
3				24		21		21		7		
12	21	5	14	3	20	26	21		11	3	20	18
3		25		12		12		2		6		7
10	1	3 I	4 F	15	26	21		12	19	12	11	26
26		18		26		2		24		19		12
21	25	26	2		21	17	20	12	19	3	10	19

A B C D E ~~F~~ G H ~~I~~ J K L M N O P Q R S T U V W X Y Z

1	2	3 I	4 F	5	6	7	8	9	10	11	12	13
14	15	16	17	18	19	20	21	22	23	24	25	26

25

1		10		20	22	24	11	12		14		11
22	7	12	5	22		9		17	12	12	7	25
21 J		24		8	15	16	17	14		1		20
15 O	13	11	12	5		12		12		17	26	12
17 L				12		22	15	7	11	22		
26	5	13	26	14	12	17		24		7	22	20
5		26								12		12
4	12	17		3		13	16	1	6	24	26	22
		17	26	12	4	12		22				24
24	2	26		7		17		18	22	17	24	22
22		5		15	7	26	12	17		15		5
10	22	4	16	12		5		12	19	22	17	11
12		24		14	7	12	22	14		23		24

A B C D E F G H I ~~J~~ K ~~L~~ M N ~~O~~ P Q R S T U V W X Y Z

1	2	3	4	5	6	7	8	9	10	11	12	13
14	15 O	16	17 L	18	19	20	21 J	22	23	24	25	26

26

7	2	3	11	■	21	2	2	7	2	12	2	■
■	24	■	3	■	3	■	21	■	26	■	9	■
16	10	4	3	11	7	■	25	13	7	4	11	2
■	11	■	■	■	14	■	21	■	6	■	18	■
18	11	17	17	3	7	16	8	■	12	13	12	2
■	23	■	21	■	■	■	11	■	7	■	■	■
3	11	2	2	11	11	■	17	1	11	16	4	26
■	■	■	26	■	22	■	■	■	2	■	13	■
2	11	19	7	■	4	13	10	16	12	7	16	8
■	22	■	16	■	3	■	2	■	■	■	20	■
2	12	7	8	19	21	■	10	16	7	24	10	11
■	1	■	3	■	7	■	21	■	1	■	1	■
■	21	14	5 Y	2 S	19 M	21	3	■	15	11	11	3

A B C D E F G H I J K L ~~M~~ N O P Q R ~~S~~ T U V W X ~~Y~~ Z

1	2	3	4	5	6	7	8	9	10	11	12	13
	S			Y								
14	**15**	**16**	**17**	**18**	**19**	**20**	**21**	**22**	**23**	**24**	**25**	**26**
					M							

27

7	17	9	24	■	10	19	14	24	24	14	6	■
■	26	■	14	■	8	■	20	■	8	■	17	■
22	4	8	2	21	18	■	3	8	2	26	5	9
■	24	■	■	■	26	■	17	■	1	■	14	■
8	2	7	1	2	21	14	9	■	14	2	9	25
■	8	■	8	■	■	■	14	■	16	■	■	■
1	25	15	18	26	9	■	9	24	18 O	8 R	7	25
■	■	■	23	■	14	■	■	■	4	■	18	■
13	8	14	14	■	3	19	4	15	6	4	9	19
■	14	■	3	■	8	■	8	■	■	■	12	■
3	15	18	24	19	14	■	18	13	13	3	17	24
■	4	■	14	■	24	■	26	■	4	■	14	■
■	3	17	6	21	14	15	9	■	11	17	9	25

A B C D E F G H I J K L M N Ø P Q R̸ S T U V W X Y Z

1	2	3	4	5	6	7	8	9	10	11	12	13
							R					
14	**15**	**16**	**17**	**18**	**19**	**20**	**21**	**22**	**23**	**24**	**25**	**26**
				O								

28

■	12	■	24	■	24	■	15	■	21	■	15	■
15	26	25	23	25	15	■	19	10	26	15	5	15
■	1	■	10	■	15	■	24	■	24	■	26	■
17	1	10	20	■	26	1	23	26	5	26	1	2
■	26	■	■	■	2	■	25	■	19	■	17	■
14	24	11	11	25	1	26	1	2	9	16	■	■
■	15	■	25	■	■	■	■	■	10	■	8	■
■	■	3	22	10	14 M	26 I	1 N	25	1	5	9	16
■	25	■	22	■	24	■	4	■	■	■	4	■
15	13	4	26	1	5	25	11	■	7	24	14	15
■	4	■	6	■	5	■	2	■	24	■	14	■
5	24	6	17	9	25	■	25	14	3	9	10	16
■	9	■	15	■	11	■	15	■	25	■	18	■

A B C D E F G H ~~I~~ J K L ~~M~~ ~~N~~ O P Q R S T U V W X Y Z

1	2	3	4	5	6	7	8	9	10	11	12	13
N												
14	**15**	**16**	**17**	**18**	**19**	**20**	**21**	**22**	**23**	**24**	**25**	**26**
M												I

29

■	12	■	11	■	21	■	8	■	16	■	16	■
22	25	11	13	21	22	■	17	1	17	7	9	22
■	25	■	19	■	14	■	20	■	9	■	21	■
22	21	3	5	■	17	20	21	9	16	12	19	21
■	12	■	■	■	9	■	9	■	11	■	22	■
12	9	9	21	22	16	11	13	8	2	5	■	■
■	22	■	3	■	■	■	■	■	2	■	18	■
■	■	26	10 H	11	23	22	11	14	12	2	2	5
■	4	■	11 I	■	11	■	13	■	■	■	12	■
24	7	11	18 B	18	2	21	1	■	4	12	15	21
■	16	■	11	■	19	■	7	■	17	■	21	■
6	17	22	16	2	21	■	14	10	17	11	9	22
■	13	■	22	■	1	■	21	■	1	■	22	■

A ~~B~~ C D E F G ~~H~~ ~~I~~ J K L M N O P Q R S T U V W X Y Z

1	2	3	4	5	6	7	8	9	10	11	12	13
									H	I		
14	**15**	**16**	**17**	**18**	**19**	**20**	**21**	**22**	**23**	**24**	**25**	**26**
				B								

30

10	■	25	■	3	■	16	■	19	■	18	■	9
26	25	26	12	10	19	24	■	4	19	10	22	23
19	■	19	■	6	■	26	■	23	■	8	■	10
20	9	12	19	21	■	19	1	18	26	23	18	20
25	■	8	■	17	■	■	■	10	■	■	■	6
■	7	12	26	25	9	17	26	8	10	26	20	20
2	■	23	■	■	■	19	■	■	■	24	■	25
12	26	2	12	26	20	20	6	13	26	24	15	■
26	■	■	■	5	■	■	■	26	■	6	■	2
16	19	24	20	26	24	15	■	12	26	2	26	24
23	■	23	■	12	■	19	■	14	■	25	■	18
12	6	13	26	25	■	2	12 R	6 I	11	6	10	21
14	■	26	■	20	■	20	■	10	■	9	■	20

A B C D E F G H ~~I~~ J K L M N O P Q ~~R~~ S T U V W X Y Z

1	2	3	4	5	6	7	8	9	10	11	12	13
					I						R	
14	15	16	17	18	19	20	21	22	23	24	25	26

31

15	23	21	7	11	23	19		26	12	2	25	5
23		1		6		15		7		20		6
5	1	14	23	5		23	22	12	19	6	9	14
8		6		2		5		8		10		13
3	1	2	8 T	7 O	15 R	5		5	10	12	1	8
12				5		18				23		
20	6	2	25	23	19		5	16	1	5	21	5
		13				12		23				1
20	23	1	5	8		16	1	15	2	13	23	19
7		16		4		25		24		23		19
2	1	16	5	6	17	23		12	9	19	12	23
12		23		20		23		15		14		5
21	7	19	23	20		16	1	18	21	23	9	8

A B C D E F G H I J K L M N ~~O~~ P Q ~~R~~ S ~~T~~ U V W X Y Z

1	2	3	4	5	6	7 O	8 T	9	10	11	12	13
14	15 R	16	17	18	19	20	21	22	23	24	25	26

32

3	26	2	19	23	3	■	5	4	2	11	11	5
9	■	12	■	19	■	13	■	3	■	2	■	21
21	17	1	19	5	■	3	17	8	19	14	23	5
2	■	■	■	6	■	7	■	15	■	19	■	6
26	21	5	6	14	19	3	6	■	6	12	19	19
5	■	25	■	21	■	14	■	5	■	3	■	14
■	4	3	22	17	21	17 D	3 A	6 T	20	14	19	■
14	■	14	■	19	■	2	■	3	■	22	■	3
2	3	24	5	■	5	20	25	25	2	5	19	17
6	■	1	■	18	■	5	■	1	■	■	■	8
20	22	19	10	20	3	1	■	21	5	5	20	19
22	■	14	■	6	■	15	■	22	■	19	■	22
17	19	5	21	5	6	■	3	16	13	3	5	6

~~A~~ B C ~~D~~ E F G H I J K L M N O P Q R S ~~T~~ U V W X Y Z

1	2	3	4	5	6	7	8	9	10	11	12	13
		A			T							
14	**15**	**16**	**17**	**18**	**19**	**20**	**21**	**22**	**23**	**24**	**25**	**26**
			D									

33

	10		12		22		25		9		7	
18	20	19	23	21	12		1	19	15	12	11	7
	21		14		22	9	9		21		24	
16	11	20	7		26		4		1	21	21	13
	11			16	12	19	23	14			7	
20	7	12	18	21		25		21	5	19	14	7
		18		25	1	19	22	21		22		
13	11	9	1	12		21		14	9	16	12	2
	21			23	9	1	14	3			15	
7	22	21	4		26		12		6	9	21	24
	20		12		21	21	11		20		1	
26	1	12	19	8	7		17	12	1 R	12 A	14	21
	7		11		21		7		24		7	

~~A~~ B C D E F G H I J K L M N O P Q ~~R~~ S T U V W X Y Z

1	2	3	4	5	6	7	8	9	10	11	12	13
R											A	
14	15	16	17	18	19	20	21	22	23	24	25	26

34

16	8	16	21	4	5	10	7	■	9	16	11	8
17	■	25	■	18	■	16	■	22	■	26	■	22
22	25	1	18	1	■	26	16	25	16	10	18	21
18	■	5	■	19	■	18	■	18	■	16	■	13
24	16	23	7	■	21	5	25	6	16	4	4	18
■	■	16	■	10	■	25	■	18	■	■	■	8
21	11	1	1	18	16	■	12	16	10	7	16	19
5	■	■	■	24	■	20	■	7	■	4	■	■
11	1	11	24	4	5	10	7	■	2	18	25	21
21	■	20	■	18	■	18	■	24	■	15	■	8
9	5	22	25	1	16	1	■	22	14	22	8	11
16	■	4	■	16	■	26	■	15	■	8	■	25
1	16	7	13	■	10	16	8 L	11 A	3 X	18	25	26

~~A~~ B C D E F G H I J K ~~L~~ M N O P Q R S T U V W ~~X~~ Y Z

1	2	3 X	4	5	6	7	8 L	9	10	11 A	12	13
14	15	16	17	18	19	20	21	22	23	24	25	26

35

11	7	1	22	25	■	21	24	1	5	25	5	15
■	23	■	17 C	■	8	■	18	■	18	■	26	■
9	3	20	7 O	24	15	5	15	■	3	11	8	22
■	25	■	6 W	■	7	■	5	■	17	■	1	■
10	5	3	9	7	25	■	3	9	25	5	15	■
■	■	■	5	■	5	■	22	■	■	■	5	■
14	7	9	19	■	17	7	7	■	13	24	19	7
■	4	■	■	■	25	■	18	■	7	■	■	■
■	4	24	18	12	1	■	3	18	12	9	5	22
■	5	■	5	■	23	■	20	■	25	■	18	■
16	18	5	6	■	5	5	9	12	15	3	22	22
■	17	■	5	■	9	■	2	■	7	■	24	■
19	5	4	15	3	2	22	■	22	25	5	5	19

A B ~~C~~ D E F G H I J K L M N ~~O~~ P Q R S T U V ~~W~~ X Y Z

1	2	3	4	5	6	7	8	9	10	11	12	13
					W	O						
14	15	16	17	18	19	20	21	22	23	24	25	26
			C									

36

19	21	7	22		2		25		6	4	9	23
9		1		11	21	20	18	14		20		21
9	19	18	7		14		14		19	15	6	5
14		7	1	20	24		18	5	14	3		9
	19		18		15	20	23		9		16	
26	21	2	24	14	3		8	15	20	17	9	5
	2			9				21			14	
2	1	6 O	5 D	5	3		25	9	12	20	14	9
	3		6		9	4	9		9		3	
5		24	6	8	20		23	6	2	9		2
15	6	20	15		15		5		2	14	20	24
20		10		16	14	9	9	5		2		9
13	20	18	24		3		5		24	9	20	12

A B C ~~D~~ E F G H I J K L M N ~~O~~ P Q R S T U V W X Y Z

1	2	3	4	5	6	7	8	9	10	11	12	13
				D	O							
14	15	16	17	18	19	20	21	22	23	24	25	26

37

■	21	■	16	■	24	■	■	■	13	■	17	■
13	15	24	25	18	15	17	■	20	15	7	18	23
■	24	■	2	■	5	■	11	■	4	■	15	■
6	18	2	22	■	1	5	2 C	25 I	1 D	25	4	12
■	24	■	5	■	■	■	25	■	■	■	1	■
■	■	17	3	5	26	5	1	■	12	15	19	19
■	17	■	5	■	6	■	25	■	11	■	14	■
8	15	11	1	■	25	4	2	18	23	5	■	■
■	23	■	■	■	17	■	■	■	20	■	8	■
5	23	20	11	24	22	5	1	■	19	18	15	3
■	18	■	10	■	14	■	24	■	25	■	11	■
15	4	9	25	16	■	21	18	25	4	5	24	14
■	17	■	1	■	■	■	16	■	12	■	3	■

A B ~~C~~ ~~D~~ E F G H ~~I~~ J K L M N O P Q R S T U V W X Y Z

1 D	2 C	3	4	5	6	7	8	9	10	11	12	13
14	15	16	17	18	19	20	21	22	23	24	25 I	26

38

	21		6		21		18		16		17	
11	10	14	13	21	10		13	22	17	2	9	10
	12		22		26		19		11		24	
2	13	22	25	6	23	22	4		10	3	17	26
	23		6				8				9	
17	22	19	23		17	8 R	18 O	26 M	17	19	23	25
			22		11		5		23			
14	18	8	4	23	7	10	22		8	13	26	15
	3				23				26		10	
21	19	18	5		21	23	1	10	17	2	9	10
	17		10		10		10		23		18	
9	23	22	10	17	8		21	18	9	23	11	21
	9		11		21		19		21		20	

A B C D E F G H I J K L ~~M~~ N ~~O~~ P Q ~~R~~ S T U V W X Y Z

1	2	3	4	5	6	7	8	9	10	11	12	13
							R					
14	**15**	**16**	**17**	**18**	**19**	**20**	**21**	**22**	**23**	**24**	**25**	**26**
				O								M

39

9	11	17	17	21	7		9	15	24	21	7	23
	10		1		23		21		24		8	
23	1	11	9	18	15	9	7		11	12	20	15
	3		15		9		15		19		15	
23	15	9	18		17	11	16	4	11	6	15	18
			1		15						26	
	24	21	19	21	5	24	15	7	7	24	13	
	11						16		20			
7	5	20	17	17	21	16	12		2	11	9	22
	23		24		18		9		2		21	
17	15	11	20		15	25	11 A	24 L	20	11	5	15
	9		14		11		25		19		26	
20	7	15	14	20	24		15	19	17	9	13	1

~~A~~ B C D E F G H I J K ~~L~~ M N O P Q R S T U V W X Y Z

1	2	3	4	5	6	7	8	9	10	11	12	13
										A		
14	15	16	17	18	19	20	21	22	23	24	25	26
										L		

10

■	21	■	4	■	11	■	10	■	18	■	26	■
20	19	1	24	7	12	20	21	■	2	13	3	11
■	10	■	1	■	2	■	25	■	24	■	20	■
14	10	5	11	10	5	■	1	20	1	3	19	■
■	22	■	3	■	20	■	20	■	■	■	7	■
4	20	11	10	■	8	2	23	6 L	24 I	15 G	12	11
■	■	■	21	■	■	■	■	■	19	■	■	■
21	5	10	10	19	24	19	15	■	16	20	20	25
■	10	■	■	■	9	■	1	■	3	■	17	■
■	13	6	20	20	25	■	20	2	1	5	24	15
■	13	■	8	■	2	■	2	■	24	■	21	■
18	6	2	15	■	7	2	21	21	20	11	11	20
■	20	■	23	■	11	■	20	■	21	■	21	■

A B C D E F ~~G~~ H ~~I~~ J K ~~L~~ M N O P Q R S T U V W X Y Z

1	2	3	4	5	6	7	8	9	10	11	12	13
					L							
14	**15**	**16**	**17**	**18**	**19**	**20**	**21**	**22**	**23**	**24**	**25**	**26**
	G									I		

41

8	4	9 H	21 A	24 L	8	4	14	■	■	15	2	13
4	■	21	■	13	■	8	■	2	■	■	■	7
23	8	6	6	8	4	14	■	21	■	6	■	21
13	■	■	8	■	■	9	■	15	12	2	17	23
5	■	■	21	5	13	■	20	■	■	11	■	13
13	11	9	2	■	21	■	17	■	16	1	8	■
16	■	■	22	21	17	20	21	3	9	■	■	11
■	25	13	16	■	24	■	4	■	17	13	23	2
21	■	14	■	■	25	■	14	4	19	■	■	21
26	2	2	18	13	■	3	■	■	4	■	■	17
2	■	16	■	24	■	9	19	4	1	13	17	16
7	■	■	■	15	■	2	■	2	■	17	■	13
13	26	26	■	■	10	19	21	3	17	21	8	4

~~A~~ B C D E F G ~~H~~ I J K ~~L~~ M N O P Q R S T U V W X Y Z

1	2	3	4	5	6	7	8	9	10	11	12	13
								H				
14	15	16	17	18	19	20	21	22	23	24	25	26
							A			L		

42

14	1	5	5	7	11	■	25	17	20	3	19	19
6	■	20	■	10	■	25	■	13	■	18	■	6
18	20	8	11	7	16	18	■	7	16	18	7	20
25	■	11	■	16	■	1	■	10	■	7	■	7
■	1	22	7	25	■	25	6	20	6	20	1	26
15	■	7	■	■	■	13	■	6	■	■	■	7
3	16	11	3	26	9	■	8	16	4	8	16	22
1 A	■	■	■	6	■	1	■	■	■	16	■	25
17 C	6	21	5	6	9	25	■	6	1	25	18	■
4	■	13	■	25	■	13	■	24	■	8	■	3
8	20	1	18	7	■	7	12	7	23	24	18	25
16	■	26	■	16	■	25	■	20	■	8	■	7
22	20	7	1	25	9	■	2	1	16	11	7	20

~~A~~ B ~~C~~ D E F G H I J K L M N O P Q R S T U V W X Y Z

1	2	3	4	5	6	7	8	9	10	11	12	13
A												
14	**15**	**16**	**17**	**18**	**19**	**20**	**21**	**22**	**23**	**24**	**25**	**26**
			C									

43

2	23	2	10		25	1	24	10	10	12	2	13
24		16		24		20		2		5		14
10	14	1	20	9	2	10		7	1	11	2	9
5		18		9		2		1		12		24
1	20	26	12	18		13	15	10	1	11	13	
17				2		26				2		6
17	2	26	12	13	15		6	24	10	9	2	10
13		10				8		17				2
	9	24	5	24	19	2		18	21	10	12	7
17		22		13		13		24		14		3
18	2	2	3	13		26	12	5	22 P	24 A	20 N	12
14		4		2		2		2		13		20
2	23	2	20	26	12	9	2		13	26	24	19

~~A~~ B C D E F G H I J K L M ~~N~~ O ~~P~~ Q R S T U V W X Y Z

1	2	3	4	5	6	7	8	9	10	11	12	13

14	15	16	17	18	19	20	21	22	23	24	25	26
						N		P		A		

11

■	25	■	26	■	25	■	25	■	8	■	2	■
25	10 H	15 O	23 V	26	9	■	8	18	1	26	9	22
■	3	■	11	■	11	14	26	■	3	■	15	■
21	1	15	9	11	14	■	3	■	19	15	17	24
■	26	■	■	■	26	1	1	■	■	■	26	■
15	13	13	9	22	■	26	■	21	11	26	1	22
■	■	18	■	3	24	2	26	9	■	19	■	■
25	8	26	14	4	■	3	■	22	15	18	7	10
■	1	■	■	■	26	9	19	■	■	■	18	■
16	11	9	7	■	3	■	11	19	12	11	12	26
■	20	■	15	■	25	11	5	■	15	■	11	■
1	26	19	15	23	26	■	26	6	18	11	24	26
■	13	■	4	■	13	■	13	■	7	■	2	■

A B C D E F G ~~H~~ I J K L M N ~~O~~ P Q R S T U ~~V~~ W X Y Z

1	2	3	4	5	6	7	8	9	10	11	12	13
									H			
14	**15**	**16**	**17**	**18**	**19**	**20**	**21**	**22**	**23**	**24**	**25**	**26**
	O								V			

45

■	15	■	19	■	24	■	19	■	23	■	21	■
4	18	24	8	5	6	■	4	24	22	5	1	17
■	5	■	5	■	24	19	25	■	19	■	5	■
26	5	5	22	■	10	■	5	■	2	19	22	5
■	12	■	■	■	22	19	15	■	■	■	20	■
18	17	5	14	19	■	1	■	23	22	19	21	5
■	■	23	■	10	14	20	3	17	■	13	■	■
4	7	24	24	25	■	23	■	13	24	7	5	6
■	19	■	■	■	19	14	17	■	■	■	16	■
3	1	24	23	■	20	■	24 O	■	3	1	10	9
■	5	■	22	■	13	19	6 D	■	19	■	20	■
19	4	18	24	22	5	■	5	9	21	20	11	5
■	11	■	15	■	6	■	1	■	11	■	17	■

A B C ~~D~~ E F G H I J K L M N ~~O~~ P Q R S T U V W X Y Z

1	2	3	4	5	6 D	7	8	9	10	11	12	13
14	15	16	17	18	19	20	21	22	23	24 O	25	26

46

2	4	9	3	2	17	■	2	7	25	22	8	2
17	■	24	■	3	■	3	■	10	■	3	■	8
24	10	16	■	24	3	9	15	10	9	2	21	13
20	■	3	■	8	■	6	■	■	■	17	■	21
1	25	23	26	10	■	25	23	2	11	25	24	20
2	■	■	■	24	■	21	■	9	■	10	■	■
■	24	20	19 M	25 I	23 N	25	2	15	25	23	26	■
■	■	23	■	3	■	3	■	15	■	■	■	3
14	10	15	9	21	3	24	■	20	3	24	21	2
3	■	21	■	■	■	25	■	2	■	3	■	11
15	24	3	18	25	23	20	2	2	■	16	13	20
12	■	5	■	10	■	2	■	20	■	16	■	15
2	20	20	25	23	26	■	3	2	2	25	2	8

A B C D E F G H ~~I~~ J K L ~~M~~ ~~N~~ O P Q R S T U V W X Y Z

1	2	3	4	5	6	7	8	9	10	11	12	13
14	15	16	17	18	19 M	20	21	22	23 N	24	25 I	26

47

■	6	■	9	■	18	■	20	■	21	■	18	■
17	21	18	14	1	23	■	19	18	3	18	8	5
■	5 G	■	18	■	23	■	8	■	13	■	2	■
24	21 U	8	4	■	21	8	15	1	14	2	1	15
■	20 L	■	■	■	1	■	19	■	1	■	14	■
14	19	24	4	21	14	7	21	23	20	16	■	■
■	14	■	19	■	■	■	■	■	20	■	13	■
■	■	18	8	4	14	19	22	4	19	13	20	16
■	17	■	5	■	1	■	19	■	■	■	19	■
7	21	4	20	18	25	1	15	■	26	19	8	11
■	1	■	18	■	18	■	5	■	19	■	11	■
13	14	7	8	12	1	■	1	10	4	7	20	23
■	16	■	5	■	9	■	14	■	1	■	16	■

A B C D E F ~~G~~ H I J K ~~L~~ M N O P Q R S T ~~U~~ V W X Y Z

1	2	3	4	5	6	7	8	9	10	11	12	13
				G								
14	15	16	17	18	19	20	21	22	23	24	25	26
						L	U					

48

16	21	6	9	23	26	11	14		4	1	9	20
11		19		9		2		12		5		9
17	19	14	11	2		1	11	15	13	4	15	24
10		22		22		17		9		7		25 B
11	2	17	7		25	15	4	12	12	4	20	17 I
		19		8		22		26				19
12	4	18	19	9	12		25	11	20	4	19	18
15				12		12		14		15		
6	1	16	7	9	17	15	16		20	17	13	7
17		9		7		6		17		18		23
16	6	25	3	11	12	7		14	15	9	24	9
11		20		14		12		4		24		19
14	17	11	7		16	5	11	20	8	17	19	18

A ~~B~~ C D E F G H ~~I~~ J K L M N O P Q R S T U V W X Y Z

1	2	3	4	5	6	7	8	9	10	11	12	13
14	15	16	17 I	18	19	20	21	22	23	24	25 B	26

49

5		10		7	16	17	2	15		22		3
23	25	3	12	20		12		4	3	3	26	22
22		7		18	12	20	8	3		7		25
15	2	21	10	18		14		7		15	2	11
13				3		3	7	15	3	12		
16	7	22 S	16 I	26 D	3	22		11		16	9	3
7		16								3		7
17	21	15		1		3	24	25	23	22	3	26
		15	2	21	26	22		3				21
22	8	16		20		9		13	3	6	3	12
23		7		12	3	20	9	15		3		16
19	16	17	2	15		25		3	20	15	3	7
15		22		22	25	3	7	26		22		17

A B C ~~D~~ E F G H ~~I~~ J K L M N O P Q R ~~S~~ T U V W X Y Z

1	2	3	4	5	6	7	8	9	10	11	12	13
14	**15**	**16**	**17**	**18**	**19**	**20**	**21**	**22**	**23**	**24**	**25**	**26**
		I						S				D

50

8	11	5	22		6	26	15	3	3	15	17	
	17		24		11		18		19		22	
3	10	11	17	15	3		21	24	6	9	15	6
	15				5		5		13		11	
12	22	5	21	23	26	15	3		15	26	13	3
	15		26 L				15		22			
5	17	5	24 O	13	3		17	5	4	15	3	12
			6 B		19				15		14	
6	24	13	6		22	15	3	5	17	19	19	13
	1		15		4		11				15	
3	12	11	22	16	15		26	24	4	2	11	13
	5		15		24		3		5		23	
	21	11	17	15	20	7	11		4	19	25	3

A ~~B~~ C D E F G H I J K ~~L~~ M N ~~O~~ P Q R S T U V W X Y Z

1	2	3	4	5	6	7	8	9	10	11	12	13
					B							
14	15	16	17	18	19	20	21	22	23	24	25	26
										O		L

51

7		24		5	25	19	11	8		14		8
17	9	15	19	25		14		11	18	11	13	24
8		23		13	15	25	14	21		8		15
6	20	25	13	9		2		24		24	20	1
20				11		11	15	14	3	26		
25	7	19	11	22	11	8		26		3	25	24
24		20								11		15
17	5	21		14		22	11	4 V	25 I	8 S	11	22
		22	14	11	15	14		11				19
8	9	25		21		26		14	10	25	21	17
17		24		15	23	25	21	16		14		3
12	17	14	20	7		21		11	4	17	9	11
15		26		11	22	16	11	22		21		8

A B C D E F G H ~~I~~ J K L M N O P Q R ~~S~~ T U ~~V~~ W X Y Z

1	2	3	4 V	5	6	7	8 S	9	10	11	12	13
14	15	16	17	18	19	20	21	22	23	24	25 I	26

52

5	9	20	12	■	21	12	8	9	15	5	8	■
■	25	■	15	■	13	■	25 M	■	21	■	19	■
13	6	10	14	25	26	■	17 U	5	9	4	17	12
■	13	■	■	■	26	■	11 D	■	23	■	5	■
6	10	14	6	6	9	5	15	■	23	13	15	8
■	12	■	10	■	■	■	12	■	9	■	■	■
13	11	16	17	21	12	■	8	5	12	12	1	12
■	■	■	5	■	2	■	■	■	8	■	13	■
13	6	12	11	■	6	14	8	9	23	9	5	15
■	14	■	12	■	12	■	9	■	■	■	9	■
18	10	14	21	9	5	■	23	21	13	3	12	10
■	7	■	12	■	11	■	12	■	17	■	8	■
■	6	12	21	17	8	12	11	■	24	9	23	22

A B C ~~D~~ E F G H I J K L ~~M~~ N O P Q R S T ~~U~~ V W X Y Z

1	2	3	4	5	6	7	8	9	10	11	12	13
										D		
14	**15**	**16**	**17**	**18**	**19**	**20**	**21**	**22**	**23**	**24**	**25**	**26**
			U								M	

Solutions

1

	B			B	
F	U	S	I	O	N
	R			X	
	N				H
G	E	I	S	H	A
	R				D

2

S	H	E	A	F	
	E			A	
	R			L	
C	O	B	B	L	E
A		O		E	
B		B	A	N	

3

A	P	P	A	L	L
L		U		E	
O	I	L		A	
U		P	I	N	
D			N		
			K		

4

S		Q		F	
E	Q	U	A	L	
A		A		E	
R	I	D	D	E	N
C				T	
H	A	T			

5

A	B	S	O	R	B
	I			E	
	L	O	A	N	
	L			T	
	O	F	F	A	L
	W			L	

6

	S	U	C	H	
	T		I		
	O		C	U	T
U	R	E	A		H
	E		D		A
	Y	E	A	R	N

7

C	H	E	E	K	Y
	O		V		
	P		E		
M		A	R	M	
U		I			
M	I	M	I	C	

8

		H		F	
	B	I	S	O	N
C		L		R	
L	I	L	A	C	
O				E	
D	E	R	I	D	E

9

I	R	I	S		
	I		I		M
	G		Z		E
	H	A	Z	E	L
	T		L		O
		W	E	A	N

10

	S		L		
M	O	R	O	S	E
	N		C		N
N	A	T	A	N	T
	R		T		R
		L	E	V	Y

11

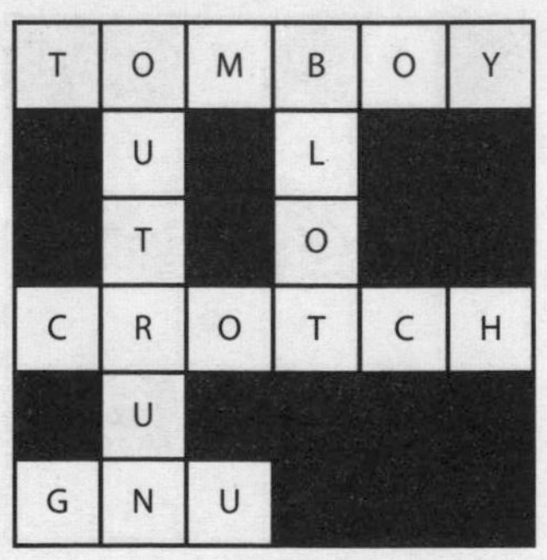

T	O	M	B	O	Y
	U		L		
	T		O		
C	R	O	T	C	H
	U				
G	N	U			

12

C	L	O	S	E	
U		U			
F	E	T	C	H	
F		I		O	
		N	E	W	T
H	O	G			

13

F	A	N			
L		I			
U	N	C	O	R	K
M		H			I
E	V	E	N		L
					O

14

S	O	L	E	M	N
	C			A	
S	U	C	K	L	E
	L			I	
	A			C	
	R	U	N	E	

15

B		W			
U	P	O	N		
F		O			
F	I	L	L	E	T
E			A		
R	U	M	B	A	

16

A	F	O	R	E	
	A		U		W
	D		S	H	E
M	I	T	E		D
	N				
	G	L	A	Z	E

17

P		F			
O	M	I	T		
T		L		G	
I	G	L	O	O	
O		Y		A	
N			S	L	Y

18

	S		F		
O	C	H	R	E	
	A		E		A
F	L	A	N	G	E
	D		Z		R
		T	Y	P	O

19

B					
U	N	D	O		
R		R		P	
L	E	A	F	Y	
A		M		R	
P	L	A	N	E	T

20

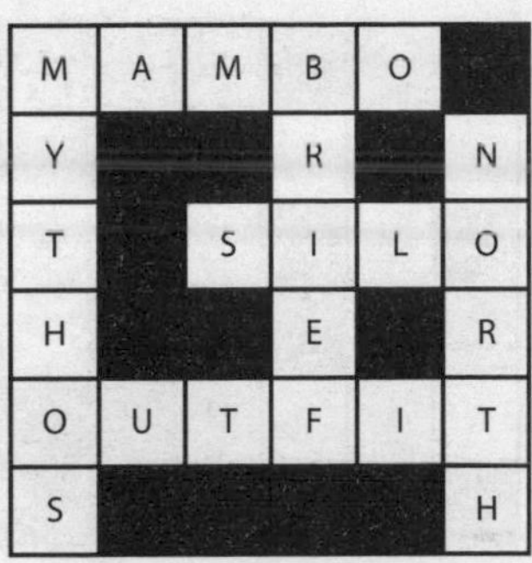

21

22

23

S	H	U	T		
A			H	U	T
D	E	W	Y		O
I			M	A	P
S			E		
M					

24

			T		
G	O	L	E	M	
	P		M		U
C	A	M	P	U	S
	L		L		E
		V	E	E	R

25

			V	A	T
J	A	Y			E
	M		P	O	X
	P		I		T
C	L	U	M	P	
	E		P		

26

		S		A	
	P	L	A	N	T
P		U		C	
A	L	I	G	H	T
Y		C		O	
	P	E	A	R	

27

		P	U	F	F
W		E		U	
R	E	B	E	L	
Y		B		L	
		L	A	Y	
D	R	Y			

28

I	N	V	E	S	T
	Y		S		U
	L	O	C	U	S
	O		A		K
S	N	I	P	E	
			E		

29

P	H	I			B
	I		S		A
	D	R	I	E	R
	E		X		M
					A
D	A	M	P	E	N

30

S				C	
O	R	D	E	A	L
U		R		L	
R		A	R	M	S
C	A	W			O
E			H	U	B

31

				G	
	S	P	A	R	
		O		O	
J		L	A	W	N
O		K		T	
T	E	A	C	H	

32

M	I	D	S	T	
A		O		U	
C	O	G		N	
E			F	I	X
				N	
	D	O	U	G	H

33

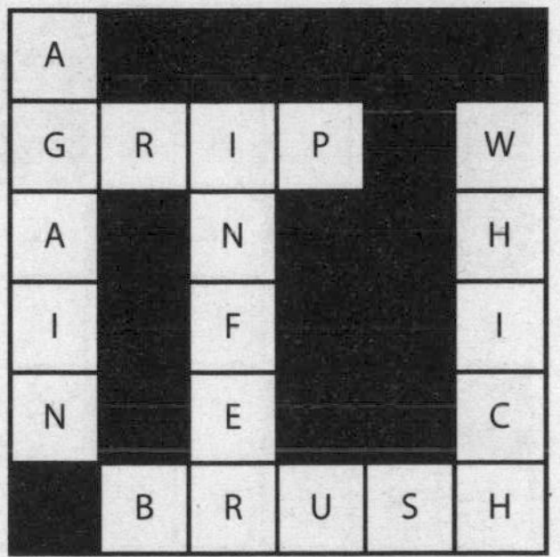

A					
G	R	I	P		W
A		N			H
I		F			I
N		E			C
	B	R	U	S	H

34

			I		B
P	A	T	T	E	R
	U		E		A
	T	U	M	M	Y
	O			A	
		F	O	W	L

35

	A	P	P	L	E
O			Y		
G	R	I	T	T	Y
R			H		
E	N	V	O	Y	
			N		

36

C					D
O	B	L	I	G	E
M			N		N
E	X	P	E	L	
D			R		
Y		S	T	O	P

37

	G				S
S	E	A			T
	E		B		A
	S		O	A	R
V	E	I	N		R
			D	A	Y

38

		T		H	
A	O	R	T	A	
N		I		N	
G	R	A	N	D	
E		G		L	
L		E	Y	E	D

39

			T		
	B	O	I	L	
	R		C		
P	E	A	K	E	D
	V		E		O
H	E	A	R	S	E

40

	C		V		
	O	V	A	L	
	U		N		S
E	G	O	I	S	T
	A		T		A
P	R	A	Y	E	R

41

			C		
R	E	S	U	M	E
	A		P		
	T	I	P	S	Y
	E		E		
	N	U	D	E	

42

G		S			
R	A	P			E
A		I			G
P	A	R	I	N	G
H		A		O	
		L	O	R	D

43

		S			
V	I	T	A	L	
E		A		U	
X	Y	L	E	N	E
		L		G	
			F	E	Z

44

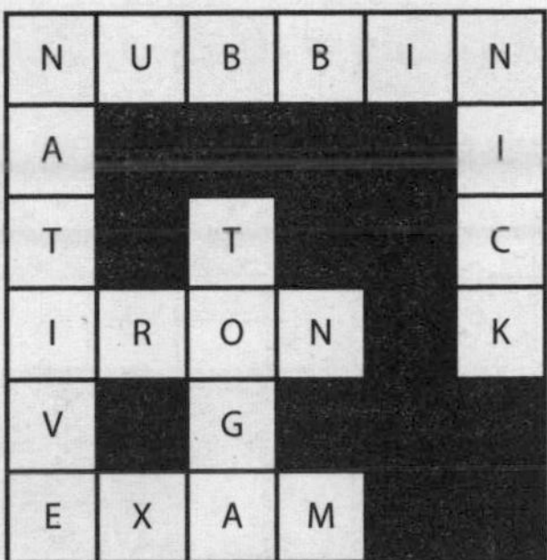

45

C	E	L	L	A	R
	X			C	
	T	W	I	T	
	R			I	
R	A	V	I	N	G
				G	

46

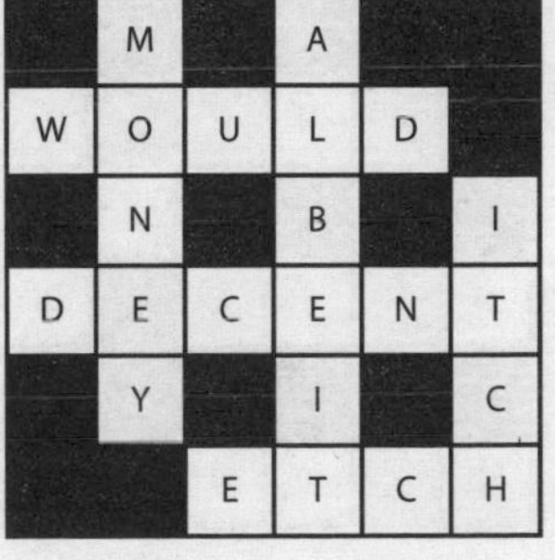

47

48

B	I	T	T	E	R
A			A		H
N	E	A	P		E
Y			I		A
A	W	A	R	D	
N					

49

		P		B	
	B	E	A	R	
E		W		O	
M	O	T	I	O	N
I		E		M	
T	O	R	N		

50

C	O	S	H		
E		O			I
R	O	T	T	E	N
A			O		K
T	R	A	S	H	Y
E			S		

51

					H
S	T	U	B		U
	R		Y	E	N
D	U	K	E		K
	N				
S	K	I	N		

52

F	O	P		S	
L		L		U	
U		A	R	M	Y
F		Z		M	
F	L	A	M	E	
Y				R	

53

				A	
C	H	O	O	S	Y
	A			S	
	R	E	C	A	P
	E			Y	
S	M	U	G		

54

S					U
C	L	E	V	E	R
O		M			N
R		I	R	K	
E	A	R		I	
			O	D	D

55

	A	S	P		
A		T			
L	I	O	N		D
O		A			O
F	U	T	I	L	E
T					S

56

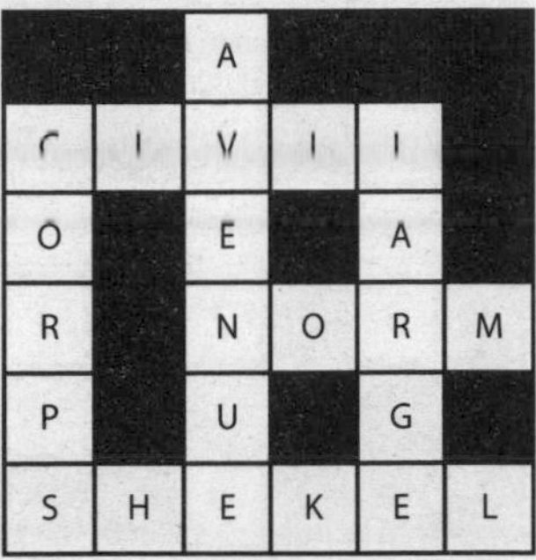

57

P	A	R	O	D	Y
A		I		O	
I	N	F	A	M	Y
L		E		A	
			W	I	N
				N	

58

59

				L	
B	R	U	T	A	L
	A			Y	
	D	R	O	O	P
	A			U	
	R	A	N	T	

60

W	H	I	F	F	
	I		A		
A	S	T	U	T	E
K			N		V
I					E
N	U	K	E		

61

	C	U	P		
	H		I		S
S	U	B	M	I	T
	B		P		I
		S	L	U	R
			Y		

62

			A	I	R
B	A	S	S		
	X		C		B
J	O	K	E		L
	N		N		I
		A	T	O	P

63

A					F
B	E	F	O	U	L
O		L			O
D	R	I	P		A
E		N			T
		G			Y

64

		C	U	R	D
F	O	E			
I		N			
L	I	T	T	L	E
T			O		
H	A	T	R	E	D

65

C	A	V	I	A	R
L			V		U
U		B	Y	T	E
B	E	E		I	
		T		L	
				T	

66

S		W			K
T	H	I	N		N
U		T			E
M			O	I	L
P			P		L
Y	O	U	T	H	

67

S		A			
C	O	B		G	
A		J	U	R	Y
R		E		O	
F	A	C	I	A	L
		T		N	

68

H	U	G			
O		I	D	L	E
A		M		I	
X	Y	L	E	M	
		E		B	
P	A	T	R	O	L

69

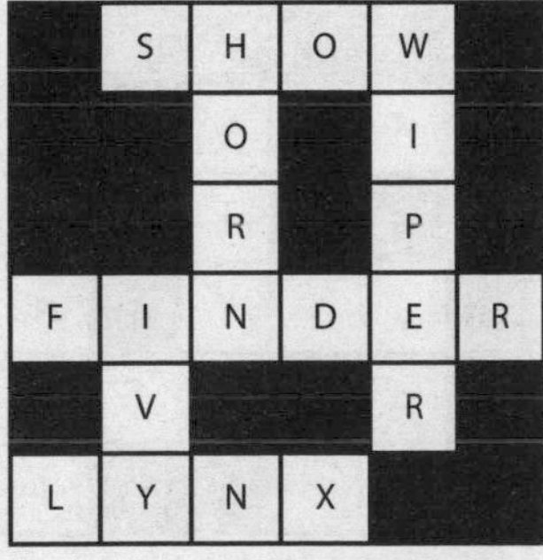

	S	H	O	W	
		O		I	
		R		P	
F	I	N	D	E	R
	V			R	
L	Y	N	X		

70

V			L		
O	T	T	E	R	
D			T		P
K	I	N			A
A		I			N
	B	L	A	S	T

71

J		F			
E		A			
T	H	R	I	V	E
	O			I	
S	U	L	T	A	N
	R			L	

72

	M		S	U	M
B	E	E	P		O
	R		O	R	B
	E	M	U		
			S		
	O	V	E	R	T

73

	F	A	C	T	
	L		H		
N	U	D	I	T	Y
O			N		E
S		D	A	F	T
H					

74

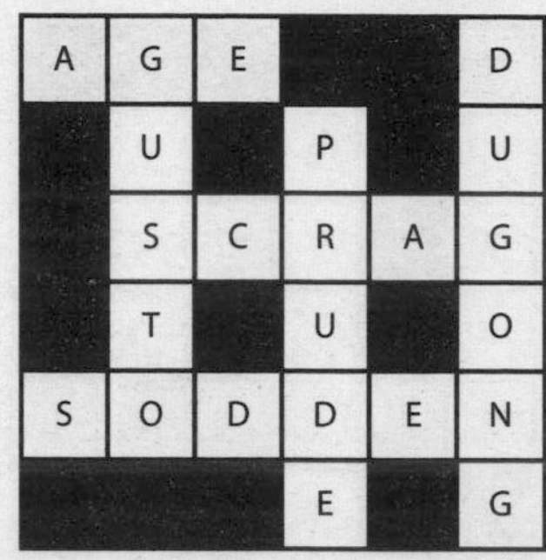

A	G	E			D
	U		P		U
	S	C	R	A	G
	T		U		O
S	O	D	D	E	N
			E		G

75

C	A	U	S	A	L
	R			R	
S	M	I	R	K	
	F		I		
	U		O		
	L	U	T	E	

76

E					S
B	R	E	D		O
B			I	N	N
	R	E	V		N
	U		A	L	E
I	M	P			T

77

H	E	C	T	I	C
O		O			H
B	O	W			U
B			V	A	N
Y					K
			N	A	Y

78

	O		P		
	K	E	R	N	
	A		O		B
E	Y	E	F	U	L
E			I		U
L	A	T	T	E	R

79

		D			
G	R	I	E	V	E
R		G		I	
U			B	E	E
N	E	W			R
T					A

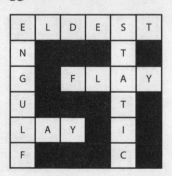

80

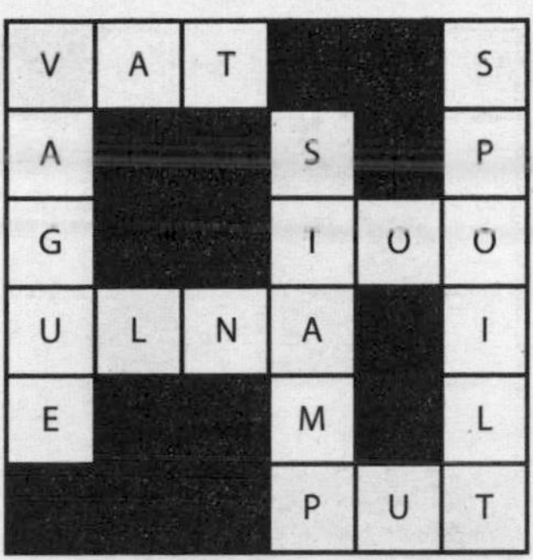

V	A	T			S
A			S		P
G			I	O	O
U	L	N	A		I
E			M		L
			P	U	T

81

	A	C	U	T	E
		H		H	
		O		O	
B	O	R	I	N	G
E		A		G	
G		L			

82

			A	S	P
S	K	Y		A	
	O			I	
L	A	B	E	L	
	L		R		
W	A	L	R	U	S

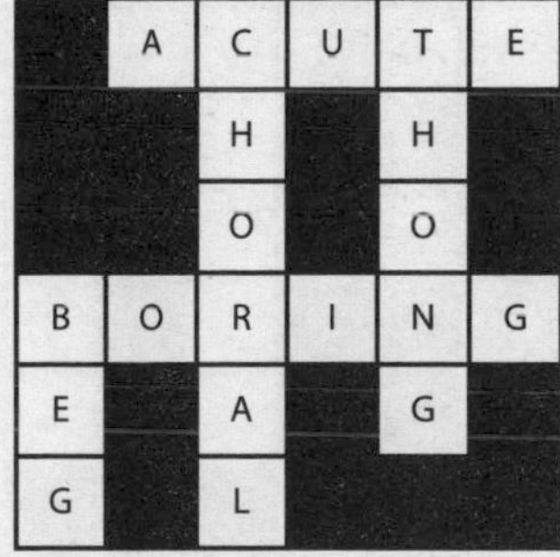

83

E	L	D	E	S	T
N				T	
G		F	L	A	Y
U				T	
L	A	Y		I	
F				C	

84

I	N	S	E	C	T
		C			A
	G	R	U	E	L
S		O			E
O		L			
P	A	L	S	Y	

85

S	H	R	E	W	
C			T		A
U			H	O	D
L			O		A
L	O	S	S		G
					E

86

	F				B
C	O	M	B		A
	R		O		C
W		G	A	W	K
R	U	E		E	
Y		L	A	D	

87

D	U	G	O	U	T
O					
N	A	K	E	D	
E			V		F
	T	W	I	N	E
			L		D

88

C	O	L	U	M	N
O			L		O
G	A	U	C	H	O
E			E		S
N			R		E
T	O	P			

89

S					
T	E	A	R	Y	
U			O		P
D	U	M	B		U
		A			T
		P	E	A	T

90

O	W	E		S	
	O		S	A	Y
H	O	P		V	
O		H		A	
B	E	I	N	G	
O				E	

91

C					
O	B	O	E		J
F					O
F	U	R	R	O	W
I					L
N	E	X	T		

92

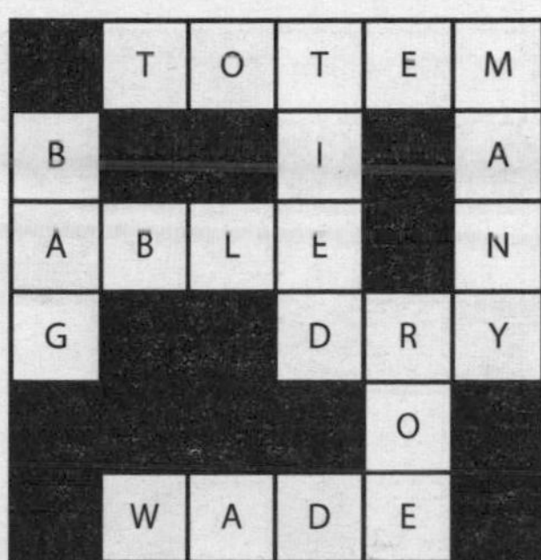

	T	O	T	E	M
B			I		A
A	B	L	E		N
G			D	R	Y
				O	
	W	A	D	E	

93

G	U	M			
N			M		
U	N	T	I	D	Y
	E		X		O
F	E	Z			U
			F	U	R

94

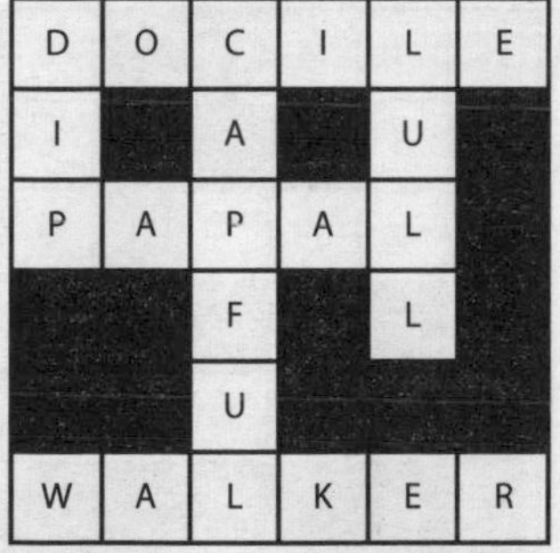

D	O	C	I	L	E
I		A		U	
P	A	P	A	L	
		F		L	
		U			
W	A	L	K	E	R

95

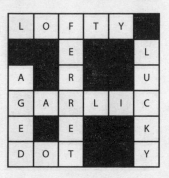

U	P	S	E	T	
N		T		A	
Z		E	D	G	Y
I		P			
P	A	P	E	R	
		E			

96

L	O	F	T	Y	
		E			L
A		R			U
G	A	R	L	I	C
E		E			K
D	O	T			Y

97

F	U	R			
	P		B		
E	S	S	A	Y	
	I		S		F
A	D	M	I	R	E
	E		N		Y

98

		S	E	E	P
	G		N		E
L	E	A	F		A
	N		O	A	R
F	E	L	L		L
			D	A	Y

99

H	A	M			B
	G				L
	O	F	F		U
A		E			S
S	T	E	N	C	H
H					

100

			J	U	S
A	S	K			A
	C				G
	R	A	T	I	O
	E			L	
S	W	I	R	L	Y

101

	T	H	I	S	
		E		L	
G	U	L	L	E	T
R		D		W	
E					
W	I	N	D		

102

	J		S	U	N
C	O	I	L		O
	B		I	O	N
J			D		E
A	S	T	E	R	
W					

103

		S	T	E	P
S			I		
C	H	E	C	K	
A		A		E	
M		R		G	
P	O	L	E		

104

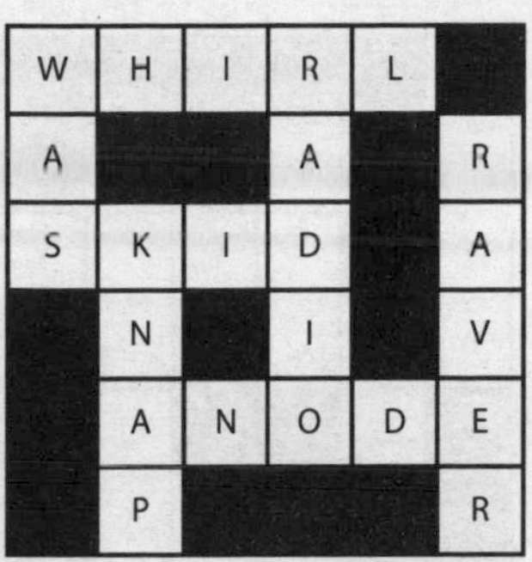

105

	M	A	S	T	
	I			O	
A	N	T		O	
	E		E	K	E
A	R	C			L
			O	A	F

106

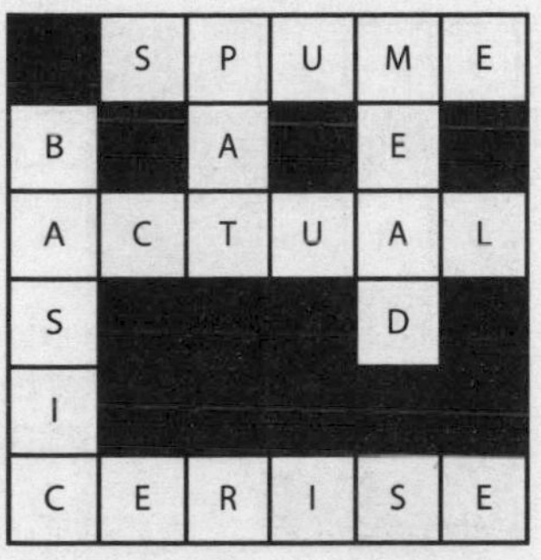

107

108

V	E	R	G	E	
E			O		C
T			B	R	A
	J	O	Y		N
		U			O
W	O	R	S	E	N

109

G					
A	I	D		S	
L		A	R	T	Y
A	D	D		O	
	E			U	
	N	E	S	T	

110

	G		H	A	Y
	L	I	E		E
	O		R		W
	B	L	E	W	
		E		A	
S	P	E	N	D	

111

J	A	I	L		S
A					L
Z	O	O			I
Z		H	A	L	T
		M		U	
			E	G	O

112

	S		V		
I	N	L	A	I	D
	A		S		I
S	C	A	T	H	E
	K			O	
		B	E	E	N

113

	H			A	
S	E	D	A	T	E
	R			O	
P		U		N	
E		S	E	A	
A	C	E		L	

114

		G	U	S	T
	O			E	
A	N	T	H	E	R
	C		U		I
L	E	S	S	E	N
			K		D

115

G	H	O	S	T	
I				O	
F	A	R	M	E	R
T		O		D	
		A			
	I	D	I	O	T

116

	K	N	O	W	N
	H			O	
P	A	R	C	E	L
	K		O		E
S	I	M	P	L	E
			E		K

117

A	G	L	O	W	
	R			A	
	A		P	R	Y
	F		I		A
	T	I	N		W
			T		N

118

A	L	T	A	R	
	A			A	
	N			Z	
F	E	L	L	O	W
I		I		R	
T	A	P	E		

119

				F	
S	U	P	P	L	Y
H		A		A	
O		G	A	S	
O	D	E		H	
K				Y	

120

			N	A	G
S	O	L	O		U
P			D		T
I	N	C	U	R	
L			L		
L	A	T	E		

121

V	E	A	L		
I		N			
S	A	G		O	
I		R	I	B	
T	O	Y		E	
			E	Y	E

122

C	A	C	H	E	
O		R			
U		E		D	
G	R	A	V	E	
H		K		M	
	P	Y	L	O	N

123

		Q			J
	D	U	D		O
		O			T
L	A	T	E	N	T
E		E			E
G			J	A	R

124

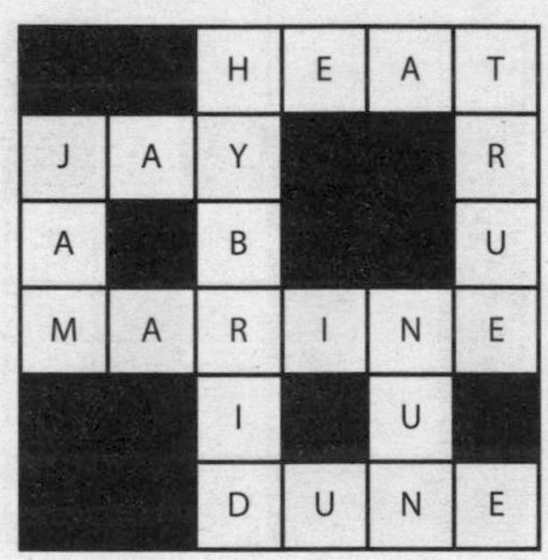

		H	E	A	T
J	A	Y			R
A		B			U
M	A	R	I	N	E
		I		U	
		D	U	N	E

125

		O			T
R	U	B	Y		W
A		L			E
F	O	O	T		N
T		N			T
		G	O	R	Y

126

			D	U	N
C	O	M	A		I
	N		R		P
B	E	S	E	T	
U		P		A	
S	T	A	N	D	

127

S	T	O	D	G	Y
H				U	
U		W		R	
S	T	A	T	U	S
H		S			
		P			

128

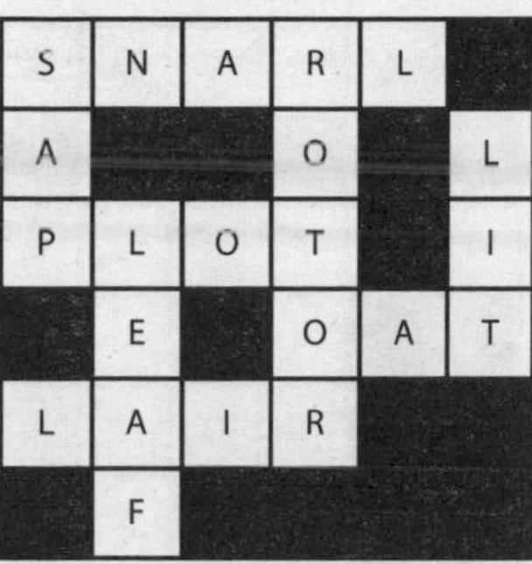

129

S	W	I	F	T	
	I		A		
S	T	A	N	C	E
	T				
	E	L	B	O	W
	D				

130

131

132

D	E	C	A	M	P
E		O		I	
L	O	V	I	N	G
L		E		I	
	I	N	T	O	
				N	

133

S	C	H	E	M	E
	A			U	
D	R	E	S	S	Y
		A		L	
		T	O	I	L
				N	

134

	L		H		
D	E	T	A	C	H
	A		L		E
	D		O	W	N
L	E	D		A	
	R		A	X	E

135

S	P	R	I	N	G
	O		B		O
	R	H	I	N	O
	T		S		F
	A				
C	L	O	P		

136

F	O	R	T		B
I			U		A
F	O	R	B	I	D
T		A		B	
Y	E	S		E	
		P	O	X	

137

		O	L	D	
S			I		
P	A	C	K		
Y			I	N	K
			N		
S	O	U	G	H	T

138

	W	O	O	D	
	E			A	
B	L	O	W	Y	
	T		A		S
			N		O
M	U	T	T	O	N

139

A		U			
T	U	N	E		
E		L		H	
	H	A	Z	E	
		C		A	
	P	E	A	R	L

140

	P	R	O		
A		I			S
C	O	M	B	A	T
H			O		A
E	L	I	X	I	R
					T

141

	H	A	S		
	E		L		
C	L	O	U	T	
	L		S		D
			H	E	Y
Q	U	A	Y		E

142

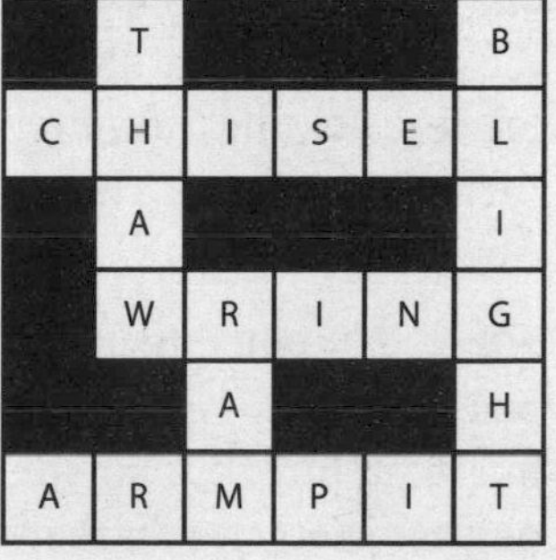

	T				B
C	H	I	S	E	L
	A				I
	W	R	I	N	G
		A			H
A	R	M	P	I	T

143

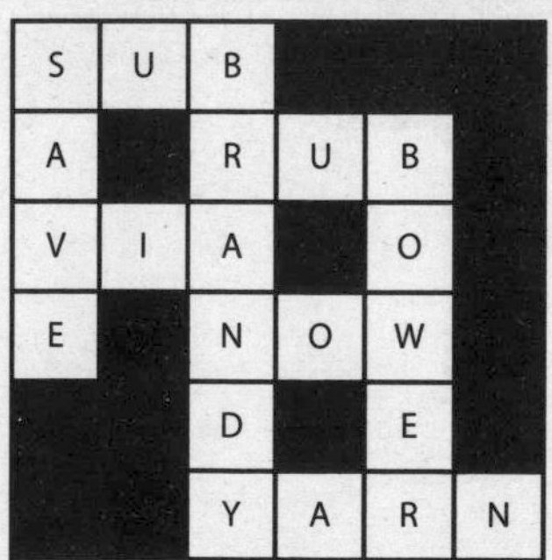

S	U	B			
A		R	U	B	
V	I	A		O	
E		N	O	W	
		D		E	
		Y	A	R	N

144

W	A	C	K	Y	
	C		I		
	R		W		
T	E	P	I	D	
A		A		U	
R	E	N	N	E	T

1 ahoy, ephor, **geography**, geophagy, gherao, gopher, graph, hare, harp, harpy, heap, hear, hero, hoar, hoary, hoer, hogg, hogger, hoggery, hope, hoper, hora, hoya, hype, hyper, hypo, opah, phage, raphe, rhea, yeah, yogh.

2 ceil, cel, clef, clerk, elf, elk, fickle, file, filer, fleck, flick, **flicker**, flier, ilk, lei, lek, lick, lie, lief, life, lifer, like, relic, rickle, riel, rifle, rile.

3 either, eth, ether, heir, hen, her, here, herein, hie, hin, hint, hire, hit, inhere, **neither**, nether, nth, the, thee, theine, their, then, there, **therein**, thin, thine, three.

4 bevy, brevity, byre, byte, eyot, ivory, obesity, obey, oyes, oyster, rosy, ryot, sobriety, storey, story, stye, toey, trey, troy, tyre, tyro, **verbosity**, verity, very, vestry, yeti, yore.

5 clod, clot, cloy, coil, cold, colt, coly, dicot, diol, **docility**, doily, doit, dolt, idiocy, idiot, idol, lido, loti, oily, otic, tody, toil.

6 cess, cesspit, cite, emit, epic, issei, item, mesic, mess, metic, misstep, mite, pectic, pest, pietism, piste, sceptic, **scepticism**, sect, seismic, semi, sept, septic, sice, sipe, site, smectic, smite, spec, spice, spite, stem, step, stipe, stipes, temp, time, times, tmesis.

7 act, actor, arc, arco, car, carr, carrot, **carroty**, carry, cart, cat, cay, coat, cor, cot, coy, cry, oca, oracy, orc, orca, racy, roc, taco, torc, trocar.

8 **caseload**, clad, clade, clod, closed, coda, code, cold, dace, dale, deal, decal, dolce, dole, dosa, dose, ecad, laced, lade, lead, load, lode, olde, salad, salade, scad, scald, scold, sled, soda.

9 acme, ahem, amped, amuck, beam, bema, bump, bumph, came, camp, champ, chum, chump, dame, damp, decamp, dumb, dump, haem, hemp, hump, humpback, **humpbacked**, humped, kame, kemp, mace, mache, mack, make, mead, much, muck, puma, umph.

10 deform, demo, doe, doer, dome, dorm, erode, foe, for, ford, fore, form, forme, **freedom**, fro, froe, from, mod, mode, more, ode, ore, orf, orfe, redo, rod, rode, roe.

11 darn, dean, denar, dene, dense, earn, endear, erne, nard, near, need, needs, nerd, rand, ranee, redan, rend, sand, sander, sane, sedan, send, sender, sene, **serenade**, serene, snare, sneer.

12 blouse, bole, bolus, bone, bonus, bosun, boule, ebon, leno, lobe, lone, lose, louse, **nebulous**, noble, nose, nous, obelus, onus, ousel, slob, sloe, snob, sole, sone, soul.

13 fetor, fore, fort, forte, froe, orfe, otter, retort, retro, **retrofit**, riot, rioter, rort, rote, roti, rotifer, rotter, tiro, toft, tore, torr, tort, torte, tote, trio, trot.

14 atop, oar, oat, opt, otto, poo, poor, port, pot, potato, potto, pro, proa, roo, root, rot, rota, **taproot**, taro, tarot, too, toot, top, topo, tor, toro, tort, tot, troop, trot.

15 bump, **bumptious**, impost, miso, mist, moist, most, muso, must, muti, omit, opium, ostium, simp, smut, sputum, stomp, stum, stump, submit, sumo, sump, tomb, tump, umbo, upmost.

16 add, ahi, aid, ail, ash, dad, dah, dais, dal, dash, dhal, dial, hail, haldi, lad, **laddish**, lah, lash, lias, sad, said, sail, sal, shad, siddha.

17 beedi, berried, bide, bier, bird, birder, birr, bride, brier, derive, devi, dire, dive, diver, drier, drive, driver, eider, rebid, reive, reiver, ride, rider, rive, river, **riverbed**, rivered, vibe, vide.

18 bend, bide, bile, bine, blend, **blindside**, deli, deni, desi, diel, dine, idle, indie, inside, isle, lend, lenis, lens, lied, lien, line, lined, nide, nisei, send, side, sidle, sine, sleb, sled, slide, snide.

19 filo, flow, foil, fowl, how, howl, low, lowish, oil, owl, owlish, show, silo, slow, soh, soil, sol, sow, who, wolf, **wolfish**.

20 acme, amice, calm, came, camel, **camellia**, cami, claim, clam, clime, email, lama, lame, lamia, lime, llama, mace, macle, mail, male, malice, mall, meal, mela, melic, mica, mile, mill.

21 adhan, ahead, aleph, alpha, anhedral, daphne, dhal, dharna, haar, hade, hale, haler, hand, handle, handler, hard, harden, hardpan, hare, harp, head, heal, heald, heap, hear, help, henna, herald, herd, herl, lahar, panhandle, **panhandler**, raphe, rhea.

22 earn, elan, lane, larn, lean, learn, lunar, lune, nave, navel, near, neural, raven, renal, run, rune, ulna, ulnar, **unravel**, unreal, urn, van, vane, venal, vernal.

23 impi, **implosion**, limp, lisp, loop, oops, pion, plosion, poison, polio, polis, polo, pons, pool, poon, simp, slip, sloop, slop, snip, snoop, spin, spoil, spool, spoon.

24 aboral, abort, alba, arbor, barry, baryta, blat, bloat, blot, boar, boart, boat, bolo, bolt, booay, boor, boot, booty, bora, bort, boyar, boyo, brat, bray, broo, labor, **laboratory**, lobar, lobo, oblatory, obol, robot, tabla, taboo, tabor, toolbar.

25 ace, acer, acre, arc, car, care, carer, carr, carry, carve, carver, **carvery**, cave, caver, cavy, cay, crave, craver, cry, cryer, race, racer, racy, rec, vac, varec.

26 dank, darn, drunk, dunk, durn, junk, junky, **junkyard**, knar, kuna, nard, nark, narky, nary, rand, randy, rank, unary, undy, yank, yarn, yuan.

27 amah, amir, arch, aria, cami, chai, chair, char, charm, cram, haar, hair, haram, harm, maar, machair, maha, marc, march, **mariachi**, mica.

28 aright, aweigh, earwig, eight, gait, gaiter, garth, gate, gather, gear, ghat, girt, girth, gîte, grate, great, grit, hegira, rage, right, targe, target, tiger, tight, triage, trig, twig, wage, wager, **watertight**, weigh, weight, wight, wright.

29 clonk, clunk, coke, conk, deck, dock, duck, duke, dunk, kendo, keno, koel, lock, luck, lunk, neck, nock, nuke, undock, unlock, **unlocked**.

30 able, alibi, bail, bailer, bailie, bale, baler, ball, baller, bare, bear, beira, bell, bier, bile, bill, biri, birl, blare, blear, brae, brail, brill, **illiberal**, label, labile, liable, libel, liberal, libra.

31 alap, apnea, apnoea, jalap, **jalapeño**, japan, jape, leap, lope, napa, nape, neap, nopal, nope, opal, open, paan, paean, paeon, pale, palea, pane, panel, peal, pean, penal, peon, plan, plane, plea, pole, pone.

32 **eminent**, emit, item, meet, mete, mien, mine, mite, née, neem, nene, net, nine, nite, tee, teem, teen, tein, ten, tenné, tie, time, tine.

33 amir, amrit, arum, atrium, imam, **immature**, irate, maim, mare, marmite, mart, mate, mater, mature, meat, muriate, ramie, rate, ream, tame, tamer, tare, team, tear, terai, tram, umami, umma, urate, urea, uremia.

34 defer, deft, feed, fend, fender, fern, fete, fetor, fetter, fond, font, food, foot, footer, ford, fore, fort, forte, free, freon, fret, fretted, froe, frond, front, often, orfe, reef, roof, **tenderfoot**, toft.

35 ace, acer, acme, acre, amice, arc, cam, came, cami, car, care, **ceramic**, circa, ciré, craic, cram, cream, crema, crim, crime, erica, ice, mac, mace, macer, marc, mic, mica, race, **racemic**, rec, rice.

36 ceil, cilium, clime, clique, clue, culm, ileum, ilium, kelim, kilim, lick, lieu, like, lime, luce, luck, melic, melick, mickle, mile, milieu, milk, muckle, mule, **quicklime**.

Lexica Solutions

Polygon Solutions

Scrabble™ Challenge Solutions

Word Watch Solutions

Codeword Solutions

37 ant, apt, aunt, daunt, dunt, dust, **dustpan**, nut, nuts, pant, past, pat, punt, put, spat, stand, stud, stun, stupa, tad, tan, tap, tapu, tau, tun, tuna, tup, unapt, **upstand**, ustad.

38 bourse, brose, burse, bus, debus, desorb, dose, douse, druse, ours, rebus, rose, **rosebud**, rouse, ruse, sob, sober, sod, sorb, sore, sou, sour, sub, sue, suer, surd, sure, urbs, use, used, user.

39 elfin, fell, fellow, felon, felony, file, fill, filly, filo, fine, fino, floe, flow, foil, foley, folly, fowl, inflow, info, lief, life, lowlife, olefin, wife, wifely, wolf, **yellowfin**.

40 deft, delft, felid, felt, fetid, feud, field, file, filet, filo, flit, floe, flout, flue, fluid, flute, fluted, foetid, foil, fold, foul, fuel, futile, left, lief, life, lift, loft, lofted, **outfield**, tofu.

41 bode, body, **bodysurf**, bodysurfer, border, bordure, bored, budo, debur, deburr, debus, defy, derby, derry, desorb, dobe, doer, dory, dose, dour, douse, drey, drub, druse, dryer, dyer, feud, ford, fyrd, order, ordure, redo, robed, rode, rosebud, rude, rudery, suborder, surd, used.

42 age, agree, are, bag, bar, bare, barège, barge, bargee, barre, bear, bearer, bra, brae, brag, eager, eagre, ear, era, gab, gar, garb, gear, **gerbera**, grab, rag, rage, rager, rare, rear, rebar.

43 albino, anti, baton, **biathlon**, bint, bitonal, blain, blin, halon, hint, hobnail, into, lino, lint, lion, loan, loin, nail, noil, obtain, talon, than, thin, tian, tonal.

44 **accentuate**, acetate, acne, actuate, acutance, acute, ante, attune, cane, catena, cent, cetacean, cetane, cuneate, cute, enact, neat, neta, nett, tacet, tante, tauten, teat, teen, tenace, tenet, tent, tune, tutee.

45 ace, acme, amice, amicus, **caesium**, cam, came, cami, case, cause, cesium, cue, cum, ecu, ice, mac, mace, mesic, mic, mica, miscue, music, sac, sauce, scam, scum, sec, sic, sice, sumac.

46 agism, agist, ambit, bait, bast, bats, bias, **bigamist**, gait, gambit, iamb, imagist, mast, sati, sigma, stab, stag, stigma, tabi, tibia.

47 allium, alum, **halloumi**, haulm, hilum, holm, homa, limo, loam, luma, mail, mall, maul, miaul, mill, milo, moil, mola, molal, moll, mull, mullah.

48 army, mare, maser, mass, massé, massy, mayo, mayor, **mayoress**, mesa, mess, messy, morass, moray, more, mosey, moss, mossy, ramose, ream, roam, same, samey, seam, seamy, smear, smeary, soma, some.

49 argot, arrow, art, gar, gator, gora, groat, grot, grow, oar, orra, rag, **ragwort**, rat, raw, roar, rort, rot, rota, row, tar, taro, tor, torr, trog, trow, war, wart, wort.

50 bell, belly, **bellyflop**, bole, boll, fell, floe, flop, foley, folly, lobe, loll, lolly, lope, pelf, pleb, ploy, pole, poll, polly, poly, yell, yelp.

51 aglet, eaglet, eat, elate, eta, gat, gate, gelt, get, gleet, lat, late, leat, leet, legate, let, tael, tag, tale, tea, teal, tee, teg, valet, vat, **vegetal**, veleta, vet.

52 acute, cruet, curare, curate, cure, curer, curt, cute, ecru, facture, farceur, faucet, **fracture**, furcate, recur, returf, truce, true, tufa, turf, urate, urea.

53 ceil, cill, cine, cline, clip, epic, incline, lien, line, linen, linn, lipline, nice, nine, pein, pencil, **penicillin**, penni, pile, pill, pine, plié

54 eruv, ire, per, peri, perv, pew, pie, pier, pure, **purview**, rep, rev, ripe, rive, rue, vie, view, viper, weir, wipe, wiper, wire

55 euro, insure, inure, issue, issuer, **neurosis**, nous, nurse, onus, ours, **resinous**, roué, rouse, ruin, rune, ruse, serious, serous, sinus, sorus, sour, souse, suer, sunrise, sure, urine, ursine, user.

56 enrol, keno, koel, krone, kroon, leno, lone, loner, look, looker, loon, lore, lorn, nook, nork, oner, **onlooker**, orle, roko, role, rone, rook.

57 beer, beet, belt, belter, bent, beret, betel, blue, bluet, blunt, blur, blurt, brunet, brunt, brut, brute, bunce, bunt, buret, burl, burn, burnet, butler, celeb, club, cube, curb, lube, rebec, rebel, rebut, rube, ruble, treble, tube, tuber, tubercle, tubule, **turbulence**.

58 aldol, dale, deal, dell, dhal, dhol, dhole, dhow, dole, doll, dowel, dwale, dwell, hade, **hallowed**, head, heald, hold, lade, ladle, lead, lewd, load, lode, olde, wade, waldo, weld, woad, wold.

59 acned, candy, caned, cede, chad, dace, dance, dancey, dank, dean, decay, deck, deke, dene, deny, dyke, dyne, ecad, **hackneyed**, hade, hand, handy, head, heady, heed, keyed, knead, naked, need, needy.

60 ashet, atheist, ease, east, estate, haste, hate, heat, **hesitate**, saithe, sate, sati, seat, seta, shea, staithe, stat, state, tase, tash, taste, tatie, tease, teat, testa, that, theta.

61 glut, **glutton**, gout, gut, lot, lout, not, nut, out, tog, tolu, ton, tong, tot, tout, tug, tun, tut, unto.

62 acid, acidy, acrid, airy, aria, arid, arnica, cadi, cairn, canid, cardia, cariad, carina, dairy, diary, dinar, diya, drain, nadir, naiad, naira, radian, **radiancy**, raid, rain, rainy, rancid, rani, riad, rind.

63 aioli, allusion, alluvion, also, avulsion, illusion, liaison, lilo, lino, lion, llano, loan, loin, louis, naos, noil, nous, nova, onus, oval, salon, salvo, silo, soil, sola, soul, **villainous**, villous, vino, vinous, viol, viola, violin, vision, visional, voila.

64 allium, alum, amid, ampul, ampulla, damp, dump, impala, lama, lamia, lamp, limp, llama, luma, lump, maid, mail, mall, maul, miaul, mild, mill, mull, **palladium**, pallium, palm, plum, puma, ulama.

65 derv, **dervish**, desh, deshi, desi, devi, die, dire, dis, dish, div, dive, diver, divers, drive, edh, herd, hide, hider, ide, red, rid, ride, shed, sherd, shred, side, vid, vide.

66 ace, acer, acre, arc, calque, car, care, carl, caul, cel, claque, clear, clue, cru, cruel, cue, cur, cure, curl, ecru, ecu, lac, lace, **lacquer**, luce, lucre, race, rec, ulcer.

67 gelt, gilet, gill, gilt, gist, gîte, glissé, glue, glut, glute, guess, guest, guile, guilt, **guiltless**, guise, gules, gulet, gull, gullet, gusset, gust, gutless, legit, ligule, luge, slug.

68 esse, feint, **feistiness**, fess, fesse, fete, fine, finesse, finite, fitness, infest, inset, issei, ness, nest, nisei, nite, seif, seine, seise, seisin, sene, seniti, sense, sensei, sensitise, sent, sente, sess, sine, site, stein, teen, tein, tenesi, tense, tine.

69 entry, erk, ken, kern, key, kyte, nerk, net, nuke, rent, ret, rue, rune, rye, ten, tern, trek, trey, true, tune, tuner, turkey, **turnkey**, tyke, tyre, ute, yen, yet.

70 engross, ergo, ergot, gens, gent, gesso, goer, gone, goner, gore, gorse, goss, gross, grot, ogre, ogress, snog, song, **songster**, strong, tong, trog.

71 arbor, bare, barf, barre, barrio, barrow, bear, beira, bier, **biowarfare**, biro, birr, boar, boer, bora, bore, borer, bower, braai, brae, braw, brew, briar, brief, brier, brio, brow, fiber, fibre, fibro, forb, forbear, forerib, rebar, robe.

72 cep, desh, dye, edh, espy, hep, hey, hype, pec, psyche, **psyched**, sec, she, shed, spec, syce, yeh, yes.

73 amble, balm, beam, bema, blame, **embattle**, lamb, lame, male, malt, mate, matt, matte, meal, meat, meet, mela, melt, metal, mete, mettle, tame, team, teem.

74 adman, admin, airman, amid, amir, anima, army, **dairyman**, damar, damn, diram, dram, drama, maar, maid, maidan, main, mana, mania, many, mardy, marina, maya, mind, miry, myna, myriad, ramin, rimy, yardman.

75 else, erst, est, ester, lest, reset, rest, see, seel, seer, **seltzer**, sere, set, sleet, steel, steer, stele, stere, streel, teres, terse, zest, zester.

76 ego, elm, erg, ergo, gel, gem, germ, goer, golem, gore, leg, **legroom**, loge, lore, mole, more, morel, ogle, ogler, ogre, olé, ore, orle, reg, rem, roe, role.

77 lilo, limo, limp, lisp, loll, mill, milo, moil, moll, pill, **plimsoll**, polis, poll, sill, silo, slim, slip, slop, soil, spill, spoil.

78 elfish, fell, file, flesh, fleshly, fleshy, hell, isle, jell, jellify, jelly, **jellyfish**, lief, life, lisle, lyse, seif, self, sell, shelf, shell, shelly, sley, yell.

79 fig, fight, filth, filthy, fit, flight, **flighty**, flit, gift, gilt, git, hilt, hit, lift, lig, light, lit, tig.

80 deni, dine, done, dope, **downpipe**, endow, nide, node, nope, open, opine, pein, peon, pepo, pied, pine, pipe, pone, pope, wend, wide, widen, wine, wipe.

81 abed, adnate, awned, band, bandsaw, bated, bawd, bead, bend, data, date, dawn, dean, debt, dent, dewan, nada, sand, sedan, send, stand, stead, **sweatband**, tend, wada, wade, wand, wasted, wend.

82 engine, ennui, gen, gene, genie, **genuine**, gin, gnu, gun, **ingénue**, inn, née, neg, nene, nine, nun, uni.

83 abhor, above, arvo, aver, bare, bear, beau, behavior, **behaviour**, beira, boar, bohea, bora, brae, brave, bravo, hair, hare, have, haver, hear, hoar, hora, obeah, rave, rehab, rhea, urea, uvea, vair.

84 becoming, begin, begum, being, benign, bice, bine, bing, binge, bingo, biog, biome, bogie, boing, bonce, bone, bong, bonnie, bougie, bounce, bouncing, bunce, bunco, bung, bunion, comb, combe, combi, combine, cube, ebon, gibe, gobi, gumbo, imbue, mobe, numb, umbo, **unbecoming**.

85 coil, coin, col, con, cos, icon, ion, ionic, lino, lion, loin, noil, oil, scion, **silicon**, silo, soil, sol, son, sonic.

86 amuse, arum, assume, mare, marque, **marquess**, maser, masque, masquer, mass, massé, masseur, mesa, mess, mure, muse, muss, ramus, ream, same, seam, serum, smear.

87 cere, cheer, chef, chief, chin, chine, ching, cine, ciré, cringe, enrich, fence, fencer, fencing, fennec, fiche, fierce, finch, generic, genic, **greenfinch**, hence, inch, nice, niche, niece, rice, rich, richen.

88 else, erst, esse, ester, leer, leet, less, lessee, lesser, lest, reel, reset, rest, rete, seel, seer, sere, sleet, steel, steer, stele, stere, streel, teres, terse, tree, **treeless**, tress.

89 aloo, alow, also, anoa, anodal, dado, dodo, doona, dosa, dowd, down, download, laddoo, ladoo, load, loan, loon, naos, nodal, saddo, salon, saloon, **sandalwood**, saola, slow, snood, snow, soda, sola, soldo, solo, sool, soon, swoon, waldo, woad, wold, wood, woodland, wool.

90 abed, able, bald, bale, baud, bead, beadle, beau, bedel, blade, bleed, blue, cable, celeb, club, cube, daub, daube, debacle, **educable**, lube.

91 alow, bawl, below, blow, bowel, bowl, elbow, halwa, howe, howl, owlet, tawa, thaw, thew, towable, towel, wale, weal, wealth, welt, weta, whale, **whaleboat**, what, wheal, wheat, whet, whoa, whole.

92 aloo, alow, calk, clap, claw, cloak, clop, coal, cola, cool, copal, cowl, kola, lack, lock, loco, look, loop, opal, pawl, plock, plook, plow, polka, polo, pool, walk, wool, **woolpack**.

93 eft, err, fie, fire, firer, fitter, fret, **fritter**, ire, ref, refit, ret, rife, rite, tie, tier, tire, titer, titfer, titre, tret, trier, trite.

94 outsit, **outstrip**, pious, pistou, pitot, posit, poui, prosit, protist, puri, purist, riot, rösti, roti, sirup, spirt, spit, sprit, spruit, stir, strip, suit, suitor, tiro, topi, tourist, trio, trip, tripos.

95 cement, cementite, cent, centime, cite, emetic, eminent, emit, enceinte, entente, entice, **enticement**, intent, item, meet, mentee, mete, metic, mint, mite, mitt, mitten, nett, nite, teem, teen, tein, tenement, tenet, tenné, tent, time, tine, tint.

96 hilus, hut, lotus, louis, lout, **loutish**, lush, lust, oust, out, shout, shul, shut, sluit, slut, sou, soul, south, suit, thou, thus, tolu, tui, tulsi, tush.

97 arrive, aver, avert, avian, aviate, invert, naive, **narrative**, native, nave, rave, raven, raver, ravin, ravine, rive, river, rivet, tavern, taverna, vain, vair, vane, variant, variate, varna, vein, vent, venti, vert, vina, vine.

98 cor, core, corf, corse, cos, course, cru, crus, cruse, cue, cur, cure, curse, eco, ecru, ecu, focus, **focuser**, force, fresco, orc, rec, **refocus**, roc, score, scour, scurf, sec, source, sucre.

99 alb, alp, bap, bay, boa, byplay, lab, lap, lay, loa, opal, pal, paly, pay, play, **playboy**, pya, yap, yay.

100 alow, anew, lawn, **lawnmower**, lower, meow, mewl, mower, owner, rowan, rowel, rowen, wale, wane, ware, warm, warn, weal, wean, wear, woman, worm, worn, wren.

101 beedi, belie, bice, bid, bide, bile, cedi, ceil, **decibel**, decile, deli, dib, dice, die, diel, edible, elide, ice, iced, ide, idle, lei, lib, lid, lie, lied.

102 bedel, bedew, bedim, beedi, belie, below, beside, besom, bide, bile, biome, bleed, blow, bode, boil, bold, bole, bolide, bowel, bowl, bowsie, demob, **disembowel**, dobe, dweeb, edible, elbow, embed, imbed, limb, limbo, lobe, lobed, mobe, mobile, obelise, obese, semibold, sleb, slob, womb, womble.

103 **airship**, aphis, apish, asp, hap, harp, hasp, hip, pah, pair, par, parish, pas, pash, phi, pia, pish, psi, rap, rasp, rip, sap, sharp, ship, sip, spa, spahi, spar.

104 adept, adit, **aptitude**, audit, date, diet, duet, edit, etui, pate, peat, petit, pietà, pita, pitta, pitted, putt, tape, tapu, tatie, taupe, taut, teat, tepid, tide, tied, update.

105 crud, crude, cruise, crus, cruse, cuisse, curd, cure, curie, curse, cursed, cursive, curve, cuss, cussed, **discursive**, discus, disuse, diuresis, druse, duress, ecru, eruv, issue, issuer, rude, ruse, scud, sucre, suds, sudser, suer, suicide, surd, sure, used, user, versus, virus, viscus.

106 bib, big, bio, biog, bis, bob, bog, bogus, bub, bubo, bug, bus, **gibbous**, gibus, gob, gobi, obi, sib, sob, sub.

107 almond, aloo, dolma, dolman, dolor, drool, ladoo, land, lard, lardon, lardoon, larn, load, loam, loan, loom, loon, lord, lorn, marl, modal, mola, molar, mold, **moorland**, moral, nodal, normal, oral.

108 awry, denary, deny, dewy, dray, drey, dyer, dyne, eyra, nary, nerdy, randy, ready, runway, unary, **underway**, undy, unready, unwary, waney, wary, weary, wynd, yard, yare, yarn, yawn, yean, year, yearn, yuan.

109 arvo, aver, avow, even, ever, nave, nerve, névé, never, nova, oven, **ovenware**, over, overawe, rave, raven, reave, rove, vane, veena, veer, wave, waver, weave, weaver.

110 ape, ave, daven, dean, den, deva, due, dune, dupe, end, nape, nave, neap, ned, nude, pane, pave, pea, pean, pen, **unpaved**, upend, uvea, vane, vaned, vend.

111 adept, cadet, caped, chad, chased, dace, dash, date, death, depth, desh, **despatch**, detach, ecad, hade, head, heptad, scad, shad, shade, shaped, shed, spade, stead.

112 ace, acne, act, actin, ait, ani, ant, ante, anti, antic, axe, axenic, can, cane, cant, cat, eat, eina, enact, eta, exact, **inexact**, neat, neta, tan, tax, taxi, tea, tenia, tian, tinea.

113 cert, cite, erect, kept, kite, pert, peter, picket, **picketer**, pricket, receipt, recite, rete, retie, rite, terce, tick, ticker, tier, tierce, tike, tire, tree, trek, trice, trick, trike, trip, tripe.

114 hoop, hotpot, hotspot, oops, phot, photo, pooh, poor, port, posh, post, potshot, potto, psst, shop, **shortstop**, spoor, sport, spot, stoop, stop, strop, thorp, topo, topos, tops, tosspot, troop.

115 aah, aga, agma, aha, amah, ana, anna, gam, hag, ham, hang, **hangman**, mag, maha, man, mana, manga, manna, naan, nag, naga, nan, nana.

116 able, bagel, bale, balk, ball, bell, black, **blackleg**, blag, bleak, cable, calk, call, cell, cella, cleg, gable, gale, gall, glacé, kale, label, lace, lack, lake, leak, leal, legal.

117 berm, blur, brume, bur, burl, burse, lemur, lumber, lur, lure, mure, rebus, rem, rub, rube, ruble, rue, rule, rum, rumble, ruse, serum, **slumber**, slur, suer, sure, umber, urbs, user.

118 alum, amuse, emulous, louse, luau, lues, luma, lumme, maul, **mausoleum**, moue, mouse, mule, muse, museum, muso, oleum, omasum, ousel, slue, slum, soul, summa, sumo, ulema, umma, usual.

119 ache, aching, chai, chain, change, **changeling**, channel, chela, chile, chin, china, chine, ching, each, haggle, hail, hale, hang, hangi, hanging, heal, henna, higgle, hinge, inch, inhale, leach, lech, lehnga, lengha, lichen, neigh, niche, nigh.

120 blue, blur, brume, bum, bummer, bur, burl, emu, lemur, leu, lube, lum, lumber, lumme, lur, lure, mule, mum, mumble, **mumbler**, mure, rub, rube, ruble, rue, rule, rum, rumble, umbel, umber.

121 actin, action, anti, antic, atonic, cant, canto, cation, coat, coati, coot, into, iota, octavo, ontic, onto, otic, ovation, taco, tian, toco, tonic, toon, vatic, **vocation**.

122 beer, beet, belie, belt, belter, bemire, bent, beret, berm, betel, bier, bile, bine, bint, bireme, biri, birl, bite, biter, blin, brim, brine, ember, libertine, limb, limber, niblet, nimble, rebel, timber, **timberline**, timbre, timbrel, treble, tremble, tribe.

123 agist, aright, gait, garish, garth, gash, ghat, girt, girth, gist, gratis, grist, grit, right, shag, sigh, sight, stag, **straight**, tight, trig.

124 derv, devoré, devote, devotee, dove, drove, even, event, eventer, ever, evert, nerve, névé, never, oven, over, **overextend**, overt, reeve, revet, rove, trove, veer, vend, vender, vendor, veneer, vent, vented, vert, vertex, veto, vetoer, vexed, vexer, vortex, vote, voter.

125 aegis, agile, aisle, espial, gill, glia, glial, ileal, isle, lapis, lias, lipa, lipase, lisle, lisp, pail, pial, pile, pilea, pill, pillage, plié, sail, sepia, silage, sill, sipe, slip, spiel, spile, spill, **spillage**.

126 estufa, fault, **faultless**, fetus, flatus, flue, flute, fuel, full, fuse, fuss, lues, lust, lute, luteal, saltus, salut, salute, sauté, slue, slut, suet, sulfa, sulfate, talus, tufa, tule, tulle, tussle.

127 **envision**, envoi, eosin, inosine, ionise, neon, nine, nisei, nisi, noise, none, noni, nose, oven, ovine, sine, sone, vein, venison, vine, vino, vision.

128 any, arm, army, arum, jam, jar, jay, jumar, **juryman**, man, many, mar, may, myna, nary, nay, ram, ray, unary, yam, yarn, yuan.

129 cere, ceroc, ciré, coerce, **coercive**, core, corvée, cove, cover, crevice, ever, over, recce, reive, rice, rive, rove, veer, vice, vireo, voice, voicer.

130 agree, cage, cargo, charge, charger, coverage, crag, eager, eagre, ergo, gear, ghee, gherao, goer, gora, gore, grace, grave, graver, greave, grocer, grove, ogee, ogre, overage, **overcharge**, racegoer, rage, rager, recharge, roger, verge, verger.

131 aching, agin, ani, awn, can, chain, chin, china, ching, **chinwag**, gain, gin, gnaw, hang, hangi, hin, inch, nag, nigh, wain, wan, whang, whin, win, winch, wing.

132 erhu, flesh, flesher, flush, flusher, fresh, heel, here, herl, hers, herself, huff, huffer, hurl, lush, reshuffle, rush, sheer, shelf, shuffle, shuffler, shul, usher.

Lexica Solutions

Polygon Solutions

Scrabble™ Challenge Solutions

Word Watch Solutions

Codeword Solutions

133 ace, bloc, cab, cable, cap, cape, capo, cel, cep, clap, clop, coal, cob, coble, col, cola, cole, cop, copal, cope, eco, lac, lace, oca, pace, pec, place, **placebo**.

134 cor, court, crop, croup, cru, cupro, cur, curt, orc, our, **outcrop**, outro, poor, port, pour, pro, roc, roo, root, rot, roup, rout, rut, tor, torc, toro, tour, troop, uproot.

135 boor, bort, broo, brut, burp, burr, burro, outro, poor, port, pour, prob, prop, purport, purr, robot, root, rort, rotor, roup, rout, toro, torpor, torr, tour, troop, troppo, turbo, **turboprop**, uproot.

136 ant, arson, man, manor, mason, matron, moan, morn, naos, nor, norm, not, notam, ransom, rant, roan, roman, san, santo, snort, snot, son, sonar, tan, tarn, ton, tons, **transom**.

137 actor, cannot, cant, canto, canton, cantor, cart, carton, cartoon, coat, **concordant**, concordat, coot, craton, croton, dart, doctor, donator, drat, natron, octad, odorant, onto, rant, ratoon, root, rota, taco, tandoor, tarn, taro, toad, toco, tondo, toon, torc, tornado, toro, trad, tronc.

138 ensue, lens, lune, lunette, nest, nestle, nett, nettle, nutlet, nuts, sene, sent, sente, stent, stun, stunt, teen, telnet, tenet, tense, tent, tune, unset, **unsettle**.

139 allusive, avulse, eluate, elusive, elute, etui, ileus, lieu, lues, lust, lute, luteal, salut, salute, sauté, slue, sluit, slut, suave, suet, suit, suite, talus, **televisual**, tule, tulle, tulsi, utile, uvea, uveal, value, vatu, vault, villus, visual, vitellus.

140 atopy, **autopsy**, oaty, pasty, patsy, pay, payout, posy, pouty, pya, say, soapy, soupy, soy, soya, spay, spy, stay, sty, toy, typo, yap, you, yous.

141 able, bagel, bagger, baggy, bale, baler, bare, barge, barley, bear, beggar, **beggarly**, beggary, belay, berg, beryl, blag, blagger, blare, blear, bleary, brae, brag, bray, byre, gable, garb, garble, grab, gybe.

142 adman, afar, alar, alarm, anal, damar, damn, darn, dram, drama, farad, fail, farm, farman, **farmland**, flam, flan, lama, land, lard, larn, maar, malar, mana, marl, nada, nard, rand.

143 aim, air, amir, ani, arm, bairn, bam, ban, bar, barm, barn, bra, brain, bran, iamb, main, man, mar, mbira, **minibar**, nab, rai, rain, ram, ramin, rani, ria.

144 isle, kiln, kinless, kiss, lenis, lien, like, liken, line, link, silk, silken, sine, sink, sinless, skein, skin, **skinless**, slink.

1 FRAILTY
J4 across (79).
HANDSOME
D10 down (91).

2 RECHARGE
C7 across (52).
GIGABYTE
A8 across (135).

3 JUBILEE
D8 across (48).
ABLAZE
A8 across (91).

4 PHOTOBOMB
H7 across (69).
TWENTY
I8 across (37).

5 HELIPAD
E5 down (52).
WIDTH
F6 down (28).

6 VARIETY
E4 across (94).
BATHCUBE
E5 down (84).

7 BIVALVE
B10 down (23).
DRUMBEAT
A8 across (117).

8 JODHPURS
A8 down (75).
BORZOI
C15 down (68).

9 CORNFLOUR
A7 across (45).
TOPAZ
C9 across (23).

10 PYRITES
E11 down (48).
UPHELD
G12 down (30).

11 EARACHE
F4 down (91).
DIPLOMAT
E6 down (65).

12 JIGSAW
A7 down (39).
ADENOIDS
A15 down (90).

13 EQUABLY
F9 across (55).
HOWZAT
D8 across (57).

14 WALNUT
A8 across (41).
MASTIFF
D8 across (36).

15 PIMENTO
K5 across (44).
DINGHY
D4 down (36).

16 GRANULE
L6 across (74).
VINEYARD
K4 across (110).

17 KEEPNET
F8 across (38).
SOUPCONS
A15 down (108).

18 EQUERRY
A10 down (47).
GATEAUX
A13 down (46).

19 PROPHECY
H8 across (72).
TROOP
D11 down (31).

20 MILKSOP
E11 down (60).
BYPATH
F6 down (31).

21 KNEECAP
E4 down (84).
PUBLICAN
D6 down (78).

22 UKULELE
H7 across (12).
INSOMUCH
A8 across (135).

23 LOGJAM
F7 across (42).
UNFROZE
A14 down (78).

24 SUNDEW
C15 down (36).
HEBE
A12 down (35).

25 COWGIRL
E11 down (52).
GAZEBO
E7 down (46).

26 DIPLOMA
E5 across (129).
MYSTICAL
E10 down (79).

27 LOWLAND
C7 across (48).
NITPICKY
A15 down (171).

28 FAJITAS
C7 across (58).
XENON
C13 down (49).

29 CYGNET
A8 down (47).
ROBOTIC
C11 down (38).

30 AUGMENT
E5 down (40).
ZIPWIRE
F4 down (48).

31 FROMAGE
F10 down (96).
SURVEYOR
E4 down (86).

32 SKYWARD
C10 down (33).
MARIGOLD
A8 across (108).

Lexica Solutions
Polygon Solutions
Scrabble™ Challenge Solutions
Word Watch Solutions
Codeword Solutions

33 ADEQUACY
F7 across (43).
TELEX
A15 down (51).

34 EARTHWARD
A8 down (51).
MANKIND
D7 across (42).

35 MOPHEAD
E5 down (60).
PAVLOVA
D4 down (32).

36 TOECLIP
F12 down (84).
SHAMROCK
I4 across (85).

37 URANIUM
B9 down (11).
PROHIBIT
A15 down (135).

38 JEWELLED
B10 down (35).
EXOTIC
E10 across (50).

39 EGGCUP
H10 across (47).
SHADOWY
C9 down (44).

40 LARCENY
K5 across (48).
MIMICRY
L4 across (38).

41 BITUMEN
E5 across (111).
MISWROTE
H4 across (76).

42 SILKWORM
B7 across (54).
SEAFARER
A15 down (99).

43 EQUIVOCAL
D7 across (33).
STANZA
B14 down (70).

44 FLIPFLOP
A8 across (66).
GUFFAW
B7 down (37).

45 ROGUISH
E5 down (44).
TOWROPE
F5 across (40).

46 ORBITAL
D5 down (85).
ICEBOUND
K5 across (102).

47 HOEDOWN
B9 down (34).
DYNAMICS
A8 across (144).

48 JOVIAL
D8 across (63).
VORTEX
D10 across (53).

49 OVERSEWED
H7 across (50).
DEPEND
A15 down (29).

50 MUDBATH
E11 down (60).
ICEBOX
E10 down (39).

51 BENEATH
E4 across (88).
CORDUROY
J4 across (66).

52 ATROPHY
F7 across (30).
BUOYANCY
A15 down (162).

53 SEQUOIA
F8 across (36).
MAXIM
G8 across (39).

54 KIDNAP
H10 across (45).
EPERGNE
A14 down (36).

55 BIPOLAR
K5 across (44).
RHYTHM
L4 across (42).

56 MOPHEAD
F9 across (93).
BAGPIPES
D5 across (80).

57 OBVIOUS
F9 across (30).
GUNSHIPS
A8 across (126).

58 JERSEY
B10 down (48).
WIZARDRY
A8 down (75).

59 JOBSWORTH
A8 down (75).
TEASHOP
C9 across (41).

60 COHABIT
E5 down (56).
RUBDOWN
F12 down (32).

61 BUGBEAR
F4 across (82).
ACRIMONY
J5 across (67).

62 ACCIDENT
F7 across (25).
EYEPATCH
A15 down (162).

63 CHEQUE
C14 down (40).
HOWZAT
A7 across (49).

64 IMAGINARY
H7 across (48).
FOREARM
A11 down (41).

Lexica Solutions
Polygon Solutions
Scrabble™ Challenge Solutions
Word Watch Solutions
Codeword Solutions

1 **TERENA** (b) (A member of) an Arawak group of South American Indians of the Southern Mato Grosso in Brazil. Also, the language of this group. 1928: "In the Terena tribe we have a typical group of forest Indians who are fast adopting civilised ways."

2 **BARRELET** (b) A little barrel or cask. The diminutive of "barrel". 1699; "Range them in the Jarr or Barrelet with Herbs and Spice."

3 **SOBRANYE** (b) The parliament or national assembly of Bulgaria. Adaptation of the Bulgar name. 1923: "In spite, however, of his declaring the elections invalid, the Grand Sobranye met and occupied itself with the difficult task of finding a prince willing to accept the thorny crown which Prince Alexander had laid down."

4 **BRACKMARD** (a) A horseman's short sword. Adaptation of the French "braquemart", a short broad sword. 1874: "The brackmard or cutlass has a straight flat wide blade, that is pointed and very sharp at either edge."

5 **NIN** (c) In Liverpool working-class use: grandmother. Adaptation of the Welsh "nain". 1966: "Every true wacker has three relations, viz 'Me Mar, Me Nin, an Me Anti-Mury".

6 **PARIETINES** (a) Fallen or ruined walls; ruins. Adaptation of the Latin "parietinae", feminine plural of "parietinus", of or belonging to walls. 1621: "We have many ruins of such baths found among those parietines and rubbish of old Roman towns."

7 **ICONIAN** (c) Of or pertaining to Iconium (modern Konya), a town in Asia Minor where St Paul preached, or to the church established there (Acts xiii, 5, xiv 1-7). 1899: "There were strife and jealousy between the Antiochean Church and the Iconian Church about precedence and comparative dignity."

8 **PEPLOS** (c) An outer robe or shawl worn by women in ancient Greece, usually of rich material and design, hanging in loose folds and sometimes drawn over the head; specifically, that woven yearly for the statue of the Goddess Athene at Athens, embroidered with mythological subjects, and carried in procession to her temple at the greater Panathenaea. 1875: "O child, put from thine eyes/ The peplos, throw it off, show face to sun!"

9 **TALEA** (b) A repeated rhythmic pattern in late-medieval isorhythmic motets. From the Latin, literally, a stick or cutting. 1963: "The structural skeleton of the movement is sixteen rotations of the melody, containing fifteen rotations of the rhythmic pattern or talea."

10 **COLOPHONY** (c) The dark or amber- coloured resin obtained by distilling turpentine with water. Toponym from "Colophonia resina", resin of Colophon (a town in Lydia). Formerly also called Greek pitch (Pix Graeca). 1831: "Colophony or Dry Resin is the resinous part of the turpentine remaining in the still after the extraction of the essential oil by distillation."

11 **TAOVALA** (c) In Tonga, a piece of fine matting worn round the waist over a "vala" or Tongan kilt (and without which one is not considered properly dressed). Traditionally worn by the male (with the exception of the Queen as monarch). It should be torn in several places, to show that the wearer does not set himself above his fellows.

12 **COMICES** (a) An assembly. Adaptation of the Latin "comitia". Cf. "notice", etc. 1600: "The chief priest immediately held the comices."

13 **BLUDGER** (a) A prostitute's pimp. Shortened form of "bludgeoner". 1960: "They are strikingly different to the white prostitutes who ply their trade for coloured bludgers."

14 **WARPISS** (c) To cast or throw off; to put aside. Old French from the Germanic root "werp-", to chuck. 1444: "God forbid that ye should, for a little money that their Englishmen have promised you, warpiss your good name."

15 **BRETELLE** (a) Each of the ornamental shoulder-straps extending from the waist-belt in front to the belt behind of a woman's dress. French for a strap or sling; in the plural, braces. 1932: "Two bretelles in front are knotted at the centre front of the corsage."

16 **ZEPHYR** (a) A light shirt worn by athletes. From Zephyr, the west wind, considered (erroneously) to be light. 1887: "When the athlete has got a pair of the best shoes, a zephyr, and a pair of silk or merino drawers, he has got all the stock-in-trade to win half-dozen championships."

17 **LAMA** (b) Gold or sliver cloth, originally made in Spain. Adaptation of the Spanish, literally "plate". 1818: "A gold embroidered lama lama drapery. Borders of silver lama on crimson satin."

18 **SPES** (c) A hope or expectancy, especially of some future benefit. Also in various Latin phrases. Latin. 1952: "The taxpayer's answer to that is, first of all, that this is not property at all but a mere spes or hope of getting something."

19 **MORGANATIC** (c) The distinctive epithet of that kind of marriage by which a man or exalted rank takes to wife a woman of lower station, with the provision that she remains in her former rank, and that the issue of the marriage have no claim to succeed to the possessions or dignities of their father. Apparently an adaptation of

the Old High German for "Morning Gift". A morganatic marriage is sometimes called "a left-handed marriage", because in the ceremony the bridegroom gave the bride his left hand instead of his right.

20 **SULLAN** (b) Of or pertaining to Sulla and his party, or the laws and political reforms instituted by him. The eponym of the Roman general and dictator, Lucius Cornelius Sulla (c. 138-78BC). 1892: "Caesar fled in disguise into the mountains of Samnium. Here he was pursued and captured by the Sullan bloodhounds, who were everywhere."

21 **IARFINE** (b) One of the four branches of the Irish clan structure comprising the men in the third grade of relationship to the chief. Irish "iar" means "after". 1921: "If the Iarfine and the Indfhine existed as communal family groups, the explanation is to be found in the reluctance to disturb the family holdings when the Derbfhine had run its course."

22 **SEMINIUM** (b) The first principle of anything; germ; etc. Adaptation of the Latin for procreation, also race, stock, breed. 1822: "It is difficult if not impossible to account for the quickening of the lurking seminium of the poison at this time rather than at any other."

23 **LATOUR** (c) Elliptical toponym for "Chateau Latour", the vineyard where it is produced. A red Bordeaux wine from the Haut-Medoc district of France. 1967: "Full-bodied and hard when young, Latour develops into something firm, rich, and noble.

24 **SIPE** (a) The act of percolating or soaking through, on the part of water or other liquid; the water, etc, which percolates. Old English "sipian", with Teutonic cognates. 1894: "There is no inflow or spring here apparently, so the water is only sipe."

25 **RATAFIA** (c) A drink, now applied especially to a type of aperitif made from grape juice and brandy. Cheers! 1973: "I was interested to learn that ratafia is an aperitif made in Champagne by mixing brandy with unfermented champagne grape juice. I have 'essence of ratafia' which is made from bitter almonds."

26 **CATSO** (b) Cripes! Good grief! An adaptation of the Italian "cazzo", the membrum virile. Used as an interjection: "What! God forbid! Tush!" Also, a rogue or scamp. 1708: "Catso! Let us drink."

27 **PROSOPAGNOSIA** (b) An inability to recognise a face as that of any particular person. Greek for "face + ignorance". 1976: "She can read slowly and complains of inability to recognise faces: people are recognised by their vioices."

28 **CROCKARD** (a) A kind of foreign money, decried as base under Edward I. Anglo-French, of uncertain origin. 1769: "Pollards and crockards, which were foreign coins of base metal."

29 **CULPON** (b) A piece cut off, a cutting; a portion, strip, slice, bit, shred. Adaptation of the Old French "colpon". "Coupon" is cognate with it. Also, as verb, to cut into pieces. 1606: "Superstition is like some serpents, that though they be culponed in many cuts, yet they can keep some life in all."

30 **WHIPPOORWILL** (b) Popular name in US and Canada for a species of Goatsucker, "Antrostomus (Caprimulgus) vociferus". Echoic from the bird's note. "Mark Twain", "Huckleberry Finn", 1884: "Whippoorwill and a dog crying about somebody that was going to die."

31 CENATION (c) Dining, supping. Adaptation of the Latin "cenatio", dining-room, etymologically, noun of action from "cenare", to dine. 1646: "The rooms of cenation in the summer."

32 TOCHUS (b) The backside, buttocks; the anus. Adaptation of the Yiddish "tokhes", adaptation of the Hebrew "tahat", beneath. 1951: "I don't go for all these fancy conferences and I don't kiss anybody's tochus."

33 SWENG (a) A stroke, blow; also applied widely to various kinds of violent action, eg a fall at wrestling, a swing, a military assault. The Old English word. "The Siege of Jerusalem", 1400: "Eleven hundred Jews in the mean while Swalten, while he sweng last by sword & by hunger."

34 LOGIAN (b) Containing the Logia of Jesus. Adaptation of the Greek. 1909: "To call the source we are considering simply 'the Logian document' cannot, I think, be open to the same objection."

35 SURICATE (b) An animal of the genus "Suricata", especially "S. zenik" or "S. tetradactyla", a viverrine burrowing carnivore of Cape Colony; the meerkat or zenik. Adaptation of the native African word. 1800: "The suricate is distinguished by a long, short-pointed nose."

36 MANCALA (c) A board game, originally Arabic but now common throughout Africa and Asia, played by two players on a special board, the object of which is the capture of the opponent's pieces. 1952: "Anthropologists use the term mancala for any similar game played on a board in which the pattern usual for board-games is replaced by two, three or four rows of holes deep enough to contain a number of pieces at the same time."

37 BADINEUR (c) One who indulges in badinage or raillery. From the French badin, silly. Pope, Letter to Swift, 1734: "Rebuke him for it as a badineur, if you think that more effectual."

38 YALI (b) A type of house found on the shore of the Bosporus. Adaptation of the Turkish for a shore or waterside residence, from the Greek aigialos, the seashore. 1978: "Not the tourist Istanbul, but the out-of-the-way places, the yalis, and the small markets beyond the zouks."

39 AGBA (b) A West African tree (Gossweilerodendron balsamiferum), also, its timber. Yoruba. 1952: "The desk for Unilevers, designed by Charles Kenrick, in agba, with a black bean top and hardboard case."

40 AURICLE (a) The external ear of animals. Formerly restricted to the lower lobe or "lap" of the human ear. From the Latin auricula, diminutive of auris, the ear. 1874: "The auricle has as its functions the reception, reflection, and condensation of the waves of sound."

41 POLISSON (b) An urchin or scamp; an ill-bred and uncouth person. French. 1915: "Instead of the polisson manner for which he used to be celebrated, he is now quiet and well-behaved, like anybody else."

42 CHONDRE (b) One of the small rounded grains which enter into the composition of some stony meteorites. Adaptation of the Greek "Chondros", a groat, grit, or lump of salt. 1882: "In these [deep-sea] deposits occur 'chondres', or spherical internally radiated particles referred to bronzite."

43 RAVINEMENT (b) An unconformity in river or shallow marine sediments caused by interruption of deposition by erosion. Adaptation of the French "ravinement", gullying. 1969: "In the field an unconformity can be proved because the erosion surface or ravinement is conspicuous."

44 CATHETUS (c) A straight line falling perpendicularly on another straight line or surface. Adaptation of the Greek for "let down". 1676: "Having the cathetus of the first and common hypotenuse given, to find the cathetus of the simple angle."

45 CLUSTERFIST (c) A clumsy-fisted fellow; a clown, boor, lout. Also, a close-fisted fellow, a niggard. 1658: "The Charter, which was no where extant but in the Noddles of these clusterfists."

46 PUKATEA (b) A tall forest tree, "Laurelia novae-zelandiae", of the family Monimiaceae, native to New Zealand; also the timber obtained from this tree. 1949: "Tree burial was resorted to in the thickly forested Urewera country. Natural hollow trees such as the pukatea were utilized when available."

47 CISSOID (b) A curve of the second order, invented by Diocles. The cusp of the cissoid resembles the re-entrant angles of an ivy-leaf. From the Greek for "ivy-like". 1879: "If a parabola roll on an equal one, the locus of the vertex of the moving parabola will be the cissoid." Eh? Ed.

48 POUSADA (a) An inn or hotel in Portugal, especially one of a chain administered by the State. Portuguese "pousada", resting- place; "pousar", to rest. 1949: "Just outside the main gate of Elvas is one of the nicest of the Government pousadas or inns."

49 PENTATONIC (c) A scale with five different notes to the octave. From the Greek. 1936: "In China the development from the non-semitonal to the seven-note scale is certainly traceable, even though the old pentatonic always remained the foundation of its music."

50 GRANDEE (a) A Spanish or Portuguese nobleman of the highest rank. Spanish "grande", for a Grand (Person). 1833: "A muleteer bestrides his beast of burden with the air of a grandee."

51 RAMBLAGE (a) The right to ramble over land in addition to passing across it, chiefly in the phrase "right of ramblage". From "ramble". 1887: "The public will not only be able to claim right of way but also right of ramblage over the whole of the headlands down to the shores."

52 FLAUGHTBRED (c) With the arms spread out like the wings of a flying bird; hence, eagerly. From a variant of "flocht". Scottish. 1768: "Flaughtbred upon his face, and there he lay."

53 DOWF (a) Dull, flat; wanting in spirit or energy; inactive, spiritless. Of sound: dull, flat, hollow. Also douf. Perhaps an adaptation of the Old Norse daufr. "Her dowf excuses make me mad."

54 DEADOH (a) and (b) Dead drunk. And deeply asleep. Nautical colloquialism. Masefield, "Sard Harker", 1924: "He slept, as sailors say, dead-oh."

55 EURAQUILO (b) A stormy wind from the NE or NNE blowing in the Levant. Latin Eurus is the East wind, Aquilo is the North wind. 1582: "A tempestuous wind that is called Euraquilo."

56 PUBBY (c) Of the nature and character of a public house. 1959: "It retains a pleasant pubby atmosphere and there's a good, mildly chaotic restaurant upstairs."

57 CHANNER (a) To mutter, grumble, murmur, fret. Also jawner. cf jaunder. Onomatopoeic? 1802: "The cock doth craw, the day doth daw,/ The channerin worm doth chide." Do worms mutter?

58 JISM (b) Energy, strength. Also, semen, sperm. Slang, originally US. Origin unknown. 1969: "You've got to walk around downtown Newark dripping jism down your forehead."

59 COLOBIN (b) A monkey of the African genus Colobus, distinguished by the absence or rudimentary development of the thumb. Adaptation of the Greek kolobos, docked, curtailed. 1840: "The black Colobin. Ursine Colobin. White-thighed Colobin."

60 LUES BOSWELLIANA (b) A disease of admiration; a biographer's tendency to magnify his subject. 1834: "Biographers, translators, editors, – all, in short, who employ themselves in illustrating the lives or the writings of others, are peculiarly exposed to the Lues Boswelliana, or disease of admiration."

61 BASHLIK (b) A kind of hood with long side-pieces worn by Russians in inclement weather as a protective covering for the head. Also, transferred, a light covering for the head, worn by women in the US. Adaptation of the Russian "bashlyk". 1882: "Hanging between the shoulders, and knotted around the neck, is the bashlik or hood, worn during bad weather."

62 VIEWY (b) Of persons: Given to adopting speculative views on particular subjects; inclined to be unpractical or visionary. 1885: "Lord Shaftesbury was no viewy or screaming philanthropist; he was a man of hard sense."

63 BARKLE (c) To cake, encrust (with dirt). D.H. Lawrence, "Sons & Lovers", 1913: "Aven't you got a drink, Missis, for a man when he comes home barkled from the pit?"

64 WHOPSTRAW (a) A country bumkin. From dialect "to make up straw into bundles". Clare, "The Village Minstrel", 1811: "The bumtiuous serjeant struts before his men,/ And 'clear the road, young whopstraws!' will he say."

65 TIRRA-LIRRA (a) A representation of the note of the skylark, or of a similar sound uttered as an exclamation of delight or gaiety. Echoic. Cf. Old French "tureluru". Tennyson, "The Lady of Shalott", 1832: " 'Tirra-lirra', by the river/ Sang Sir Lancelot."

66 JOCKER (c) A tramp who is accompanied by a youth who begs for him or acts as his catamite. Also, a male homosexual. North American slang. 1972: "Roxie hustles the guys who want a queen, and the kid goes after the ones who want a jocker. The jocker would probably become a queen himself."

67 TOWAI (b) A large New Zealand timber tree, "Weinmannia racemosa", N.O. "Saxcifragaceae", also called by colonists "Black Birch". Not to be confused with "tawhai", (irritatingly) another kind of birch. 1883: "Towai – A large tree; trunk two to four feet in diameter, and fifty feet high."

68 **HOMEY** (a) Or "homie". An Englishman; a British immigrant to New Zealand, especially one newly arrived. 1970: "An English accent. How hard it was to remember that it was as natural to a homey as your own accent was to you.

69 **SLOYD** (c) A system of manual instruction or training in elementary woodwork, originally developed and taught in Sweden. Adaptation of the Old Norse sloego. 1888: "In Sweden sloyd or elementary woodwork is taught with considerable success to children of both sexes."

70 **ASIGMATIC** (c) Not sigmatic, formed without sigma, the Greek letter S. 1893: "The one asigmatic tense that is not digammated is generally admitted to have dropped a sigma."

71 **SIDEWINDER** (b) Any of several small rattlesnakes, especially Crotalus cerastes. 1888: "The New Mexicans have named this animal the 'side-winder', because of the slightly lateral motion which they have in passing forward."

72 **BARRETTE** (b) The crossbar of a fencing foil or the hilt of a rapier. French diminutive of barre, a little bar. Also a bar for supporting a woman's back hair; also, a hair ornament. 1952: "Girls with jewelled barrettes in their new-washed hair."

73 **VESTIARY** (b) Of, pertaining or relating to, clothes or dress. Hence, the vestry of a church. From the Latin "vestis", clothing. 1870: "Some VESTIARY materials have become more abundant and lower in price."

74 **AUBUSSON** (a) Tapestry made at Aubusson, especially a carpet made of this. The toponym of a manufacturing town, Department Creuse, France. 1927: “Wasn’t that the dreadful hairy, smelly one [sc. a Russian conspirator] who spoilt your AUBUSSON?”

75 **VIVERRINE** (b) Resembling or related to the civet, or the civet family, specifically, belonging to the subfamily Viverrinae. In specific names, as VIVERRINE cat, dasyurus, opossum. 1885: “A VIVERRINE phalanger from Australia.”

76 **DEANESS** (a) A female Dean or wife of a Dean. 1848: “A large party today (Saturday) at the Master of Pembroke’s and ditto in the evening at the DEANESS of Christ Church (Mrs Gaisford).”

77 **VALGUS** (b) A variety of club-foot in which the foot is turned outwards (or inwards). From the Latin for bandy-legged. 1884: “The second expedient is only used for valgus, and consists in fixing a pad under the sole of the foot.”

78 **JIVA** (a) In Hindu and Jain philosophy: Life, the soul, the self; the vital principle. Sanskrit for living being, life, the highest personal principle of life. 1951: “Some vegetables, such as trees, are provided with a collectivity of jivas.”

79 **VOUTRY** (a) Adultery. The aphetic version of “avoutry”. 1382: “Thy sinfulness, thy voutries, and the hideous guilt of thy fornications.”

80 **INCHE** (c) In Malaysia, a prefixed title signifying respect, used for persons with no other special distinction; equivalent to "Mr". Adaptation of the Malay "enche'", master, mistress. 1972: "Inche Ghafar clarified today (Friday) that he had not made any offer for the formation of a coalition government."

81 **ROUGHBACK** (b) One of several flatfishes with rough skins, especially the long rough dab, "Hippoglossoides platessoides". 1903: "Long Rough Dab, Rochie, Roughback, Fluke is not looked upon with much favour as an article of food."

82 **FLATION** (b) Blowing or breathing. Latin "flare" merans to blow; hence "flation-em". 1708: "The pnoee, or Flatus, is by the Fathers supposed to continue so long, and no longer, than the Act of Spiration, or Flation, lasts."

83 **RATOON** (a) To cut down (plants) in order to induce them to send up new shoots. 1925: "Reports indicate that ratooned cotton has suffered. Ratooned plants produce a much earlier crop than new plants and Zululand had ratooned a considerable quantity this year."

84 **FRACEDO** (a) Putrefying heat. From the Latin "fracidus", after the analogy of "dulcedo", sweetness. 1677: "Some Insects have an Origination by very strength and fracedo of the Earth and Waters quickened by the vigorous Heat of the Sun."

85 NAVICULA (c) An incense-holder in the form of a boat. The diminutive of the Latin "navis", a ship. 1884: "There was a procession through the new clergy-house, with crosses, candles, thurible and navicula."

86 ERIA (b) The silkworm that produces this silk, "Attacus ricini". Also "eri". 1944: "The rearing of eri is much easier than that of any other silk worm."

87 ONDE (a) To breathe. Also, perhaps, to sniff or smell. Midland and southern form of northern "ande". 1440: "These beasts ondes on him to warm him with."

88 CHEESA (b) An explosive stick. Adaptation of the Zulu dialect "tshisa", to cause to burn. Also Xhosa. 1915: "In South Africa cheesa sticks are used, which consist of stiucks of cordite with ammonium oxalate and shellac. They have recently been authorised in England."

89 FLOSCULATION (c) A flower (of speech); a literary embellishment or ornament. 1651: "That with literary flosculations I should endeavour to adorn his memorial."

90 SPHAIRISTIKE (c) A type of tennis first played in 1873 which was later developed and turned into lawn tennis. Adaptation of the Greek "skill at playing with the ball". Sphairistike developed because of bouncy rubber balls and mechanical lawn-mowers. It changed its name because people would mispronounce it as though it had three syllables, just as ignoramuses today pronounce "Nike" as though she were a monosyllable.

91 FRITHSTOOL (a) A place of safety, a refuge; a seat, usually of stone, was formerly placed near the altar in some churches, which afforded inviolable protection to those who sought privilege of sanctuary. 1829; "The frithstool is hewn out of a solid stone, with a hollow back."

92 TELEDU (a) The stinking badger, a small nocturnal burrower of Java and Sumatra. The native name. 1965: "The teledu is well able to defend itself by means of the offensive secretions of its large anal glands."

93 ZAMANG (c) A large ornamental leguminous tree (Pitheocolobium Saman, suborder of Mimoseae) of tropical South America, having a spreading head of branches of immense extent. The native name. 1852: "The zamang is a species of mimosa; the leaves of this giant of nature are as small and delicate those of the silver-willow."

94 CREPIS (b) A plant of a large genus of herbs so called, belonging to the family Compositae and including a few cultivated species. Adaptation from the Greek, Theophrastus's name for another plant. 1948: "Most species of crepis are weeds and all have flowers like small dandelions."

95 VORAX (b) Voracious, ravenous. hungry. Adaptation of the Latin "vorax", devouring. 1535: "This Alexander of Badzenoch was called all his days 'The vorax wolf'."

96 BURKE (b) To evade, to shirk, to avoid. 1931: "The problem, as it concerns the investor, of the holding company and its accounts is one which it is not wise to burke."

1

Q		A		P	A	C	E	R		R		S
U	M	B	R	A		A		E	X	E	R	T
A		L		S	C	R	A	P		G		U
S	W	E	A	T		O		A		U	R	N
H				E		L	O	Y	A	L		
I	N	V	A	D	E	S		S		A	R	C
N		O								R		O
G	U	Y		Z		B	L	O	U	S	O	N
		A	R	O	M	A		R				F
J	O	G		N		K		A	L	I	B	I
O		I		I	D	E	A	L		T		R
T	E	N	O	N		R		L	O	C	U	M
S		G		G	U	S	H	Y		H		S

2

I	S	L	E		I	S	S	U	I	N	G	
	Q		E		M		P		N		O	
B	U	R	L	A	P		O	U	T	L	A	Y
	E				E		U		E		D	
D	E	S	C	A	L	E	S		R	I	S	K
	Z		H				E		J			
D	E	T	A	C	H		S	W	E	E	P	S
			M		E				C		R	
D	O	F	F		C	I	C	A	T	R	I	X
	B		E		K		R				V	
N	E	U	R	A	L		I	N	R	O	A	D
	Y		E		E		B		O		T	
	S	A	D	I	S	T	S		D	R	E	Y

3

A	C	H	E		P	O	U	L	T	R	Y	
	R		R		A		N		E		O	
M	A	C	A	W	S		G	E	N	I	U	S
	Z				T		U		A		R	
A	I	R	S	P	A	C	E		C	A	S	K
	E		U				N		I			
T	R	I	B	E	S		T	H	O	R	A	X
			J		Q				U		V	
A	P	S	E		U	N	L	I	S	T	E	D
	R		C		I		U				R	
F	I	L	T	E	R		S	W	I	F	T	S
	S		E		E		T		R		E	
	M	O	D	E	S	T	Y		K	I	D	S

4

	S		B		A		S		G		F	
W	H	I	L	E	S		E	C	L	A	I	R
	O		O		P		X		A		E	
Z	E	S	T		E	C	T	O	D	E	R	M
	B				C		E		I		Y	
W	O	R	K	S	T	A	T	I	O	N		
	X		N						L		I	
		C	O	N	C	L	U	S	I	O	N	S
	Q		C		U		N				V	
P	U	C	K	E	R	E	D		J	O	E	Y
	I		O		T		U		O		N	
F	L	O	U	T	S		L	I	G	H	T	S
	L		T		Y		Y		S		S	

5

V	A	P	I	D		O	P	P	R	E	S	S
	R		M		P		R		I		Q	
S	E	A	B	O	R	N	E		O	P	U	S
	N		I		O		S		T		E	
J	A	B	B	E	D		E	N	S	U	E	
			E		U		N				Z	
O	W	E	D		C	A	T		T	O	Y	S
	A				T		A		H			
	F	U	N	G	I		T	O	W	E	L	S
	F		E		V		I		A		O	
F	L	O	W		E	X	O	R	C	I	S	T
	E		E		L		N		K		E	
O	S	P	R	E	Y	S		U	S	U	R	P

6

B		S		B		J		S		P		R
E	M	U	L	A	T	E		A	Z	U	R	E
R		N		N		S		L		M		P
E	B	B	E	D		T	R	A	V	A	I	L
T		U		I				M				A
	G	R	A	T	I	F	Y	I	N	G	L	Y
A		N				A				L		S
D	I	S	S	E	R	T	A	T	I	O	N	
E				V				I		R		F
P	E	A	F	O	W	L		A	X	I	A	L
T		C		K		O		R		O		A
L	A	T	H	E		P	L	A	Q	U	E	S
Y		S		S		E		S		S		K

7

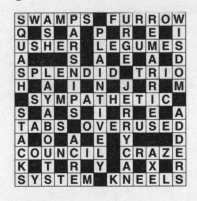

C	O	W	S	H	E	D		S	H	A	W	L
H		I		A		E		L		M		I
R	E	L	I	C		S	P	I	R	A	L	S
O		T		K		I		C		Z		P
N	E	S	T	L	E	S		E	V	I	L	S
I				E		T				N		
C	O	A	R	S	E		J	A	G	G	E	D
		M				P		Q				I
G	L	I	N	T		O	P	U	L	E	N	T
U		A		H		E		A		X		H
S	U	B	J	E	C	T		R	A	I	S	E
T		L		F		I		I		T		R
O	V	E	R	T		C	R	A	S	S	L	Y

8

S	W	A	M	P	S		F	U	R	R	O	W
Q		S		A		P		R		E		I
U	S	H	E	R		L	E	G	U	M	E	S
A				S		A		E		A		D
S	P	L	E	N	D	I	D		T	R	I	O
H		A		I		N		J		R		M
	S	Y	M	P	A	T	H	E	T	I	C	
S		A		S		I		R		E		A
T	A	B	S		O	V	E	R	U	S	E	D
A		O		A		E		Y				D
C	O	U	N	C	I	L		C	R	A	Z	E
K		T		R		Y		A		X		R
S	Y	S	T	E	M		K	N	E	E	L	S

9

	C		S		F		H		A		S	
G	H	E	T	T	O		O	R	B	I	T	S
	O		U		R	E	V		E		U	
D	R	A	B		G		E		T	A	C	K
	E			W	O	U	L	D			C	
A	S	T	E	R		S		A	X	I	O	M
		E		I	C	I	E	R		R		
Q	U	A	R	T		N		E	J	E	C	T
	P			E	D	G	E	D			H	
C	H	U	M		A		M		J	A	I	L
	E		O		I	M	P		A		N	
C	L	O	C	K	S		T	E	M	P	T	S
	D		K		Y		Y		S		Z	

10

C	O	W	S	L	I	P	S		V	I	E	W
L		E		O		O		S		M		I
I	N	A	P	T		E	X	T	R	A	C	T
C		L		H		T		A		G		T
K	I	T	S		B	R	O	C	C	O	L	I
		H		I		Y		K				E
D	O	Y	E	N	S		G	E	Y	S	E	R
E				S		E		D		T		
F	R	E	Q	U	E	N	T		Z	I	N	C
U		D		L		I		B		M		L
S	E	I	Z	I	N	G		U	V	U	L	A
E		F		N		M		N		L		N
D	A	Y	S		J	A	N	G	L	I	N	G

11

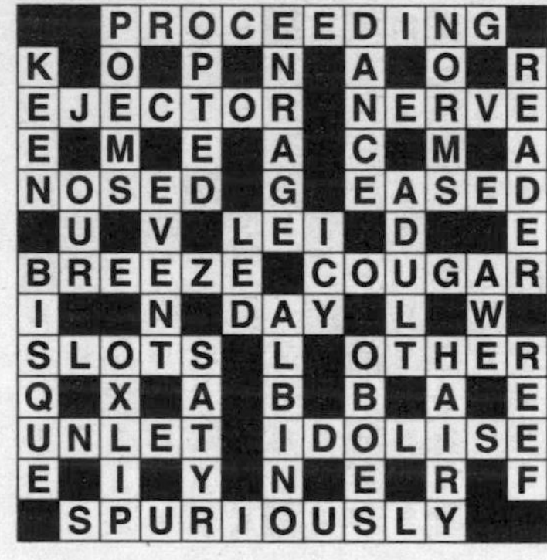

		P	R	O	C	E	E	D	I	N	G	
K		O		P		N		A		O		R
E	J	E	C	T	O	R		N	E	R	V	E
E		M		E		A		C		M		A
N	O	S	E	D		G		E	A	S	E	D
	U		V		L	E	I		D			E
B	R	E	E	Z	E		C	O	U	G	A	R
I			N		D	A	Y		L		W	
S	L	O	T	S		L		O	T	H	E	R
Q		X		A		B		B		A		E
U	N	L	E	T		I	D	O	L	I	S	E
E		I		Y		N		E		R		F
	S	P	U	R	I	O	U	S	L	Y		

12

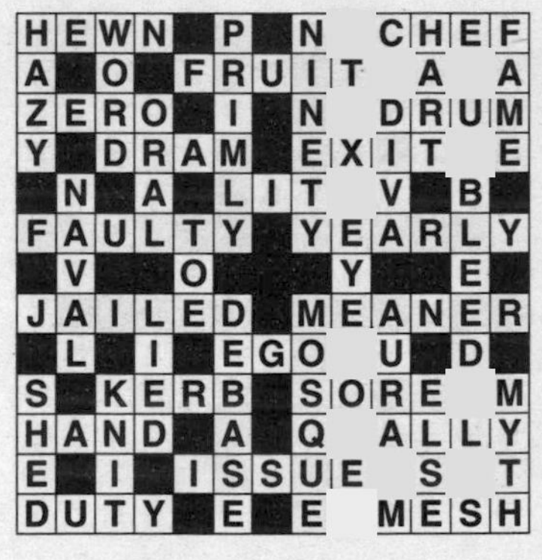

H	E	W	N		P		N		C	H	E	F
A		O		F	R	U	I	T		A		A
Z	E	R	O		I		N		D	R	U	M
Y		D	R	A	M		E	X	I	T		E
	N		A		L	I	T		V		B	
F	A	U	L	T	Y		Y	E	A	R	L	Y
	V			O				Y			E	
J	A	I	L	E	D		M	E	A	N	E	R
	L		I		E	G	O		U		D	
S		K	E	R	B		S	O	R	E		M
H	A	N	D		A		Q		A	L	L	Y
E		I		I	S	S	U	E		S		T
D	U	T	Y		E		E		M	E	S	H

13

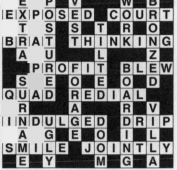

	E		P		V				W		B	
E	X	P	O	S	E	D		C	O	U	R	T
	T		S		S		T		R		O	
B	R	A	T		T	H	I	N	K	I	N	G
	A		U				L				Z	
		P	R	O	F	I	T		B	L	E	W
	S		E		O		E		O		D	
Q	U	A	D		R	E	D	I	A	L		
	R				A				R		V	
I	N	D	U	L	G	E	D		D	R	I	P
	A		G		E		O		I		L	
S	M	I	L	E		J	O	I	N	T	L	Y
	E		Y				M		G		A	

14

15

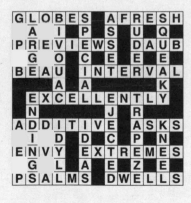

G	L	O	B	E	S		A	F	R	E	S	H
	A		I		P		S		U		Q	
P	R	E	V	I	E	W	S		D	A	U	B
	G		O		C		E		E		E	
B	E	A	U		I	N	T	E	R	V	A	L
			A		A						K	
	E	X	C	E	L	L	E	N	T	L	Y	
	N						J		R			
A	D	D	I	T	I	V	E		A	S	K	S
	I		D		D		C		P		N	
E	N	V	Y		E	X	T	R	E	M	E	S
	G		L		A		E		Z		E	
P	S	A	L	M	S		D	W	E	L	L	S

16

17

18

19

20

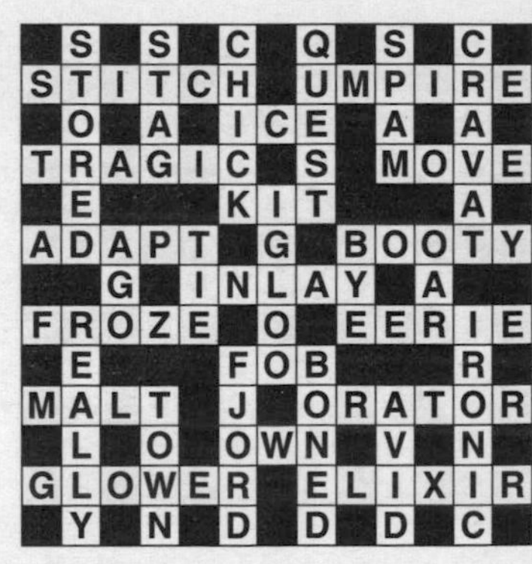

21

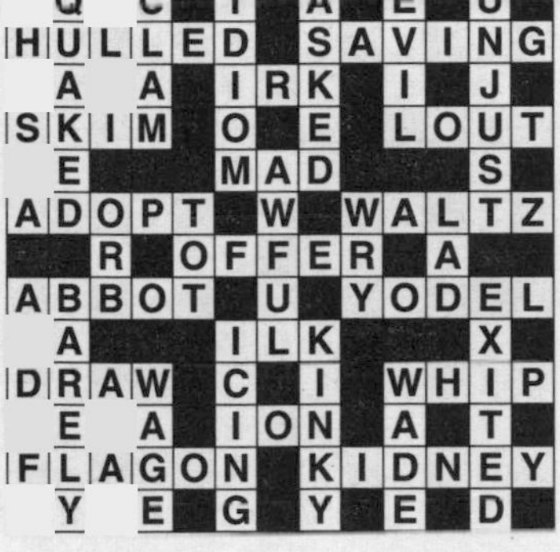

22

23

24

25

C		V		P	A	S	T	E		D		T
A	R	E	N	A		Q		L	E	E	R	Y
J		S		W	O	U	L	D		C		P
O	F	T	E	N		E		E		L	I	E
L				E		A	O	R	T	A		
I	N	F	I	D	E	L		S		R	A	P
N		I								E		E
G	E	L		Z		F	U	C	H	S	I	A
		L	I	E	G	E		A				S
S	K	I		R		L		B	A	L	S	A
A		N		O	R	I	E	L		O		N
V	A	G	U	E		N		E	X	A	L	T
E		S		D	R	E	A	D		M		S

26

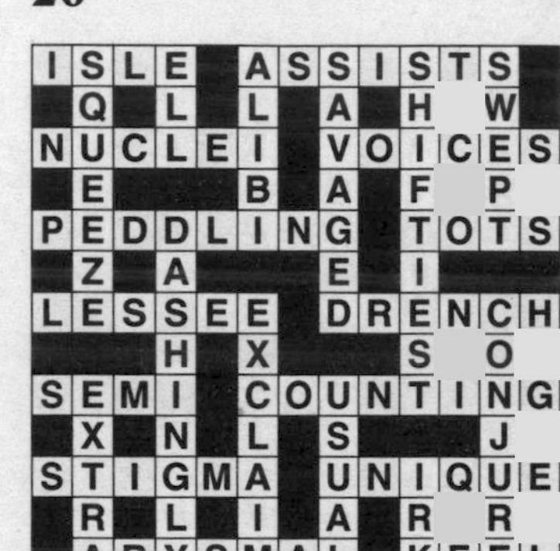

I	S	L	E		A	S	S	I	S	T	S	
	Q		L		L		A		H		W	
N	U	C	L	E	I		V	O	I	C	E	S
	E				B		A		F		P	
P	E	D	D	L	I	N	G		T	O	T	S
	Z		A				E		I			
L	E	S	S	E	E		D	R	E	N	C	H
			H		X				S		O	
S	E	M	I		C	O	U	N	T	I	N	G
	X		N		L		S				J	
S	T	I	G	M	A		U	N	I	Q	U	E
	R		L		I		A		R		R	
	A	B	Y	S	M	A	L		K	E	E	L

27

M	U	S	T		W	H	E	T	T	E	D	
	N		E		R		X		R		U	
V	I	R	A	G	O		C	R	A	N	K	S
	T				N		U		P		E	
R	A	M	P	A	G	E	S		E	A	S	Y
	R		R				E		Z			
P	Y	L	O	N	S		S	T	O	R	M	Y
			J		E				I		O	
F	R	E	E		C	H	I	L	D	I	S	H
	E		C		R		R				Q	
C	L	O	T	H	E		O	F	F	C	U	T
	I		E		T		N		I		E	
	C	U	D	G	E	L	S		B	U	S	Y

28

	Z		A		A		S		B		S	
S	I	E	V	E	S		H	O	I	S	T	S
	N		O		S		A		A		I	
K	N	O	W		I	N	V	I	T	I	N	G
	I				G		E		H		K	
M	A	D	D	E	N	I	N	G	L	Y		
	S		E						O		F	
		P	R	O	M	I	N	E	N	T	L	Y
	E		R		A		U				U	
S	Q	U	I	N	T	E	D		J	A	M	S
	U		C		T		G		A		M	
T	A	C	K	L	E		E	M	P	L	O	Y
	L		S		D		S		E		X	

29

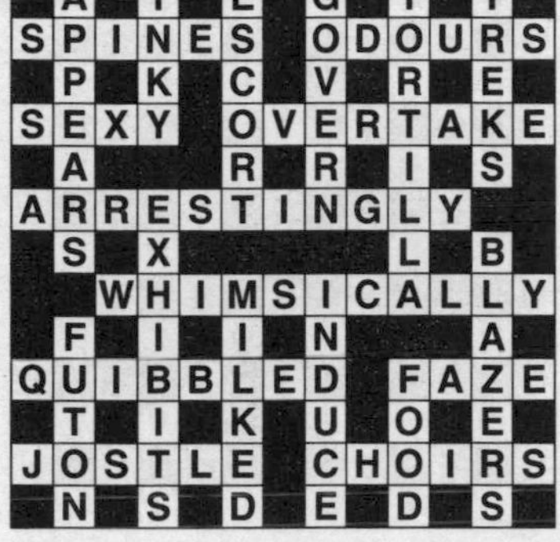
A I E G T T
SPINES ODOURS
P K C V R E
SEXY OVERTAKE
A R R I S
ARRESTINGLY
S X L B
WHIMSICALLY
F I I N A
QUIBBLED FAZE
T I K U O E
JOSTLE CHOIRS
N S D E D S

30

F T K F A U C
ETERNAL BANJO
A A I E O D N
SCRAG AQUEOUS
T D H N I
WRETCHEDNESS
P O A L T
REPRESSIVELY
E X E I P
FALSELY REPEL
O O R A M T U
RIVET PRIZING
M E S S N C S

31

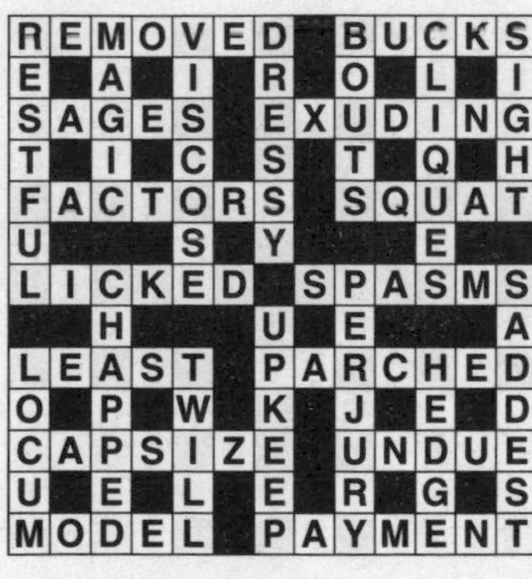
REMOVED BUCKS
E A I R O L I
SAGES EXUDING
T I C S T Q H
FACTORS SQUAT
U S Y E
LICKED SPASMS
H U E A
LEAST PARCHED
O P W K J E D
CAPSIZE UNDUE
U E L E R G S
MODEL PAYMENT

32

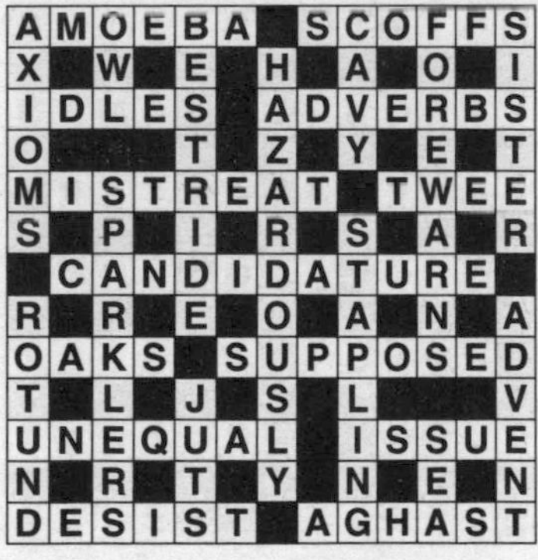
AMOEBA SCOFFS
X W E H A O I
IDLES ADVERBS
O T Z Y E T
MISTREAT TWEE
S P I R S A R
CANDIDATURE
R R E O A N A
OAKS SUPPOSED
T L J S L V
UNEQUAL ISSUE
N R T Y N E N
DESIST AGHAST

33

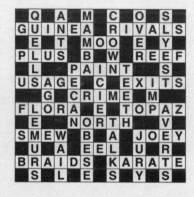

	Q		A		M		C		O		S	
G	U	I	N	E	A		R	I	V	A	L	S
	E		T		M	O	O		E		Y	
P	L	U	S		B		W		R	E	E	F
	L			P	A	I	N	T			S	
U	S	A	G	E		C		E	X	I	T	S
		G		C	R	I	M	E		M		
F	L	O	R	A		E		T	O	P	A	Z
	E			N	O	R	T	H			V	
S	M	E	W		B		A		J	O	E	Y
	U		A		E	E	L		U		R	
B	R	A	I	D	S		K	A	R	A	T	E
	S		L		E		S		Y		S	

34

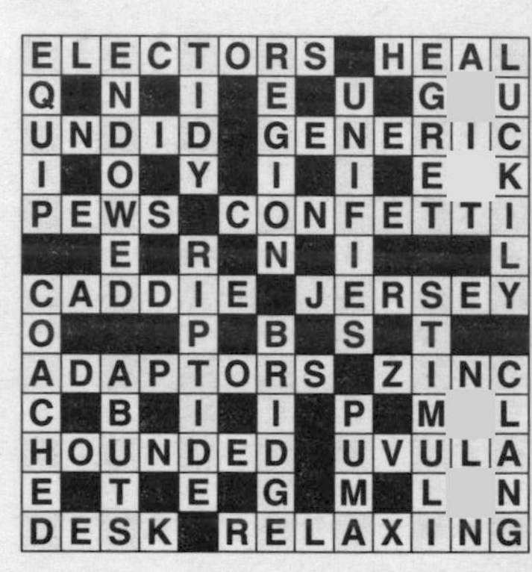

E	L	E	C	T	O	R	S		H	E	A	L
Q		N		I		E		U		G		U
U	N	D	I	D		G	E	N	E	R	I	C
I		O		Y		I		I		E		K
P	E	W	S		C	O	N	F	E	T	T	I
		E		R		N		I				L
C	A	D	D	I	E		J	E	R	S	E	Y
O				P		B		S		T		
A	D	A	P	T	O	R	S		Z	I	N	C
C		B		I		I		P		M		L
H	O	U	N	D	E	D		U	V	U	L	A
E		T		E		G		M		L		N
D	E	S	K		R	E	L	A	X	I	N	G

35

M	O	I	S	T		Q	U	I	E	T	E	R
	V		C		P		N		N		X	
L	A	B	O	U	R	E	R		A	M	P	S
	T		W		O		E		C		I	
Z	E	A	L	O	T		A	L	T	E	R	
			E		E		S				E	
H	O	L	D		C	O	O		J	U	D	O
	F				T		N		O			
	F	U	N	G	I		A	N	G	L	E	S
	E		E		V		B		T		N	
K	N	E	W		E	E	L	G	R	A	S	S
	C		E		L		Y		O		U	
D	E	F	R	A	Y	S		S	T	E	E	D

36

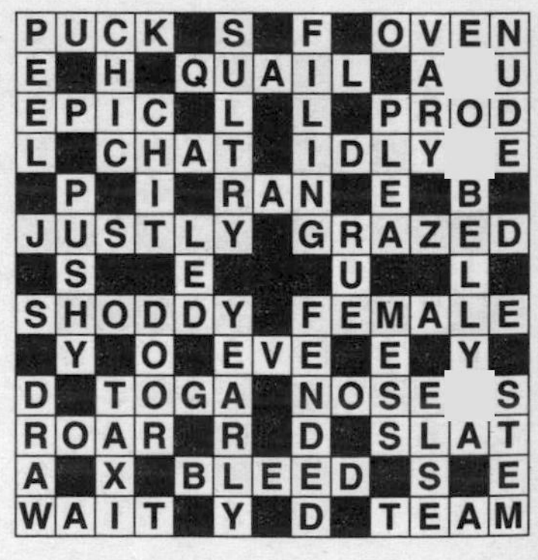

P	U	C	K		S		F		O	V	E	N
E		H		Q	U	A	I	L		A		U
E	P	I	C		L		L		P	R	O	D
L		C	H	A	T		I	D	L	Y		E
	P		I		R	A	N		E		B	
J	U	S	T	L	Y		G	R	A	Z	E	D
	S			E				U			L	
S	H	O	D	D	Y		F	E	M	A	L	E
	Y		O		E	V	E		E		Y	
D		T	O	G	A		N	O	S	E		S
R	O	A	R		R		D		S	L	A	T
A		X		B	L	E	E	D		S		E
W	A	I	T		Y		D		T	E	A	M

37

	J		P		R				F		S	
F	U	R	I	O	U	S		B	U	X	O	M
	R		C		E		A		N		U	
H	O	C	K		D	E	C	I	D	I	N	G
	R		E				I				D	
		S	T	E	W	E	D		G	U	L	L
	S		E		H		I		A		Y	
Q	U	A	D		I	N	C	O	M	E		
	M				S				B		Q	
E	M	B	A	R	K	E	D		L	O	U	T
	O		V		Y		R		I		A	
U	N	Z	I	P		J	O	I	N	E	R	Y
	S		D				P		G		T	

38

	S		H		S		O		J		A	
D	E	F	U	S	E		U	N	A	B	L	E
	Q		N		M		T		D		K	
B	U	N	C	H	I	N	G		E	X	A	M
	I		H				R				L	
A	N	T	I		A	R	O	M	A	T	I	C
			N		D		W		I			
F	O	R	G	I	V	E	N		R	U	M	P
	X				I				M		E	
S	T	O	W		S	I	Z	E	A	B	L	E
	A		E		E		E		I		O	
L	I	N	E	A	R		S	O	L	I	D	S
	L		D		S		T		S		Y	

39

R	A	B	B	I	S		R	E	L	I	S	H
	W		O		H		I		L		Q	
H	O	A	R	D	E	R	S		A	G	U	E
	K		E		R		E		M		E	
H	E	R	D		B	A	N	J	A	X	E	D
			O		E						Z	
	L	I	M	I	T	L	E	S	S	L	Y	
	A						N		U			
S	T	U	B	B	I	N	G		C	A	R	P
	H		L		D		R		C		I	
B	E	A	U		E	V	A	L	U	A	T	E
	R		F		A		V		M		Z	
U	S	E	F	U	L		E	M	B	R	Y	O

40

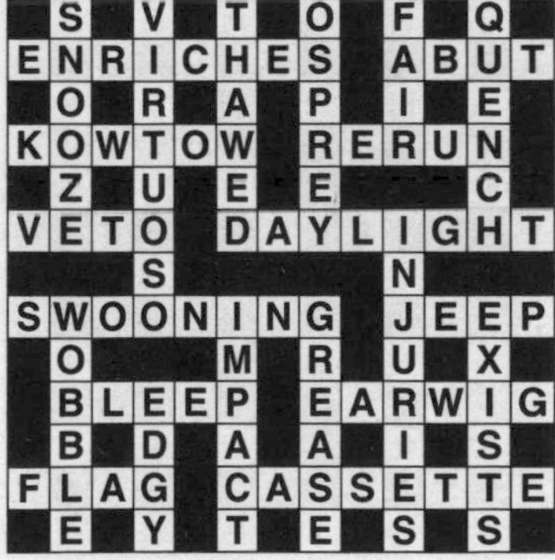

	S		V		T		O		F		Q	
E	N	R	I	C	H	E	S		A	B	U	T
	O		R		A		P		I		E	
K	O	W	T	O	W		R	E	R	U	N	
	Z		U		E		E				C	
V	E	T	O		D	A	Y	L	I	G	H	T
			S						N			
S	W	O	O	N	I	N	G		J	E	E	P
	O				M		R		U		X	
	B	L	E	E	P		E	A	R	W	I	G
	B		D		A		A		I		S	
F	L	A	G		C	A	S	S	E	T	T	E
	E		Y		T		E		S		S	

41

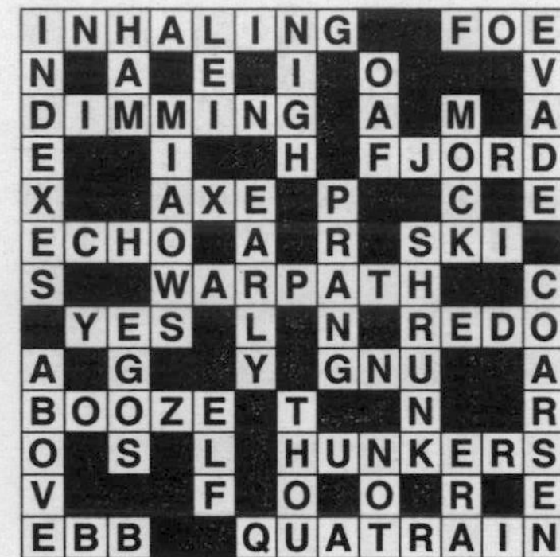

42

43

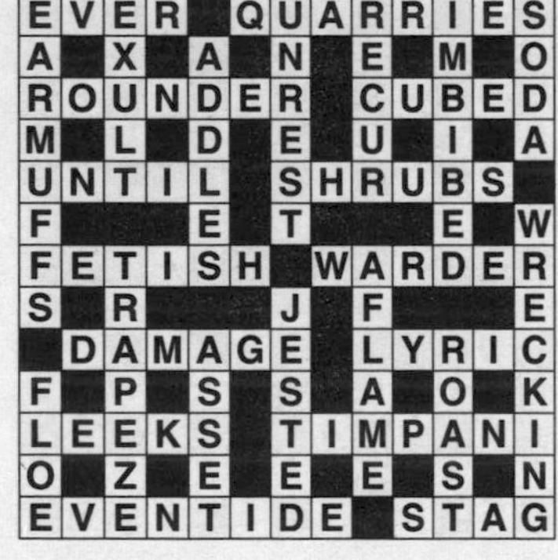

44

45

	W		A	■	O	■	A	■	G	■	C	■
S	H	O	V	E	D	■	S	O	R	E	L	Y
	E		E	■	O	A	K	■	A	■	E	■
J	E	E	R	■	U	■	E	■	B	A	R	E
	Z	■	■	■	R	A	W	■	■	■	I	■
H	Y	E	N	A	■	L	■	G	R	A	C	E
■	■	G	■	U	N	I	F	Y	■	M	■	■
S	P	O	O	K	■	G	■	M	O	P	E	D
	A	■	■	■	A	N	Y	■	■	■	Q	■
F	L	O	G	■	I	■	O	■	F	L	U	X
	E		R	■	M	A	D	■	A	■	I	■
A	S	H	O	R	E	■	E	X	C	I	T	E
■	T	■	W	■	D	■	L	■	T	■	Y	■

46

S	Q	U	A	S	H	■	S	W	I	F	T	S
H	■	R	■	A	■	A	■	O	■	A	■	T
R	O	B	■	R	A	U	C	O	U	S	L	Y
E	■	A	■	T	■	X	■	■	■	H	■	L
D	I	N	G	O	■	I	N	S	P	I	R	E
S	■	■	■	R	■	L	■	U	■	O	■	■
■	R	E	M	I	N	I	S	C	I	N	G	■
■	■	N	■	A	■	A	■	C	■	■	■	A
J	O	C	U	L	A	R	■	E	A	R	L	S
A	■	L	■	■	■	I	■	S	■	A	■	P
C	R	A	Z	I	N	E	S	S	■	B	Y	E
K	■	V	■	O	■	S	■	E	■	B	■	C
S	E	E	I	N	G	■	A	S	S	I	S	T

47

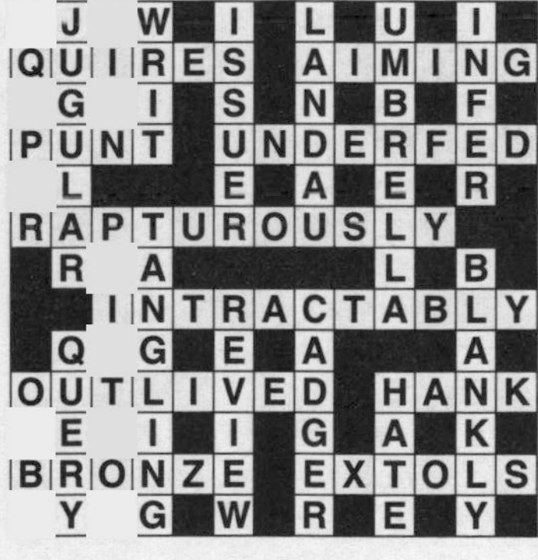

	J		W	■	I	■	L	■	U	■	I	■
Q	U	I	R	E	S	■	A	I	M	I	N	G
	G		I	■	S	■	N	■	B	■	F	■
P	U	N	T	■	U	N	D	E	R	F	E	D
	L	■	■	■	E	■	A	■	E	■	R	■
R	A	P	T	U	R	O	U	S	L	Y	■	■
■	R		A	■	■	■	■	■	L	■	B	■
■	■	I	N	T	R	A	C	T	A	B	L	Y
■	Q		G	■	E	■	A	■	■	■	A	■
O	U	T	L	I	V	E	D	■	H	A	N	K
	E		I	■	I	■	G	■	A	■	K	■
B	R	O	N	Z	E	■	E	X	T	O	L	S
	Y		G	■	W	■	R	■	E	■	Y	■

48

S	Q	U	A	W	K	E	D	■	O	P	A	L
E	■	N	■	A	■	X	■	C	■	H	■	A
I	N	D	E	X	■	P	E	R	F	O	R	M
Z	■	Y	■	Y	■	I	■	A	■	T	■	B
E	X	I	T	■	B	R	O	C	C	O	L	I
■	■	N	■	V	■	Y	■	K	■	■	■	N
C	O	G	N	A	C	■	B	E	L	O	N	G
R	■	■	■	C	■	C	■	D	■	R	■	■
U	P	S	T	A	I	R	S	■	L	I	F	T
I	■	A	■	T	■	U	■	I	■	G	■	W
S	U	B	J	E	C	T	■	D	R	A	M	A
E	■	L	■	D	■	C	■	O	■	M	■	N
D	I	E	T	■	S	H	E	L	V	I	N	G

49

J		M		N	I	G	H	T		S		E
O	P	E	R	A		R		W	E	E	D	S
S		N		B	R	A	K	E		N		P
T	H	U	M	B		Z		N		T	H	Y
L				E		E	N	T	E	R		
I	N	S	I	D	E	S		Y		I	C	E
N		I								E		N
G	U	T		Q		E	X	P	O	S	E	D
		T	H	U	D	S		E				U
S	K	I		A		C		L	E	V	E	R
O		N		R	E	A	C	T		E		I
F	I	G	H	T		P		E	A	T	E	N
T		S		S	P	E	N	D		S		G

50

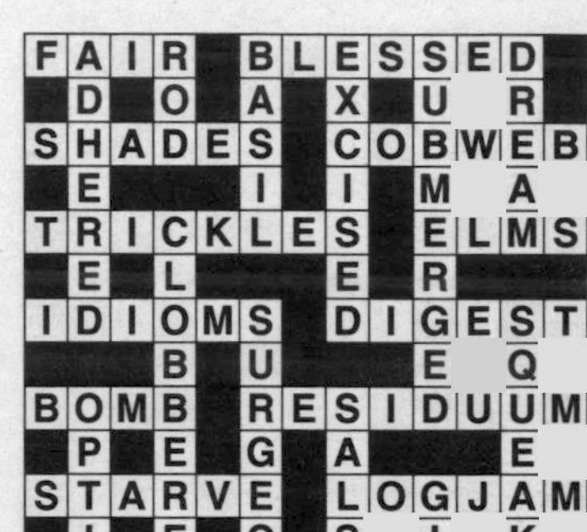

51

52

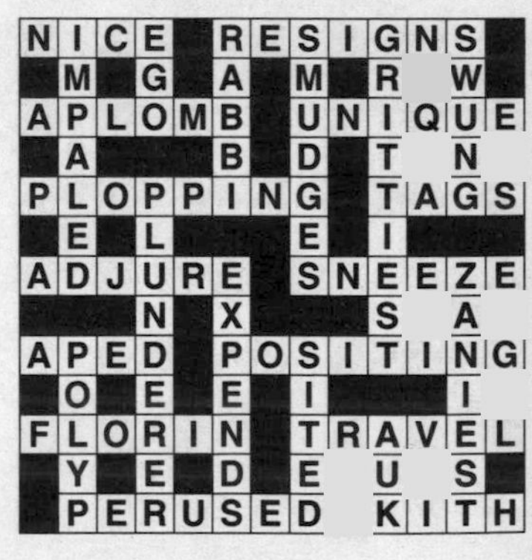